Tourism, Religion, and Pilgrimage in Jerusalem

Jerusalem is a city with a singular nature. Home to three religions, it contains spiritual meaning for people the world over; it is at once a tourist destination and a location with a complex political reality. Tourism, therefore, is an integral part of Jerusalem's development and its political conflicts.

The book traces tourism and pilgrimage to Jerusalem from the late Ottoman era, through the British Mandate, during the period of the divided city, and to the reunification of the city under Israeli rule. Throughout, the city's evolution is shown to be intertwined with its tourist industry, as tourist sites, accommodations, infrastructure, and services transform the city's structures and open spaces. At the same time, tourism is wielded by various parties in an effort to gain political recognition, to bolster territorial control, or to garner support. The city's future and the role tourism can play in it are examined. While the construction of a "security fence" will have many implications for Jerusalem's tourist industry, steps are proposed to minimize the effects of the security fence and optimize tourism.

Written by leading academics, this title will be valuable reading for students, academics, and researchers in the fields of tourism, religious studies, geography, history, cultural studies, and anthropology.

Kobi Cohen-Hattab is a Senior Lecturer at the Department of Land of Israel Studies and Archaeology, Bar Ilan University, Ramat-Gan, Israel. His main research interests are historical-geography of tourism, tourism in historical towns, holy places and tourism development, and the evolution of seaside resorts.

Noam Shoval is an Associate Professor at the Department of Geography, Hebrew University of Jerusalem. His main research interests are tourism and culture as tools for urban regeneration, tourism management in heritage cities, and the implementation of advanced tracking technologies for spatial research.

Contemporary Geographies of Leisure, Tourism and Mobility
Series Editor: C. Michael Hall, Professor at the Department of
Management
*College of Business and Economics, University of Canterbury, Christchurch,
New Zealand*

The aim of this series is to explore and communicate the intersections and relationships between leisure, tourism and human mobility within the social sciences.

It will incorporate both traditional and new perspectives on leisure and tourism from contemporary geography, e.g. notions of identity, representation and culture, while also providing for perspectives from cognate areas such as anthropology, cultural studies, gastronomy and food studies, marketing, policy studies and political economy, regional and urban planning, and sociology, within the development of an integrated field of leisure and tourism studies.

Also, increasingly, tourism and leisure are regarded as steps in a continuum of human mobility. Inclusion of mobility in the series offers the prospect to examine the relationship between tourism and migration, the sojourner, educational travel, and second home and retirement travel phenomena.

The series comprises two strands:

Contemporary Geographies of Leisure, Tourism and Mobility aims to address the needs of students and academics, and the titles will be published in hardback and paperback. Titles include:

Routledge Studies in Contemporary Geographies of Leisure, Tourism and Mobility is a forum for innovative new research intended for research students and academics, and the titles will be available in hardback only. Titles include:

Tourism, Religion, and Pilgrimage in Jerusalem

Kobi Cohen-Hattab and Noam Shoval

LONDON AND NEW YORK

First published 2015
by Routledge
2 Park Square, Milton Park, Abingdon, Oxon OX14 4RN

and by Routledge
711 Third Avenue, New York, NY 10017

First issued in paperback 2017

Routledge is an imprint of the Taylor & Francis Group, an informa business

British Library Cataloguing in Publication Data
A catalogue record for this book is available from the British Library

Library of Congress Cataloguing in Publication Data
Cohen-Hattab, Kobi.
Tourism, religion and pilgrimage in Jerusalem / Kobi Cohen-Hattab, Noam Shoval.
    pages cm – (Contemporary geographies of leisure, tourism and mobility)
    Includes bibliographical references and index.
    1. Tourism–Religious aspects–Judaism. 2. Pilgrims and pilgrimages–Jerusalem. I. Shoval, Noam. II. Title.
    G156.5.R44C65 2014
    338.4'791569442–dc23   2014003294

ISBN 13: 978-1-138-08249-6 (pbk)
ISBN 13: 978-1-138-78098-9 (hbk)

Typeset in Times New Roman
by Wearset Ltd, Boldon, Tyne and Wear

Contents

Illustrations

Figures

Table

Preface

Jerusalem is a holy city for the three monotheistic religions, a location where many of the important events chronicled in the Old and New Testaments took place. The city has been tied to ancient traditions in Judaism, Christianity, and Islam. This holiness was what brought generations of pilgrims and tourists to visit the city. Conversely, its holiness was also what made it a stage for political conflicts throughout the ages; in the past century, this has been especially evident in the frequent regime changes.

Much has been written about Jerusalem as a sacred place and as a site of conflict, a place of regime turnover and tussles between world powers and armies; these vicissitudes have been reflected in various narratives and symbols throughout the ages. However, it is surprising that until now no comprehensive volume has studied the phenomena of pilgrimage and tourism to Jerusalem.

As a religious and political center for generations rather than a port or city of commerce, Jerusalem's economic sector was heavily influenced by pilgrimage and tourism as a major economic sector and a significant factor in the political struggle for hegemony. This was true during the days of the first Jewish Temple that was built 3,000 years ago, through the contested Roman rule in Jesus's time, throughout the Crusades, and under the Ottoman Empire—and its status as a place of pilgrimage still affects its development and character today. This book aims to fill the void in the academic literature.

The two authors of this book are children of Jerusalem and feel a deep connection and a special affinity for the city. During our academic studies, we naturally found ourselves pulled toward studying the city in various ways. Thus during the second half of the 1990s, we wrote doctoral dissertations about tourism in Jerusalem and its effect on the city, both through the Geography Department of the Hebrew University of Jerusalem. Kobi Cohen-Hattab wrote his dissertation, under the supervision of Prof. Yehoshua Ben-Arieh and Prof. Yossi Katz, about tourism in Jerusalem during the British Mandate period; Noam Shoval wrote his under Prof. Arie Shachar on tourism in united Jerusalem in the late twentieth century. Over the years, we have often collaborated on research on Israel generally and Jerusalem in particular, and we recently arrived at the conclusion that our many studies on tourism in Jerusalem and the dearth of comprehensive, integrative, and wide-ranging research justified the collaboration on a book that would complete the picture. It is our hope that our research makes a significant contribution and serves as a milestone in the understanding and development of Jerusalem in the modern era.

We are indebted to the many people and organizations that supported this project. We wish to thank Tamar Soffer, chief cartographer of the Geography Department at the Hebrew University of Jerusalem, for her help in drawing most of the figures in this book and Adi Bennun, director of the Geographical Information Center at the Hebrew University of Jerusalem, for his advice on GIS-related issues. We also wish to thank Deena Glickman for her important help with the English linguistic and stylistic editing. Noam Shoval is grateful for the support of the Israel Science Foundation (grant no. 749/09), which gave the impetus for writing this book.

Finally, we wish to thank our spouses and children for their support and understanding while we were writing this book.

Kobi Cohen-Hattab and Noam Shoval
Jerusalem, Israel
January 2014

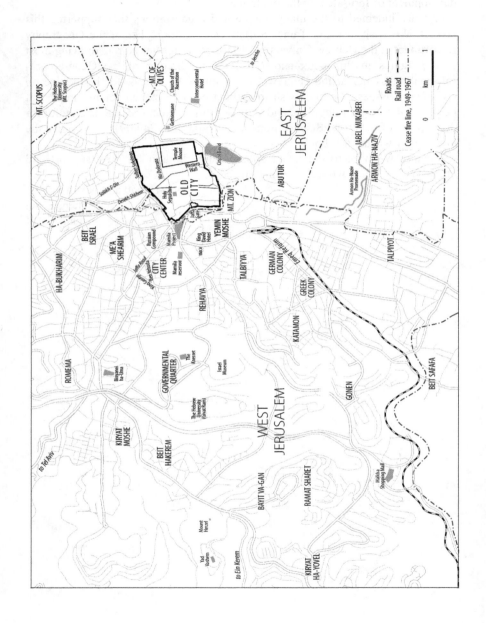

1   Introduction
Jerusalem of Heaven, Jerusalem on Earth

More than 3,000 years ago the city of Jerusalem was conquered by King David, who made it his capital. David's transfer of the Ark of the Covenant to Jerusalem, and his son Solomon's building of the Temple, transformed the city into a religious center and a focus of Jewish pilgrimage during the First Temple period. This trend grew during the Second Temple period, reaching its peak in the first century of the Common Era. Around that time, Jesus and his disciples arrived in Jerusalem as pilgrims during one of the Passover festivals. As a result of this famed journey, Jerusalem became one of Christianity's holiest sites—if not the holiest—as well as a focal point for Christian pilgrims. Approximately 600 years later, Islam, too, adopted Jerusalem as one of its sacred places, distinguishing the city in a number of religious traditions, such as Mohammed's Night Journey and the location of his ascent to heaven.

With the city's importance for the three monotheistic religions, pilgrimage has been a significant component of Jerusalem's existence in the centuries since. While Rome, Mecca, and Varanasi are mono-religious centers, Jerusalem is a multi-religious center of unique character, spiritual meaning, and universal appeal. Jerusalem, then, presents a singular case among the world's sacred places: it attracts pilgrims from a diverse and broad range of religions, nations, and cultural traditions.

But at the same time, the fact that Jerusalem is sacred to believers of three faiths and their many denominations creates spatial and organizational competition and fierce conflicts over particular rituals, sites, and itineraries.

Modern secular tourism, which took shape in Europe in the form of the "Grand Tour," began trickling into the city in the sixteenth century (Towner 1985), and appeared in Jerusalem at an ever-growing rate during the nineteenth century (Ben-Arieh 1986). The obstacles to such tourism had, until that point, been the relatively long distances to the Holy Land from the tourists' countries of origin, issues of security, and the absence of an infrastructure suited for tourism (Brendon 1991).

The shift from individual tourism to organized tourism in Jerusalem and the Holy Land can be pinpointed as the spring of 1869, when the Thomas Cook & Son company began its operations in the region with an organized tour for 30 people to Egypt and the Holy Land—a tour guided by Thomas Cook himself. By 1882, Thomas Cook & Son had brought over 5,000 tourists to Jerusalem and the

Holy Land (Brendon 1991). This trend has continually grown over the decades; in 2010, more than three million tourists and pilgrims visited Jerusalem, making it by far the place of highest attraction for tourism in Israel.

If Jerusalem's nature as a religious center is unique, its dynamic of growth and change over thousands of years has also been distinct. Visitors to the city—as well as the mechanisms and services that are part and parcel of their visits—have always had great influence on the city. Thus pilgrimage and tourism become agents in the city's evolution. This is a phenomenon that is seen from time to time with tourist cities; however, Jerusalem has, in a sense, been a destination for pilgrims for thousands of years. With this unique dynamic, Jerusalem and its tourists are worthy of study—both as an individual case and for application to other tourist locations.

In examining the distinctive relationship between Jerusalem and its tourists over the past 150 years, we focus on two central themes in the history of pilgrimage and tourism to the city. As the book advances from one period to the next, these are examined in light of geomorphological and political shifts in Jerusalem and the region.

First and foremost, we investigate the ways in which tourism and pilgrimage, as integral processes in the city, were always decisive elements in the city's growth. It is an intricate and reciprocal relationship that exists between the visitors to Jerusalem and the city as an evolving entity. Buildings and institutions were established to house the city's visitors and services were created to accommodate them; these then became part of the city's skyline and daily life. As the nature of tourism changed, so did the needs of Jerusalem's visitors—and, as a result, so did the city itself. Where tourism can, in other cities, be an instrument of change, it is a particularly significant feature in Jerusalem; its effects are immense and widespread.

The second theme explored is the connection between tourism and political conflict. In a city whose control is contested regularly, tourism has been employed implicitly and explicitly to exert authority or create change for the benefit of one party. Throughout the book, we will see tourism utilized as a means to an end—for example, to stake a claim or justify a political worldview—and we will see political considerations influencing tourism.

Pilgrimage, sacred sites, and modern tourism

In the coming chapters, we take a closer look at the city of Jerusalem, the urban trends of the past 150 years, and the development of tourism at the city's religious sites. Before we begin, we briefly review the nature of pilgrimage and tourism as well as developments in the field of tourism research.

Pilgrimage

The pilgrimage is one of humanity's most ancient phenomena and spans all religions. It consists of a circular movement of people from one place to another in a short period of time, and includes psychological, religious, sociological, and tourist dimensions, with sacred spaces at the core of the journey (Reader and Walter 1993).

Academic study of the phenomenon gained momentum in the 1970s with a series of studies composed by renowned sociologist Victor Turner. He viewed the pilgrimage as a universal religious behavior and the site of worship as a marginal location; that is to say, the destination, in his opinion, was external to the believers' usual locale.

Turner's work was an expansion of the research of Van Gennep, who had studied rites of passage. Van Gennep stated that such a ritual involved a separation from everyday life; a trek to a holy place and a stay there; and finally a return home (Van Gennep 1960). Thus Turner viewed the relationship between the holy site and the pilgrim as an excentric one, accentuating the movement from the center of society to its periphery (Turner 1973; Turner and Turner 1978). He termed the holy site "the center out there," where the pilgrim went to search for meaning in a place of chaos, a place far removed from his or her everyday existence.

Turner examined the social dimension of the pilgrimage, noting that on such a journey social solidarity formed between pilgrims. The central—or *liminal*—stage of Van Gennep's three stages was one that accompanied changes in place, age, or social role; in Turner's opinion, during this ceremonial stage the social order was wiped clean, with all relationships based on spontaneity and equality.

Mircea Eliade (1959), unlike Turner, felt that the pilgrimage was a concentric process, one in which the individual on the periphery aspired to reach a center of some kind. He coined the term *axis mundi*, the axis connecting heaven and earth, and claimed that the place of pilgrimage was, for the pilgrim, the center of the world, the place where heaven and earth met.

In the 1990s, a new approach to pilgrimage began to take shape. Erik Cohen claimed that Turner's understanding of the phenomenon was highly influenced by his experience as a Catholic. Catholicism, Cohen claimed, distinguished between the political and religious, a process which ultimately pushed religious institutions to the periphery. However, in other cultures—Eastern, in particular—no distinction was made between the religious and the political, leading to a state in which the religious and the political—the priesthood and royalty, for example—were one and the same. Cohen instead distinguished between two types of pilgrimage—the formal, which was concentric in nature, and the popular, excentric in nature (Cohen 1992b).

John Eade and Michael Sallnow further contested Turner's views; they posited that rather than consisting of social harmony, many pilgrimages were characterized by hostility and the marking of boundaries (Eade and Sallnow 1991). They also noted that the destination's significance was in the eye of the believer rather than absolute (Shachar and Shoval 1999). A pilgrimage destination, according to this view, is deemed universal when it can reflect a variety of religious outlooks and give a variety of pilgrims the desired experience.

Whether we view the pilgrimage as excentric or concentric, whether we think of the holy site as absolute or relative, whether we believe that the social order changes in the process or not, the pilgrimage is a millennia-old phenomenon of great significance. However, this significance does not relate only to the pilgrim; as we will see, the arrival of visitors in a given location greatly influences the nature of that location as well. In fact, the pilgrimage has, for centuries, served as one of the most important elements in the formation of space in various places in the world.

From pilgrimage to tourism

Several concurrent economic, social, and technological processes resulted in a sharp rise in tourism during the second half of the twentieth century (Shachar 1995). Tourism was transformed from the exclusive luxury of the elite social classes it had been for centuries (Towner 1996) into a widespread phenomenon constituting part of the lifestyle of practically everyone in the developed world. With the advent of modern tourism the nature of visits to sites of religious significance changed dramatically. Where once visitors to a given site were pilgrims, coming out of religious motivation, tourism brought with it an increase in visitors coming for other reasons, such as culture and heritage.

The majority of academic literature relates to the modern form of tourism without touching on the historical perspective (Reader and Walter 1993; Vukonic 1996). There have been, however, a number of attempts to characterize the relationship between pilgrimage and tourism. One opinion views the two as existing on a continuum, with one end sanctified and the other secular; visitors to a given place, then, will fall somewhere on the spectrum (Rinschede 1988, 75; Smith 1992, 3–4).

Recent decades have seen a significant increase in tourism that is not necessarily religious in nature alongside an increase in pilgrimage activity (Nolan and Nolan 1989; Olsen and Timothy 2006). In keeping with the effect that pilgrimage had on locations, this "touristification" of religious sites (Olsen and Timothy 2006, 104) has had serious ramifications on local populations as well (Cohen-Hattab and Shoval 2007; Collins-Kreiner 2009; Digance 2003; Gatrell and Collins-Kreiner 2006).

Tourism and its impact on urban destinations

Modern tourism constitutes a new type of travel characterized by greater access and different types of motivations. This change in the very nature of tourism is reflected in the dramatic growth in the international flow of travel: whereas in 1950 a total of slightly over 25 million tourists crossed international borders, this number reached nearly one billion in 2011.

More than 40 years ago, geographer and city planner Sir Peter Hall offered an excellent description of the rising importance of tourism in the economies and urban planning of cities. Hall claimed that the "age of mass tourism is the biggest single factor for change in the great capitals of Europe, and in many smaller historical cities too, in the last 30 years of this century" (Hall 1970, 445). Indeed, the increasing tourist flow has served to irrevocably alter many locations. Numerous airports, for instance, have been transformed from mere landing strips with small terminals into massive complexes that include shopping malls, hi-tech industrial parks, and hotels (Gottdiener 2000). Huge mega-resorts have begun to emerge, such as Las Vegas and Orlando in the U.S., the Gold Coast in Australia, Cancún in Mexico, and the Costa del Sol in Spain (Gladstone 1998; Mullins 1991). Capital cities and global financial centers have registered enormous growth, notably in business-oriented travel (Braun 1992; Law 1996). Similarly, historical cities have become magnets for tourism to such an extent that their physical and social carrying capacities are actually placed in jeopardy (Ashworth and Tunbridge 2000; Borg *et al.* 1996; Canestrelli and Costa 1991; Page and Hall 2003; Russo 2001). These issues have become factors in the broader context of visitor mobility in urban areas.

It is somewhat ironic that urban tourism is one of the most popular forms of tourism but among its least researched phenomena (Ashworth and Page 2011). Indeed, the call for more and better research is a common theme of much of the literature written over the last 20 years. Ashworth's work is seen by many as the beginning of research into urban tourism (1989). His central thesis is that urban centers are both the origins of most tourists and the destinations for many, but that most research tends to focus on tourism's impact on non-urban areas. While the volume of literature is growing (see for example the following books: Law 1993; Page 1995; Judd and Fainstein 1999; Hoffman *et al.*, 2003; Judd 2003; Page and Hall 2003; Spirou 2011), in his follow-up reflective piece, Ashworth (2003) argues that there is still insufficient research into various aspects of the urban tourism phenomenon. Pearce (2001) also notes a general increase in interest in this issue, with the phrase "urban tourism" entering the tourism lexicon. Yet he, too, feels that research is still in its early stages, and that "there is still a considerable way to go in terms of developing a coherent corpus of work, pursuing common goals and carrying out comparable studies" (Pearce 2001, 928). He cites a number of largely unexplored lines of inquiry including detailed examination of tourists' behavior as they arrive in and travel through cities, linkages between tourist nodes, and interaction between such nodes. Most recently, Ashworth and Page, discussing the paradoxes in urban tourism research, observed that "it is curious that very little attention has been given to the questions about how tourists actually use cities" (Ashworth and Page 2011, 7).

Tourism in urban areas is a spatially selective activity with tourist nodes or precincts clustered unevenly throughout a city (Pearce 2001). The number of tourist nodes depends on both the size and geomorphology of a destination. Tourist nodes can be focused around icon attractions, shopping, and business precincts or anchored by hotels (Pearce 1998). But even though tourism may be perceived as a dominant facet of such zones, in reality it may not be the primary activity and tourists may not be the central user group (Ashworth and Page

2011). Beyond this generic knowledge, though, relatively little research has been conducted examining the spatial structure of tourism in cities at a neighborhood level (Pearce 1999), with Maitland's (2008) work in London the sole exception. Research on large cities is rare and the research that does exist does not analyze the development over long periods of time.

The study of Jerusalem—a city that has been inundated by individual tourists and tour groups for hundreds of years—can contribute greatly to the literature on urban tourism and growth.

Jerusalem: a case study

An examination of Jerusalem cannot be conducted without taking into account its religious character. As we saw earlier, Jerusalem is considered holy by three different religions, thus the tourism it generates is distinctive in nature. The city's urban growth and political life are highly influenced by the type of tourism it attracts—a tourism that is tied to the way the city is perceived by its visitors.

Jerusalem on Earth and Jerusalem of Heaven

Tourism to Jerusalem—in tourism's most basic sense, leaving one's place of permanent residence and traveling extensive distances to visit another place— has had a distinct character throughout the city's long history. It is an urban tourism of a particular nature in which the city itself, its sights, its views, its buildings, its architecture, its people, its food and smells—in short, all the com- ponents of an earthly place which might attract tourists to visit it—have histori- cally had almost no meaning in engendering visits.

The last time the city was built on a monumental scale, before the present period, was during the reign of Herod the Great, when it was known for the mag- nificent Second Temple; for its multitude of impressive palaces, roads, and bridges; and for its highly sophisticated urban infrastructure. Two thousand years passed before Mayor Teddy Kollek restored some allure and a distinct physical presence to the built environment of Jerusalem. With the exception of the Dome of the Rock (built in 691 CE), which was well-known as an architectural master- piece, no attraction existed in Jerusalem—no building, palace, temple, shrine, church, mosque, garden, fountain, or other man-made structure or natural phe- nomenon—that was unique in size, shape, or design. It may simply be stated that Jerusalem was, from the Roman destruction in 70 CE and until very recently, a small, poor, neglected place, barely surviving at the periphery of various empires, with—Dome of the Rock aside—no physical attractions of any distinction.

In fact, one might say that Jerusalem as a global center for pilgrims and visi- tors was not the city on earth, the built city, but Jerusalem of Heaven on High, the spiritual image of the city as preserved and nurtured in the visitors' minds and hearts. This religious ideal was, then, a subjective paradise, envisioned dif- ferently by members of each sect.

In fact, Bowman (1991, 98–99) claims that since pilgrims in Jerusalem travel to different places at different times and establish different rituals, Jerusalem should not be regarded as one holy city, but as several holy cities—equivalent to the number of religions and denominations worshiping within. In his opinion, the coexistence of several holy cities side by side within the urban milieu leads to the conclusion that it is not the physical built environment which attracts pilgrims and visitors to Jerusalem; it is the images, the narratives, and the dreams which each pilgrim and visitor brings, manifesting in rituals and prayers at their particular sacred space in Jerusalem. Once in Jerusalem, pilgrims realize and give concrete meaning to the spiritual world they studied and dreamed of in their places of origin.

The development of pilgrim spaces in Jerusalem

Tours to Jerusalem until the second half of the nineteenth century took the form of pilgrimages, filling a moral and spiritual role for visitors (Cohen 1992a; Eliade 1969). They were not only meant to meet the needs of religious obligation; the goal of the visit to Jerusalem was to allow pilgrims to identify themselves with its history, its moral leadership, its agonies and sufferings, and its hopes of salvation and personal purification for peace on earth (Turner 1973; Turner and Turner 1978). The visit to Jerusalem was not solely a matter of intellectual contemplation or aesthetic observation. Rather, it involved fantasy, prayers, and dreams (Rinschede 1992). To borrow Urry's expression: "The city is the repository of people's memories and of the past; and it also functions as a receptacle of cultural symbols" (Urry 1995, 24). In this respect, the question of the historical sites' authenticity was only of minor significance for Jerusalem's pilgrims and visitors, as long as they believed in their sect's commonly accepted lore about the historical and religious geography of Jerusalem of the past.

This is precisely the point at which the personal spiritual experience of the individual pilgrim-visitor is molded by the socially constructed spatial pattern of specific sites which have become "sacred spaces." These spaces, designated as such by the narratives of religions and denominations in Jerusalem throughout its long history as a religious center, constitute an *omphalos* of the world, an *axis mundi*—the point of intersection between the mundane and transcendental worlds. These sacred spaces then, in time, become "pilgrim spaces."

The politics of tourist space segmentation

The segmentation of Jerusalem on Earth into several distinct "sacred spaces," which turned into "pilgrim spaces" over time and transformed into "tourist spaces" in modern times, should be viewed as a highly political process which shapes and reshapes the entire urban fabric of Jerusalem. Aside from the Crusader period of the Latin *Kingdom of Jerusalem* (1099–1187), when Jerusalem was chosen as the capital of the Latin East (Prawer 1972), Jerusalem was not the capital city of any empire, kingdom, or nation for almost 2,000 years—between the 70 CE Roman conquest and destruction of the Second Temple and 1917, when the British declared the city to be the capital of Palestine.[1] This reality left the various religions and sects to determine the physical growth and structure of the urban built environment through their actions and construction. This process was carried out in two distinct steps. First, the never-ending stream of pilgrims identified and imparted historical-religious validation to "sacred spaces"; second, visitors carried out the second step of turning a "sacred space" into a "pilgrim space" and later on into a "tourist space" (Nolan and Nolan 1992).

The sacred space included not only the sites of historical-religious signifi-cance; erected adjacent to them were headquarters of the religious organizations and institutions which tended to, cared for, and managed the holy places. Places of worship and prayer were most appropriate for the establishment of institutes of religious learning—those institutions aimed at the organized pursuit of the principles of belief and of moral behavior. The combination of a holy place and an institution of learning and contemplation is a powerful urban growth pole, stimulating development around it.

This process of urban growth around the nucleus of a sacred space stands at the base of the ecological structure of the Old City of Jerusalem: the Muslim Quarter is located around the Dome of the Rock and the Al-Aqsa Mosque; the Christian Quarter is situated around the Church of the Holy Sepulchre; the Jewish Quarter is adjacent to the Western Wall (or Wailing Wall), the sole remnant of the Temple Mount complex; and the Armenian Quarter is positioned around the St. James Cathedral.

The political nature of pilgrimages to Jerusalem was evident throughout the last 2,000 years, culminating in the nineteenth century when various European powers hastened to wrest control over the city from the weakening Ottoman Empire. This was not done using military might but by establishing physical bridgeheads in Jerusalem in the form of services to pilgrims and tourists such as churches, hospices, and hospitals, built in large complexes, reflecting a sense of majesty and erected on a quasi-monumental scale. Construction of these com-plexes required the acquisition of large tracts of land, in essence giving the various European powers a concrete stronghold in Jerusalem.

These European outposts of pilgrim and tourist services created new tourist spaces of a grand scale and appearance. These compounds, it should be noted, had a decisive influence in establishing and shaping the growth of new Jerusa-lem outside the walls of the Old City. In fact, they still constitute many of the remarkable landmarks in Jerusalem's urban landscape, having transformed gradually from services and accommodations for visitors to tourist sites worth visiting by virtue of their own aesthetic qualities and historical significance to the city's evolution (Shoval and Cohen-Hattab 2001).

The political nature of urban tourism and the impact of the developing tourist spaces on the recreation of Jerusalem's urban landscape received new impetus and meaning in the second half of the twentieth century with the national revival of the Jewish people and the persistent efforts to reinforce Jewish presence and dominance over Jerusalem. As will be seen later in the book, the city's urban landscape changed dramatically once it became the capital of the Jewish state. In the years following the 1948 war, when Jewish Jerusalem was limited to the western part of the city, new monuments were built, creating tourist spaces that were national and symbolic in nature. A compound comprised of the Knesset (parliament) building, the Israel Museum, and the Hebrew University became

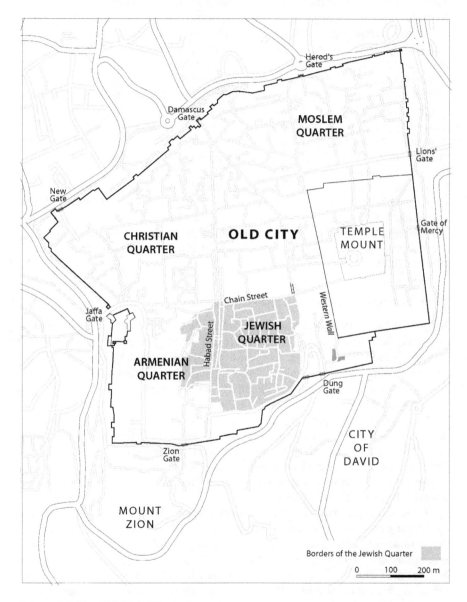

Figure 1.1 The Old City of Jerusalem.

the city's new national center; a second compound including a military cemetery and the Yad Vashem Holocaust memorial museum on Mount Herzl constitute a memorial district.

While Christian tourism has always been an integral part of the city, an in-depth examination of the patterns of Christian tourism confirms that it is tied, among other things, to the Catholic Church's shifting and ambivalent attitude to Jerusalem, and primarily to its unwillingness to make the city a pilgrimage destination competing with Rome. It appears that despite Jerusalem's holiness in Christianity, for political and economic reasons the Catholic Church promoted Rome at the expense of Jerusalem and other locales throughout history.

Jerusalem's urban development was thus highly affected by the tourist activity that took place in its borders. Shaped by the highly segmented map of various religions' and denominations' sacred spaces, the city's growth was strongly augmented by its pilgrims and visitors. Hence the argument that visiting Jerusalem, in addition to uplifting the individual spiritually and morally, fulfilled a major political role of a collective nature: the pilgrims, the visitors, and in modern times, many of the tourists, brought with them a message of material and symbolic support to their group members in the city. Pilgrims and tourists visited Jerusalem in order to identify themselves, body and soul, with their religion, denomination, or nationality. The tour of Jerusalem was thus a sort of temporary mobilization of the believers and followers, who joined the ongoing and ever-lasting struggle for a strong presence and domination of Jerusalem on Earth (Shoval 2000).

Urban tourism and urban structure in Jerusalem

Jansen-Verbeke (1985) proposed the division of urban tourism into two main components: primary elements and secondary ones. The primary elements are those attractions which bring visitors to cities; the secondary elements are the various services which provide for the tourists' needs during their visit (hotels, restaurants, travel agencies, tour operators, and the like). When the primary and secondary elements congregate spatially, a "tourism district" is created.

A number of attempts have been made in academic literature, following the well-known concept of a Central Business District, to define an area in which most primary and secondary tourism elements are concentrated as a CTD, or Central Tourism District (Burtenshaw et al. 1981). Other terms that have been suggested are Recreational Business District (Stansfield and Rickert 1970) and Tourism Business District (Getz 1991).

We would argue that the sites which are visited, observed, and worshipped at by pilgrims and tourists in Jerusalem are highly segmented and differentiated by the various religious groups and, more recently, by the national entities comprising the city. To borrow from MacCannell's terminology (1990), each group and national entity creates the set of sacred places and national monuments which are visited by pilgrims. These different sets of sites, which are shaped and defined over long periods of time, are a prime example of what might be termed "conferred authenticity," and the spatial authentication process is performed through religious belief or national symbolism as represented in a continuous stream of pilgrims and tourists to the various sets of sites (Cohen-Hattab and Kerber 2004; Smith 1992).

We assume a high congruence between the "sacred space," which later becomes a "tourist space"—defined as "a particular set of sites determined separately and differently by each religious, denominational, and national group"— and the spatial behavior of pilgrims, visitors, and tourists; we hypothesize that pilgrims have never looked at a general, universal Jerusalem "tourist space," but rather focused and limited their "tourist gaze," their worship and personal spiritual experience, to the particular sacred space as shaped and defined by their own religious denomination (Shachar and Shoval 1999). The same congruence should be expected in modern times, when the tourist space is composed of national monuments and symbols that are sharply divergent for the Jewish and Arab nationalities vying for rule of Jerusalem.

Mapping tourism in Jerusalem

If tourist spaces in Jerusalem are segmented, each occupying different areas of the city, then these areas can be identified by reviewing and mapping the itineraries and sites of visiting tourist groups. We can further hypothesize that each tourist space is composed of (1) a majority of sites which are specific and unique for a particular group of pilgrims and tourists and (2) a small number of sites that are not directly related to the religion, culture, or national heritage of a specific group, but rather are visited because of their universal appeal, symbolizing the essence of Jerusalem which is appreciated and visited by all groups.

Those sites which are common to all visitors—unrelated to religious, cultural, or national background—when mapped and demarcated will produce a tourist space of a higher order which will be defined as a "Central Tourist District." This area is the city's primary tourist space and is determined by the largest number of visits and by the extensive overlapping of the various tourist spaces.

Until recently, tourism research was conducted using time–space diaries or observing subjects. These methods were both time-consuming and imprecise. Recent technological advances, particularly Global Positioning Systems (GPS), are transforming tourism and urban research (Shoval and Isaacson 2007). GPS devices give researchers the opportunity to collect data on a continuous basis and at high resolution, giving greater volumes of data that are also extremely accurate in time and space (Shoval and Isaacson 2010). At present, the method has been implemented on various geographic scales to study such locations as theme parks (Russo *et al.* 2010), small historic cities (Shoval 2008), and large multi-functional cities (McKercher *et al.* 2012). This groundbreaking method and its implications have not been fully explored, but it does seem to constitute a revolution in the quality and quantity of data available for analysis in tourism research.

The figures below present empirical measurements of various tourist segments' time–space patterns in the Old City of Jerusalem. This study was conducted in recent years using highly accurate GPS devices. Data collection took place over four years, from 2010 until 2013. In total, 1,030 tourists were sampled: 900 in organized Jewish groups, 40 in organized Christian groups, 60 individual tourists, and 30 backpackers. Data on Muslim tourists were not collected; at the time of data collection there was almost no Muslim tourism to Jerusalem due to the contested geopolitical situation in the city.

The findings presented in Figure 1.2 below confirm our theory that Jerusalem's tourist space is highly segmented. For the study, Jerusalem's Old City was divided into squares measuring 25 by 25 meters. The colors given reflect the relative number of visitors from each tourist segment in a given square: red cells indicate that more than 60 percent of tourists visited the site; orange indicates between 31 and 61 percent; yellow indicates between 16 and 30 percent; light green indicates between 7 and 15 percent; and dark green indicates that less than 7 percent visited. The height of the color in each square represents the average time per visitor. Figure 1.2 makes clear that:

1   The organized Jewish groups concentrate their activity within the Jewish Quarter (A)—the main tourist area in the Old City and home to many archeological findings (as will be detailed later on)—and the Western Wall Esplanade area (B).
2   The Christian organized groups visit the Jewish Quarter (A) and the Western Wall (B) as well; however they also spend significant amounts of time along the Via Dolorosa (Way of the Cross; C), the Church of the Holy Sepulchre (D), and Mount Zion (E), where the Room of the Last Supper is located.
3   Individual tourists and backpackers are independent in their choices in the city and thus seem able to visit all the different parts of the Old City. They spend time in the Jaffa Gate area (F), which serves as the entry point for the individual tourists to the Old City and offers a wide array of tourist services and information offices, enabling the tourists to gain information about the various options available. They, too, visit the Jewish Quarter and the Western Wall.

Together, these two locations—the Jewish Quarter and the Western Wall—can then be identified as the Central Tourist District of Jerusalem since all tourist segments studied visit there.

This type of research, conducted on a large scale with accurate data, can be of great use in mapping tourist services and sites in any urban tourism environment. In such cases, urban planners can quickly learn about tourist activity in a city and, subsequently, better design the transport, infrastructure, services, and tourist sites themselves to function more efficiently. In the case of Jerusalem, the data collected can be used to identify crucial loci of activity and then modify such locations to optimize their capacity and operations.

Organized Jewish Groups   Organized Christian Groups

Backpackers   Individual Tourists

Figure 1.2 Distribution of tourist groups in Jerusalem's Old City.

A study of tourism in Jerusalem

Though it was founded thousands of years ago, the history of Jerusalem as a modern tourist destination truly began near the end of the Ottoman era. From the mid-nineteenth century and until the present day, Jerusalem has undergone numerous political changes. Turkish-Ottoman rule gave way to British rule (1917), followed by Jordanian and Israeli rule (the divided city between 1948 and 1967), and finally unification under Israeli rule from 1967 onwards. The numerous political shifts brought various government authorities and agencies to the city, each of which represented one of the three monotheistic religions symbolized in Jerusalem's holy sites. These changes left their mark on the spatial organization of tourism within the city in general and on tourist services in particular. And these changes, in turn, led to shifts in the growth of the city in general.

Several dates could mark the beginning of modern tourism in Jerusalem. The year 1869 was when the first organized group of tourists was brought to Jerusalem by Thomas Cook & Son. But the first signs of modern tourism could also be attributed to the early 1880s, with the opening of the first hotel outside the city walls. We chose to begin our examination of the development of tourism in the city with the mid-1800s, some 20 years prior to the appearance of Thomas Cook & Son in Jerusalem. This is due to two occurrences at that time: the appearance of privately owned hotels within the Old City, located mainly adjacent to the city gates, and the initial development of large-scale hospitality services outside the city walls—with Russia the first to engage in this activity (with the "Russian Compound" in the mid-1850s; Ben-Arieh 1986).

Jerusalem, as a popular tourist destination, is an effective laboratory for urban tourism research. However, its unique character as a place of pilgrimage for three religions and as a contested capital for two nationalities makes the city a fascinating case study in urban change, and the brandishing of tourism to further a political goal.

In the coming chapters, we examine the intricate relationship tourism has with the Jerusalem's growth and the political conflicts over the city.

The book studies four periods, according to the key geopolitical changes in the city and the region. Each of the next four chapters relates to one of these periods, with the sixth chapter taking a look at the city's future.

1850–1917—End of the Ottoman period: Chapter 2 describes the decline of the Ottoman Empire and the onset of European activities in the city, highlighting the pilgrimage services and tourist sites.

1917–1948—The British Mandate period: The third chapter examines British rule in the city and modernization's effects on tourism.

1948–1967—The divided city: In the book's fourth chapter, we take a look at the two halves of the city, under Jordanian and Israeli rule, following the 1948 war.

1967 and on—The reunited city: The fifth chapter examines the growth in tourism following the reunification of the city in 1967 and the projects used to rehabilitate and unite the city.

The city's future: The book's sixth chapter asks how tourism can contribute to Jerusalem's future and discusses the implications of the "separation fence."

Books upon books have been written about Jerusalem, a city unparalleled on many levels. For many it is a spiritual home, the center of the earth, the direct line to heaven. For others, it is symbolic of nationalistic dreams and a source of conflict. Travelers entering its gates are inspired by the historical, religious, and national symbols and sites.

But Jerusalem's unique nature also extends to the very travelers who realize a dream in coming to see its sights. They are, consciously or unconsciously, no less a part of it, effecting changes in the city's very structure and political status. This book tells their story throughout the ages.

Note

1 Palestine, the commonly accepted name for the country at the time, was known to Jews as "Eretz Yisrael" in Hebrew. Though the British recognized Hebrew as one of the official languages, they insisted that the name of the Mandate be "Palestina" in Hebrew. The Jewish settlement in the land vehemently objected. In the end, a compromise was reached in which the Mandate was written in Hebrew as "Palestina (E.Y.)."

References

Ashworth, Gregory John. 1989. "Accommodation and the Historic City." *Built Environment* 15 (2): 92–100.

Ashworth, Gregory John. 2003. "Urban Tourism: Still an Imbalance in Attention?" In *Classic Reviews in Tourism*, edited by Christopher Cooper, 143–163. Clevedon: Channel View.

Ashworth, Gregory John and John. E. Tunbridge. 2000. *The Tourist-Historic City: Retrospect and Prospect of Managing the Heritage City*. Amsterdam and New York: Pergamon.

Ashworth, Gregory John and Stephen J. Page. 2011. "Urban Tourism Research: Recent Progress and Current Paradoxes." *Tourism Management* 32 (1): 1–15.

Ben-Arieh, Yehoshua. 1986. *Jerusalem in the Nineteenth Century: The Emergence of the New City*. Jerusalem and New York: Yad Izhak Ben-Zvi.

Borg, Jan van der, Paolo Costa, and Giuseppe Gotti. 1996. "Tourism in European Heritage Cities." *Annals of Tourism Research* 23 (2): 306–321.

Bowman, Glenn. 1991. "Christian Ideology and the Image of a Holy Land: The Place of Jerusalem Pilgrimage in the Various Christianities." In *Contesting the Sacred: The Anthropology of Christian Pilgrimage*, edited by John Eade and Michael J. Sallnow, 98–121. London and New York: Routledge.

Braun, Bradley M. 1992. "The Economic Contribution of Conventions: The Case of Orlando, Florida." *Journal of Travel Research* 30 (3): 32–37.

Brendon, Piers. 1991. *Thomas Cook: 150 Years of Popular Tourism*. London: Secker & Warburg.

Burtenshaw, David, Michael Bateman, and Gregory John Ashworth. 1981. *The City in West Europe*. Chichester: John Wiley & Sons.

Canestrelli, Elio and Paolo Costa. 1991. "Tourist Carrying Capacity: A Fuzzy Approach." *Annals of Tourism Research* 18 (2): 295–311.

Cohen, Erik. 1992a. "Pilgrimage and Tourism: Convergence and Divergence." In *Sacred Journeys: The Anthropology of Pilgrimage*, edited by Alan Morinis, 47–61. Westport: Greenwood Press.

Cohen, Erik. 1992b. "Pilgrimage Centers: Concentric and Excentric." *Annals of Tourism Research* 19 (1): 33–50.

Cohen-Hattab, Kobi and Jenny Kerber. 2004. "Literature, Cultural Identity, and the Limits of Authenticity: A Composite Approach." *International Journal of Tourism Research* 6: 57–73.

Cohen-Hattab, Kobi and Noam Shoval. 2007. "Tourism Development and Cultural Conflict: The Case of 'Nazareth 2000.'" *Social and Cultural Geography* 8 (5): 701–717.

Collins-Kreiner, Noga. 2009. "The Geography of Pilgrimage and Tourism: Transformations and Implications for Applied Geography." *Applied Geography* 30 (1): 153–164.

Digance, Justine. 2003. "Pilgrimage at Contested Sites." *Annals of Tourism Research* 30 (1): 143–159.

Eade, John and Michael J. Sallnow. 1991. *Contesting the Sacred: The Anthropology of Christian Pilgrimage*. London and New York: Routledge.

Eliade, Mircea. 1959. *The Sacred and the Profane: The Nature of Religion*. San Diego, New York, and London: Haughton Mifflin Harcourt.

Eliade, Mircea. 1969. *Images and Symbols*. New York: Sheed and Ward.

Gatrell, Jay D. and Noga Collins-Kreiner. 2006. "Negotiated Space: Tourists, Pilgrims, and the Bahá'í Terraced Gardens in Haifa." *Geoforum* 37 (5): 765–778.

Getz, Donald. 1991. *Festivals, Special Events and Tourism*. New York: Van Nostrand Reinhold.

Gladstone, David L. 1998. "Tourism Urbanization in the United States." *Urban Affairs Review* 34 (1): 3–27.

Gottdiener, Mark. 2000. *Life in the Air: Surviving the New Culture of Air Travel*. Lanham: Rowman and Littlefield.

Hall, P. 1970. "A Horizon of Hotels." *New Society* 15: 389–445.

Hoffman, Lily M., Dennis R. Judd, and Susan S. Fainstein, eds. 2003. *Cities and Visitors: Regulating People, Markets, and City Space*. Oxford: Blackwell.

Jansen-Verbeke, Myriam. 1985. "Inner City Leisure Resources." *Leisure Studies* 4 (2): 141–157.

Judd, Dennis R. 2003. *The Infrastructure of Play: Building the Tourist City*. New York and London: M. E. Sharpe.

Judd, Dennis and Susan S. Fainstein, eds. 1999. *The Tourist City*. New Haven: Yale University Press.

Law, Christopher M. 1993. *Urban Tourism: Attracting Visitors to Large Cities*. London: Mansell.

Law, Christopher M. 1996. *Tourism in Major Cities*. London: Routledge.

MacCannell, Dean. 1990. *The Tourist: A New Theory of the Leisure Class*. New York: Shocken Books.

Maitland, R. 2008. "Conviviality and Everyday Life: the Appeal of New Areas of London for Visitors." *International Journal of Tourism Research* 10 (1): 15–25.

McKercher, Bob, Noam Shoval, Eric Ng, and Amit Birenboim. 2012. "Using GPS Data to Compare First-Time and Repeat Visitors to Hong Kong." *Tourism Geographies* 14 (1): 147–161.

Mullins, Patrick. 1991. "Tourism Urbanization." *International Journal of Urban and Regional Research* 15 (3): 326–341.

Nolan, Mary L. and Sidney Nolan. 1989. *Christian Pilgrimage in Modern Western Europe*. Chapel Hill, NC: University of North Carolina Press.

Nolan, Mary L. and Sidney Nolan. 1992. "Religious Sites as Tourism Attractions in Europe." *Annals of Tourism Research* 19 (1): 68–78.

Olsen, Daniel H. and Dallen J. Timothy. 2006. "Tourism and Religious Journeys." In *Tourism, Religion and Spiritual Journeys*, edited by Dallen J. Timothy and Daniel H. Olsen, 1–21. London: Routledge.

Page, Stephen J. 1995. *Urban Tourism*. London and New York: Routledge.

Page, Stephen J. and C. Michael Hall. 2003. *Managing Urban Tourism*. Harlow: Prentice Hall.

Pearce, Douglas G. 1998. "Tourist Districts in Paris: Structure and Functions." *Tourism Management* 19 (1): 49–65.

Pearce, Douglas G. 1999. "Tourism in Paris: Studies at the Microscale." *Annals of Tourism Research* 26 (1): 77–97.

Pearce, Douglas G. 2001. "An Integrative Framework for Urban Tourism Research." *Annals of Tourism Research* 28 (4): 926–946.

Prawer, Joshua. 1972. *The Latin Kingdom of Jerusalem: European Colonialism in the Middle Ages*. London: Weidenfeld and Nicolson.

Reader, Ian and Tony Walter, eds. 1993. *Pilgrimage in Popular Culture*. Houndmills, Basingstoke, Hampshire: Macmillan.

Rinschede, Gisbert. 1988. "The Pilgrimage Center of Fatima, Portugal." In *Pilgrimage in World Religions*, edited by Surinder M. Bhardwaj and Gisbert Rinschede, 65–98. Berlin: Dietrich Reimer.

Rinschede, Gisbert. 1992. "Forms of Religious Tourism." *Annals of Tourism Research* 19 (1): 51–67.

Russo, Antonio Paolo. 2001. "The 'Vicious Circle' of Tourism Development in Historic Cities." *Annals of Tourism Research* 29 (1): 165–182.

Russo, Antonio P., Salvador Anton Clave, and Noam Shoval. 2010. "Advanced Visitor Tracking Analysis in Practice: Explorations in the PortAventura Theme Park and Insights for a Future Research Agenda." In *Information and Communication Technologies in Tourism 2010*, edited by Ulrike Gretzel, Rob Law, and Matthias Fuchs, 159–170. Vienna and New York: Springer.

Shachar, Arie. 1995. "Metropolitan Areas: Economic Globalisation and Urban Tourism." In *European Tourism: Regions, Spaces and Restructuring*, edited by Armando Montanari and Allan M. Williams, 151–160. Chichester: John Wiley & Sons.

Shachar, Arie and Noam Shoval. 1999. "Tourism in Jerusalem: A Place to Pray." In *The Tourist City*, edited by Dennis R. Judd and Susan S. Fainstein, 192–200. New Haven: Yale University Press.

Shoval, Noam. 2000. "Commodification and Theming of the Sacred: Changing Patterns of Tourist Consumption in the 'Holy Land.'" In *New Forms of Consumption: Consumers, Media and Commercial Spaces*, edited by Mark Gottdiener, 251–265. Boulder, CO: Rowman and Littlefield.

Shoval, Noam. 2008. "Tracking Technologies and Urban Analysis." *Cities* 25 (1): 21–28.

Shoval, Noam and Kobi Cohen-Hattab. 2001. "Urban Hotel Development Patterns in the Face of Political Shifts." *Annals of Tourism Research* 28 (4): 908–925.

Shoval, Noam and Michal Isaacson. 2007. "Tracking Tourists in the Digital Age." *Annals of Tourism Research* 34 (1): 141–159.

Shoval, Noam and Michal Isaacson. 2010. *Tourist Mobility and Advanced Tracking Technologies*. London and New York: Routledge.

Smith, Valene L. 1992. "The Quest in Guest." *Annals of Tourism Research* 19 (1): 1–17.

Spirou, Costas. 2011. *Urban Tourism and Urban Change: Cities in a Global Economy*. New York: Routledge.

Stansfield, Charles A. and John E. Rickert. 1970. "The Recreational Business District." *Journal of Leisure Research* 2 (2): 213–225.

Towner, John. 1985. "The Grand Tour: A Key Phase in the History of Tourism." *Annals of Tourism Research* 12 (3): 297–333.

Towner, John. 1996. *An Historical Geography of Recreation and Tourism in Western World 1540–1940*. Chichester: John Wiley.

Turner, Victor. 1973. "The Center Out There: Pilgrim's Goal." *History of Religions* 12 (3): 191–230.

Turner, Victor and Edith Turner. 1978. *Image and Pilgrimage in Christian Culture: Anthropological Perspectives*. Oxford: Basil Blackwell.

Urry, John. 1995. *Consuming Places*. London: Routledge.

Van Gennep, Arnold. 1960. *The Rites of Passage*. Translated by Monika B. Vizedom and Gabrielle L. Caffee. London: Routledge and Kegan Paul.

Vukonic, Boris. 1996. *Tourism and Religion*. London: Pergamen.

2   Harbingers of modernization

Pilgrimage and tourism to Jerusalem in the late Ottoman period (1850–1917)

A visitor to Jerusalem in the mid-nineteenth century could not but notice a great commotion on a high hill north of the Old City: in this location, the Russians had begun to build the Russian Compound, later called "Nova Yerusalima" ("New Jerusalem" in Russian). The compound's design was like that of a small city; in the compound were a church, a hospital, hostels for pilgrims, and a home for the Russian consul. The entire area was surrounded by a wall whose gates were locked at night. The thousands of Russian pilgrims who would visit Jerusalem in the coming decades now had an address for their stay in the city.

In essence, the construction of the Russian Compound in Jerusalem is a microcosm, illustrating the state of Jerusalem under the Ottomans at the time. As we will soon see, the city changed immensely—with buildings, infrastructure, and tourism services—as the very face of Jerusalem transformed near the end of the Ottoman control. As we will also see, tourism at the time took on overtly political tones, as various countries encouraged their citizens to help them establish a foothold in this very desirable location.

The overwhelming majority of visitors to Palestine until the nineteenth century had been pilgrims coming out of religious motivation. New access for Western countries transformed the land into one of the central arenas for the development of modern tourism. The European and Jewish influx into Palestine helped stimulate the country's economy, which, from that point on, was exposed to the activities of economic and social groups from various communities.

The changing Middle East

In the mid-nineteenth century the Ottoman Empire began what was, in effect, an extended process of decay and decline. This period marked the end of 400 years of Ottoman rule—and 700 consecutive years of Muslim rule—in the Holy Land. Napoleon's Mediterranean campaign from Egypt to the Holy Land (1798–1799), the Egyptian conquest of the country (1831–1839), and the Crimean War (1853–1856) which pitted the Russians against the Ottomans, British, and French—all signified the Ottoman Empire's military demise and retreat as well as the European powers' increase in strength and foray into the Empire. These trends generated what was called the "Eastern Question," at whose center stood the dilemma of whether the Empire would continue to exist and what its fate would be.

The "Eastern Question" became a predicament relevant to Europe in its entirety, both because the economic interests of European countries had expanded and because of the ramifications that the Empire's fate had on the balance of powers on the continent. The European countries' entry into the Ottoman Empire's territory was not only expressed in their eating into its land; it was also seen in their acquisition of political influence, expansion of trade, and establishment of cultural and philanthropic institutions. The European countries saw these types of activities as a means through which they could expand their influence across the Empire and create a solid base for territorial demands once the Empire was finally dismantled.

In these processes, Palestine was the center of international interest. Alongside the religious, mystical, and romantic draw of the Holy Land, the European powers had begun to rediscover its strategic and military value as a country of passage, as a possible path to India, or as an Eastern border country for the Suez Canal, inaugurated in 1869. Palestine was central: part of the sudden rise in extensive geographical and archaeological discoveries on the Asian and African continents, the object of longing and inspiration for spiritual and cultural streams in the nineteenth-century Christian world. At the end of the Ottoman era, the country also became the focus of the Jewish national and cultural revival and the setting of confrontation between Arabs and Zionist Jews.

The growth of modern tourism in the region—and in Jerusalem in particular—was a central expression of the increasing influence of the Western powers and the weakening of the Ottoman Empire. This was manifest in the proliferation of pilgrimage and tourist institutions that began to appear in the city as an expression of religious and political presence, presence which carried significant and dominant weight in the urban development characterizing the city at the time.

The Holy Land: a tourist destination

The draw of the Holy Land

The Holy Land's appeal near the end of the Ottoman period—each aspect of which played a role in the formation of modern tourism in the region—fell into a number of categories:

The *religious dimension* had drawn pilgrims to the Holy Land during earlier periods. This was especially noticeable in Jerusalem, a city considered sacred to all three monotheistic religions, with many traditions tied to its historic sites. Furthermore, more sites around the country were considered sanctified as time went on, thus evolving into attractions for visitors. Though the holy sites and the nature of visitors to them changed throughout the ages, they were always a significant draw; many travelers who came wished to see them out of a sense of belonging or interest—and not only out of religious obligation.

From a *cultural perspective*, Palestine has always stood out in its extensive and extraordinary historical heritage, which arouses great interest amongst visitors. The modern era has also seen fascinating cultural encounters between a nomadic society and a sedentary one and between Mediterranean and Western culture—primarily that represented by the Zionist movement.

In terms of *geographic location*, the land is on the crossroads of continents and is characterized by a rare variety of natural regions. The country's distinctive climate—beaches coupled with the unique qualities of the Dead Sea, mountainous and lush regions next to arid and warm desert areas, sites of healing and hot mineral springs—all concentrated in one small piece of land attracted additional types of visitors: summer tourists searching for a more pleasant climate, medical tourists seeking Palestine's healing qualities, and tourists focusing on the desert regions.

The Holy Land also became an attraction for *scientific research*, which was expressed in the first survey missions that came following the opening of the land to the countries of the West in the mid-nineteenth century. These delegations were in many cases the executive arm of political elements—mostly world powers—interested in deepening and strengthening their hold on the region within the international power struggles. Thus the scientific interest was more of a tactical political move than it seemed; the opening of the Suez Canal in 1869 and the weakening of the Ottoman Empire only increased the strategic importance of the land and lent to the increased political interest in it (Cohen-Hattab and Katz 2001).

There can be no question as to the Holy Land's singular nature in the realm of tourism; from the end of the Ottoman Empire, with the advent of modern tourism, many different factors, unparalleled anywhere else in the world, injected enormous appeal to the land for visitors from the world over.

A foothold in the Holy City

The focus of the trends in the Holy Land's landscape and culture was Jerusalem, a city whose historical and theological circumstances made it sacred to members of the three monotheistic religions, a long-standing locus of sanctity. Jerusalem was, to a great degree, also the stage for the international politics and the changes in the global balance of power taking place around the world at the end of the nineteenth century. The European arrival and presence; the religious-missionary and consular activity; the improvements in technology, public services, and traffic, in tourism services, media, and lifestyle—all were expressed clearly in Jerusalem. Jerusalem, the central focus for pilgrims in the Holy Land, was the foremost location in which nations demonstrated their increasing influence on the country. The international powers' increased activity and the establishment of many consulates around the city, the paving of the Jerusalem–Jaffa road in the 1860s, and the opening of the Jaffa–Jerusalem railroad near the end of the same century stood out as acts that signaled the seeds of modernization in the city, contributing directly and indirectly to the beginning of modern tourism in the country.

It appears, then, that the weakening of the Ottoman Empire, the improvements in security and transportation conditions, and the desire of the Western powers to demonstrate their presence in Palestine in the nineteenth century were the primary factors enabling the increase in pilgrimages to the land. In the second half of the century, other visitors began to arrive as well; some were cultured European intellectuals, newly termed "tourists," who wished to learn about and see the land rather than coming from purely religious motives. As a result, support services characterizing the early modern tourism industry sprung up: hotels, restaurants, European-style and -caliber cafés, branches of travel agencies, and more (Bar and Cohen-Hattab, 2003).

Jerusalem's attractions: holy places and sites of interest

The late-Ottoman-era visitor could frequent a number of attractions, most notably those of historical and religious significance. Three main attractions stood out, though there were a number of other religious sites to visit as well.

Haram al-Sharif/the Temple Mount

On Haram al-Sharif/the Temple Mount, which even at the end of the Ottoman Empire maintained its status as the sanctified, central location of prayer for Muslims, visits by non-Muslims were forbidden until the mid-nineteenth century; however the prohibition was eased most probably as one of the results of the Crimean War (1853–1856). Growing European influence on the Ottoman Empire and reforms in the Ottoman constitution were also factors in the change (Luke 1932). A few sources note that foreigners were allowed on the mount from that time in exchange for pay; other sources indicate that even after the Crimean War entrance to the site was not necessarily allowed, and at times visitors needed a special permit from the city's pasha. Near the end of the era, it appears, acquiring a permit became a formality. However, the opening of the mount to non-Muslim visitors and trends in the Old City at the end of the Ottoman era did not lead to noticeable changes and improvements (Ben-Arieh 1984). At the end of the Ottoman era, Western visitors to the Temple Mount were advised to find Turkish soldiers to accompany them on their tour of the Dome of the Rock (Dunning 1907), and one of the guidebooks notes that the Ottoman government allowed entry of tourists to the mount only with the accompaniment of a consular representative and a Turkish soldier (Cook 1907).

The Church of the Holy Sepulchre

The Church of the Holy Sepulchre in Jerusalem, the place where, according to Christian tradition, Jesus was crucified and buried, has attracted many pilgrims and visitors ever since its establishment in the fourth century CE. In the centuries that followed, countless descriptions have related the history of the site, the division of rights in the church, the ceremonies that took place there—as well as the conflicts between the Christian communities and the chaos that reigned, at times accompanied by fisticuffs and even injuries and death.[1] The conflicts generally stemmed from competing claims of ownership by the different Christian denominations. This was especially evident at festive events and ceremonies, when masses came together in the church and in the plaza in front of it. Oftentimes the Turkish guard was barely able to restrain the agitated rioters (Ben-Arieh 1984).

A great fire at the Church of the Holy Sepulchre in 1808 served as a turning point for the site. After the fire, which destroyed the great pillars that supported the rotunda dome and caused its collapse, tensions about who would fund repairs erupted between the Orthodox, Catholics, and Armenians. In the end, the Greek

Figure 2.1 Ceremony of washing the Apostles' feet in the entry plaza to the Church of the Holy Sepulchre, between 1898 and 1914 (Matson Collection, Library of Congress).

Orthodox Church was the primary executor of the repairs, donating the majority of the money for the costs of the renovation and in so doing increasing its influence in the church and proprietorship on different parts of the building.

The Western Wall

The Western Wall is recognized as one of the remaining external walls of the Temple Mount, where both Jewish Temples stood. Until the nineteenth century, the number of Jewish worshippers at the Western Wall was limited and prayers at the site had no specific nature. With the growth of the Jewish community in Jerusalem near the end of Ottoman reign, the Wall's status grew and the prayers took on a more fixed character (Ben-Dov *et al.* 1983). The site also began to appear in tourist guidebooks, such as the 1876 Baedeker guide, which advised tourists to visit the Western Wall often, especially on Fridays at four in the afternoon and on Jewish holidays. At those times, the guide states, a heartwarming spectacle can be seen: Jews lean against the Wall, kiss its stones, and cry. The men sit before it for many hours and read from their prayer books (Baedeker 1876).

The continued growth of the Jewish population in the city, coupled with the pilgrims and visitors in the last years of the Ottoman regime, brought worshippers and visitors in growing numbers; the Wall became the central site of worship for the city's Jews.

In the second half of the nineteenth century, a number of suggestions were made to improve conditions in the plaza, including Moses Montefiore's initiative to erect a roof over the prayer plaza, which would protect and shelter the worshippers from the summer heat or winter rain, and the Baron Edmund de Rothschild's plan to purchase a neighborhood bordering on the prayer plaza (the Mughrabi quarter) and lay the groundwork for a larger prayer plaza. Ultimately, none of the proposals was executed (Levontin 1924; Yaari-Poleskin and Steinman 1930; Zuta and Sukenik 1920).

Additional religious sites in Jerusalem

Aside from the central sites that were sacred for members of the three faiths, additional holy places developed in the Old City and its environs, attracting pilgrims and tourists as well. Between the walls of the Old City, for instance, stood the Armenian monastery and St. James Church, which could house thousands of pilgrims at once (Azarya 1987; Ben-Arieh 1984). Jesus' Via Delarosa, which began in the Muslim Quarter and ended at the Church of the Holy Sepulchre, had well-known sites from Christian tradition distributed along its length. The Jewish Quarter held synagogues and houses of learning—in particular, the four Sephardic synagogues, the Ramban synagogue, and the Hurva (Beit Ya'akov) synagogue, to which the Jews of Jerusalem attributed a special sanctified status (Brinker 1941; Luncz 1916; Reiner 1999). South of the Old City near Mount Zion there were sites as well, including the Nabi Daoud mosque, David's Tomb, and the Room of the Last Supper.

Throughout the years of Muslim rule in Israel, entry to David's Tomb was forbidden to non-Muslims. Nabi Daoud was one of the prominent mosques built in Jerusalem outside of the walls, in a location identified as the tomb of David and recognized as a holy site, the entry to which was forbidden to non-Jews. Even in the nineteenth century this prohibition remained, but with time the Dajani family, proprietors of the site's endowment (Waqf), began to allow paid entry. Jews and Christians were only permitted to enter the upper hall—the Room of the Last Supper—and from there it was possible to see the tomb building in the lower hall through a window (Ben-Arieh 1986a).

East of the Old City rose the Mount of Olives, in it the ancient Jewish cemetery and at its feet the Kidron River from which, according to Jewish tradition, the resurrection of the dead would begin with the arrival of the messiah. For Jewish pilgrims, the Mount of Olives was a site that had maintained a continuity of Jewish burial for many generations. Parts of the cemetery had become historic sites of interest, such as the tombstones of Absalom and Zachariah in the valley of Jehoshaphat to the west of the mountain (Avigad 1954; Reiner 1988).

Christianity also relates great importance to the Mount of Olives. Many Christian pilgrims came to see the place where, according to tradition, crucial events related to Jesus' visit to Jerusalem during the last week of his life took place—most importantly, his ascension to heaven after the Resurrection (Limor 1978).

Jerusalem's attractions

Aside from the holy sites, other locations in the city held the interest of visitors. These included Jaffa Gate, which was the most important of the city's gates in terms of transportation and trade. The Grand New Hotel was built in the gate's inner plaza during the 1880s, and stores and cafés were opened in the plaza outside the gate. In preparation for German Kaiser Wilhelm II's visit to the city in 1898, a portion of the wall between the citadel and the gate was removed and a road was paved to the inner plaza (Carmel 1986; Carmel and Eisler 1999; Goren 1998; Yaffe 1985). At the beginning of the century the sebil (public facility for drinking water) was built and in 1907, in honor of the quarter-century of Sultan Abdul Hamid's rule, a clock tower was built above the gate (Ben-Arieh 1986a).

Alongside the city's religious and historical sites, first buds of museum culture appeared in Jerusalem at the end of the Ottoman era. Archaeological galleries and museums had existed in Jerusalem for many generations, primarily in one or two rooms in monasteries and other church institutions, but they were intended for the local Christian population and the visiting Christian pilgrims. More comprehensive museums intended for the general public and visitors appeared in Jerusalem only in the final years of Ottoman rule in the city: at the initiative of Ismail Bai, director of the Board of Education, the municipality established a general archaeological museum in 1901. It resided in a large room in the courtyard of the government school in the Bab el-Huta quarter next to Herod's Gate. In 1911, a museum was established in the Bezalel School of Art (Ben-Arieh 1986a).

The development of roads and transportation

The improvements that began in the roads and transportation in the Holy Land and around the world in the end of the Ottoman era contributed, among other things, to the growth of pilgrimages and tourism to Jerusalem (Cohen-Hattab and Katz 2001; Nance 2007). Until the nineteenth century, transportation to and from Jerusalem was on animals; in the nineteenth century, steamer lines leaving central Mediterranean ports for the beaches of Palestine began to operate (Agstner 1996; Baedeker 1912; Cook 1907; Luncz 1891). These lines brought the land closer to the western beaches and made travel both more practical and safer than it had been in the past. Improved access to Palestine was one of the most important factors in the increase in the number of pilgrims and other visitors.

At the same time, traffic to Jerusalem's sites increased, in particular through the central road coming to the city from the Jaffa port. In 1867, prior to the opening of the Suez Canal, the Turkish sultan gave orders to pave the Jerusalem–Jaffa road; when it was done, passenger carriages began to travel the route. Over the years, the road suffered weather damage and was repaired many times, and, as a result, it was much improved by the end of the 1880s (Ben-Arieh 1984). In Jerusalem itself a "central station" was opened next to Jaffa Gate for carriages, and near the end of the nineteenth century development work was executed both in the gate's inner plaza and in the plaza outside of it. Hotels, travel agencies, tour operators, and more were concentrated at Jaffa Gate, which became the center of trade and business in the city (Baedeker 1912; Ben-Arieh 1984; Hershberg 1977).

Figure 2.2 Photograph of the train in Jerusalem at the end of the Ottoman era (Matson Collection, Library of Congress).

Transportation was reinforced in 1892 with the inauguration of the Jaffa–Jerusalem railroad. The railroad began to carry tens of thousands of pilgrims and visitors between the two cities (Glass 1992; Grunwald 1978). From that time on, Palestine took part in the regional development of railroads and trains, including the Hajj railway, which began to run at the beginning of the twentieth century (Hughes 1981; Pick 1990; Tourret 1989).

The improvements in transportation alongside the increased security transformed travel arrangements to Jerusalem and increased the traffic to the city. The great escalation in the number of visitors to the city was also one of the factors in the development of the city's internal network of roads and urban wagon traffic. The first internal road paved was Jaffa Road, which reached Jaffa Gate; subsequently, other roads within the city developed (Ben-Arieh 1984).

The beginnings of organized tourism

One of the clearest expressions of the improvements in transportation to Palestine was the arrival of organized groups. Visitors were advised to travel to the land in groups both due to economic and security considerations and due to the objective difficulties involved in a private journey (Baedeker 1876). In contrast with the different groups of pilgrims—which came to Israel in the hundreds of years of the Ottoman era and continued to do so at its end—organized tourism caught on primarily as a result of the activities of large commercial travel companies such as Thomas Cook & Son and the American Express Company. These companies organized tourist journeys around the world, bringing tens of thousands of visitors to the Middle East, including Palestine (Brendon 1991; Kark 2001; Swinglehurst 1982; Withey 1997). The tourist groups did not necessarily organize on a religious basis, as characterized pilgrimages, but on social, regional, or professional bases. At times a group was even comprised of an arbitrary collection of individuals.

The pilgrim journey took place in many cases in simpler conditions, both while traveling and during the stay, and economic or social status was not a precondition for participation; the essence was the mere arrival at the holy places. In contrast, those who took part in tourist journeys were usually from the upper middle class. They attributed great importance to their conditions, comfort, and security; thus the cost of this journey was far higher (Bar and Cohen-Hattab 2003; Feifer 1985; Hershberg 1977; Shepherd 1987). Tourists and pilgrims at the time could also be distinguished from one another in their external appearance. Tourist apparel in the groups was Western and modern; in contrast, the pilgrims' was usually far more traditional. Mark Twain attested to this himself following his famous journey to the country in 1867 (Twain 1900).

During the 1860s and 1870s, the first organized journeys to Palestine took place through Thomas Cook & Son and other companies that followed its lead. In order to promote its interests and allow the secure and easy entry of tourists to the land, the company formed economic ties primarily with the people of the Western consulates in the land. Thus, for example, at the end of the nineteenth century Herbert Edgar Clark was the American vice-consul and simultaneously the representative of Thomas Cook & Son in Palestine. From 1895 he also served as the representative and director of the Clark Tourist Company in Palestine, a company founded by his brother in New York (Kroyanker 1985).

Thomas Cook & Son's journeys in Palestine were conducted on horseback and in tent camps that moved from place to place on a daily basis. The camp would be dismantled in the morning and moved to a new location to greet the passengers in the evening. The camps were well equipped, including sleeping tents with beds; dining tents with tables and chairs; and cooking tents with ovens, water tanks, and, of course, cooks. To these were added dozens of donkeys and packhorses that carried the camp's equipment. The group was rounded out by a large staff of mule drivers and servants, as well as guard dogs. The tourist companies or the tourists themselves would usually hire a translator (or dragoman; see below), who also served as tour guide (Cook 1891; Smirek 1973; Spafford-Vester 1950).

Figure 2.3 Advertisement of Cook Travel Company about a journey to Palestine (Thomas Cook Archives).

In Jerusalem, the company would generally house its tourists in a tent camp set up near Jaffa Gate, on a hilltop near Damascus Gate, or on the Mount of Olives (Avitsur 1972; Baedeker 1876; Spafford-Vester 1950). The company owned a house for the storage of equipment and tents between Julian's Way (today's King Solomon Street) and Mamilla (today's Agron Street), which also served as a guesthouse (Kark 2001). Apart from Thomas Cook & Son, a number of other tour agencies operated in Jerusalem at the end of the Ottoman era, most of which were located in the inner plaza of the Jaffa Gate and on Jaffa Road in the area near the city wall (Baedeker 1912).

The number of Christian pilgrims who came to Jerusalem increased from year to year, though the pilgrims' affiliations changed with time. According to estimates, the number reached a few thousand annually by the middle of the nineteenth century; in its second half and the early twentieth century the number reached 10,000 or even 20,000 pilgrims a year. In one case, 1,000 pilgrims even arrived together, in the group of French Catholics known as "Le Grand Caravan de Mille" (the great caravan of 1,000), which came to Jerusalem prior to the Easter holiday in 1882 (Shilony 1994). In the final decades of Ottoman rule, a surge in visits was felt, primarily of Russian pilgrims. Where in the first half of the nineteenth century the majority of the pilgrims were Greek Orthodox and Armenian, in the second half the composition began to change—in particular, the number of Russian and Catholic pilgrims grew. With the advent of modern tourism in the city the Protestant pilgrimage grew somewhat as well (Ben-Arieh 1984; Carmel 1981; Schölch 2006). The peak, it would appear, was in the year 1900, with 11,000 pilgrims; on the eve of the First World War, more than 10,000 Russian pilgrims arrived in the city each year (Hopwood 1969).

It is difficult, however, to gauge the number of tourists who came to the city at the end of the Ottoman Empire due to the fact that there was no organized registration. Sources from that time relate an increase in tourist numbers in the city with the appearance of organized tourism in the 1870s, but the data on numbers of visitors are fragmentary. Thomas Cook & Son, for instance, relates that in 1868–1882 it brought roughly 4,200 tourists to Palestine (Shepherd 1987). From general reports on the entry of pilgrims and tourists to the Jaffa port at the turn of the century, the number of tourists visiting the country was approximately 5,000 per season, and most came from America and Europe. Pilgrim traffic increased in the years prior to the First World War. Estimates put the numbers at between 15,000 and 25,000 (Kark 1984).

Modern Jewish tourism also began to develop in the country, albeit later. The first organized groups began to come to the land in the early 1890s. Groups of Jewish tourists who came to Jerusalem from Europe and England were known as the "caravans" as of the first arrival in 1890. The Jewish settlement in Jerusalem was proud of these caravans, which to their mind proved that Jews also had a part in the city's tourism. Reports indicate that these tourists bought holy objects and souvenirs from the Jewish merchants and thus contributed to the livelihood of the Jewish settlement (Ben-Arieh 1986b; Kark 2001).

The changing face of the city

The new hotel culture

Most nineteenth-century visitors to Jerusalem were pilgrims who tended to stay primarily in monasteries and their communities' public buildings. The increase in the number of pilgrims in the nineteenth century led to the establishment of church hostels in and around the Old City. The most prominent of these were the Casa Nova hostel built next to the Protestant monastery in the Christian Quarter, the Austrian hospice built in the Muslim Quarter, and the Prussian hostel of the German Protestant Johannists built next to the Muristan (Ben-Arieh 1984). The Baedeker guide in the mid-seventies gives details about accommodations in 21 Greek Orthodox monasteries in the Old City. The hostels functioned under the auspices of the churches and Western consulates and were known for their simplicity, their basic conditions, and their low prices (Baedeker 1876).

Hospitality complexes built in the late Ottoman era by the Christian communities and the European powers were only part of their effort to expand their control in the land. The pilgrim oftentimes received financial assistance in the form of a subsidy given by the country of origin for the journey, food, lodgings, and medical aid. The European countries thus made use of pilgrims as a means to increase their control. The Russian government was among the first to invest in building in Jerusalem, going so far as to establish companies that supported pilgrims and assisted them upon arrival in the land and while they toured (Hopwood 1969; Zifroni 1977). At times this was perceived by the countries and their delegates in the land as a type of crusade which, using means such as the cultivation of pilgrimages, would bring the land back into Christian hands (Schölch 2006).

Beginning in the second half of the century, hostels were built for pilgrims outside of the Old City as well. As we saw, the Russians were the first to do this, establishing a number of hostels in a complex called the "Russian Compound," located north of the Old City. These hostels were intended for the Russian pilgrims who had begun to come to the city at the time (Ben-Arieh 1986a; Kroyanker 1987).

However, the increased tourist traffic in the city also included visitors who came independently and in organized groups. Slowly, modern tourist facilities—including modern guest houses and hotels—were added to the city's landscape of monasteries and pilgrim hostels. Guidebooks from the 1850s, 1860s, and 1870s report that two to three hotels operated at the time in Jaffa Gate and Damascus Gate. The most well-known of these were the Mediterranean Hotel next to Jaffa Gate and the Damascus Hotel next to Damascus Gate. In contrast with the hospitality in monasteries and hostels, hotels were privately owned and thus the price was much greater and the service given was on a much higher level (Eliav 1991; Gibson and Chapman 1995; Glass and Kark 1991; Shoval and Cohen-Hattab 2001).

Figure 2.4 Wilson's map, 1864–1864, with the Russian Compound.

In the 1880s, large modern hotels on a European standard began to develop in Jerusalem. The Greek Orthodox built the Grand New Hotel in the Jaffa Gate plaza across from the David Citadel (Spafford-Vester 1950). In the same period, the Feil hotel, which appears to have been the first hotel erected outside the walls, was built on Jaffa Road. A number of other hotels, hostels, and boarding houses followed. In some, European-style restaurants and cafés were opened as well.

At the turn of the century, the demand for modern hotels of a European caliber kept increasing, in particular those built outside of the walls. An important milestone in this field was the establishment of the Fast Hotel. The Fast family, among the original Templars in Jerusalem and pioneers in the city's hotel industry, rented a building from the Armenian Patriarchy in 1907 and opened the first big and modern hotel built outside of the walls, on the Old City's northwestern corner (Kroyanker 1987; Press 1964).

In sections north of the city wall, where the activity of the Arab sector was primarily concentrated, almost no new lodging services opened, neither before the end of the Ottoman era nor in the British period that followed. It is possible that the reason for this was the nature of the Muslim exit from the city walls, which was essentially private and lacked an economic-commercial basis, leaving most of the economic activity within the confines of the Old City (Davis 1999; Kark and Landman 1981).

The first modern Jewish hotel in the city was established by the Kaminetz family. In 1883, Eliezer Lipman Kaminetz (1845–1916) opened a hotel in the home of a banker named Valero, in a building across from the citadel in Jaffa Gate. After several incarnations, the hotel moved to Jaffa Road, across from the Alliance school (Tidhar 1949; Weinberg 1916). The hotel, Hotel Jerusalem (in Hebrew *Beit Eshel*, an acronym for food, drink, and lodging), was considered to be on the European standard. It had luxurious and spacious rooms, good food, a bathhouse, a garden to walk in, and carriages to the guests' destinations. Important and eminent visitors to the city stayed at the hotel, including Theodor Herzl and Baron Edmond de Rothschild. Meetings between Jewish personages from abroad and politicians from the Jewish Yishuv (settlement) in Jerusalem took place at the hotel, and many of the Yishuv's VIPs celebrated their weddings there (Cohen-Reiss 1967; Frumkin 1954; Kroyanker 1987; Press 1964).

A city modernizing

At the end of the nineteenth century, electricity came to Jerusalem and positioned it on the verge of the advanced technological age, which had already been

Figure 2.5 Façade of Fast Hotel (Matson Collection, Library of Congress).

the province of European cities for a few years. Electricity appeared in Jerusalem in 1893, shortly after the arrival of the railroad. It was at the pilgrim hostel Notre Dame de France, recently built northwest of the city walls, that electricity was first installed in the city. In 1911, four locations were known to have electric lighting, including one hotel (Ben-Arieh 1986a; Kroyanker 1987), but Jerusalem was lit by oil lamps and few buildings had their own generators producing electricity until the end of the Ottoman era (Rubinstein 1992).

The evolution of Jerusalem's tourist services

Cafés and restaurants

Cafés and restaurants were intended to serve, among others, the visitors to the city, and their development was directly tied to the increase in tourist traffic. In the first half of the nineteenth century, cafés existed within the Old City, most with a distinctly Oriental style. These were simple places, often situated in squalid-looking rooms at street level, under an archway or behind a partition. In cafés, people would drink coffee and smoke a hookah (Ben-Arieh 1984). A vivid description given at the time illustrates the atmosphere in these places:

> The furnishing of the cafés was sparse: tiny stools, small tables, a number of hookahs, cups for cold water, and small coffee mugs. In the winter, people sat inside and during the summer the stools were places outside the door. At the end of the eighteen-sixties, cafés and restaurants began to appear outside the city walls, primarily near Jaffa Gate in the area next to the wall, also mostly in Oriental style.
>
> (Yehoshua 1966)

The first European hotels built outside the walls brought restaurants and cafés of a European style and standard, but were in the minority relative to their counterparts in the Old City until the end of the Ottoman era (Baedeker 1876).

Early guidebooks for tourists

Another expression of the advent of modern tourism was the appearance of guidebooks for visitors. Useful guidebooks for tourists in Syria and Palestine began to appear in the 1850s; the first of them, it appears, was a guide published by John Murray Publishing in England in 1858. When the flow of tourists to the country grew, the number of printed guidebooks—some of which were in Hebrew—increased. In order to maintain precision and current information new editions were published periodically. The primary objective of these guidebooks was to bring the reader closer to the sights of the Holy Land and provide illustration for the visitor from Western culture, as part of a general nineteenth-century trend to validate the holy writings and Christianity's historical sources. Many of these books included regional and urban maps, some to scale and with accurate sketches, and one can learn about the process of change the land underwent as well as the development of tourism at the end of the Ottoman era by reading them (Ben-Arieh 1986b).

In 1869, a first edition of the Franciscan Liévin guide was published; the first edition of the Baedeker guide dedicated to Jerusalem and its environs was printed in 1876. In the same year, the Cook guide and Luncz's book *Netivot Zion Veyerushalayim* (Paths of Zion and Jerusalem), devoted entirely to Jerusalem, were published. Thomas Cook & Son published a special handbook for travelers to the East in 1872 (Avitsur 1984; Burns 1872). Jerusalem and its sites held a crucial place in these guidebooks; in many, information about the city takes up a good portion of the guide.

The souvenir industry

The increase in pilgrimages and tourism also led to the development of the souvenir and holy objects industry—crafts that Jerusalem's residents had been engaged in for many generations and which served as an important source of income. At the end of the Ottoman era, this was one of the few industries in the city, and its products were some of the city's principal export merchandise. In the last quarter of the nineteenth century, when the number of pilgrims and tourists in Palestine and in Jerusalem in particular had grown, the scope of the gift industry in the city swelled (Ben-Arieh 1984; Finn 1877). Sources at the time note that the Russian pilgrimages created a demand for a souvenir industry, improved the state of light industry and souvenirs, and encouraged trade in the city (Shiryon 1943; Spafford-Vester 1950). The list of products is long: necklaces; crucifixes; objects of worship and souvenirs made of pearls, shells, and olivewood; mezuzah cases; candlesticks for the Jewish Sabbath; etchings of the Western Wall; etchings of saints; dried wildflowers; and more.

At the end of the Ottoman era, the central district for stores selling souvenir objects was on David Street and the passage under the Grand New Hotel. The Baedeker guide from the end of the Ottoman era lists eight souvenir shops in which the highest-quality objects could be acquired: five under the Grand New Hotel, one in the New Gate, one in the Casa Nova hostel, and one on Jaffa Road (Baedeker 1912).

Photography, which seems to have appeared in Jerusalem as early as the late 1830s, was also a developing industry with a commercial dimension, as pictures were made as souvenirs for pilgrims and tourists (Ben-Arieh 1986b; Gibson 2003; Nir 1985; Onne 1980; Perez 1988). A special milestone in this field was the development of the American Colony's photography center and souvenir shop; established by the people of the colony, it was known as the Fredrick Vester and Co. American Colony Store. The store also sold photographs taken by colony photographers. Toward the end of the nineteenth century, colony members even began publishing guidebooks, hosting tourists, and guiding tourists (Ariel and Kark 1996; Gavish 1984; Kroyanker 1985; Shoval 1996; Spafford-Vester 1950).

In the realm of souvenirs, Jerusalem's Jews lagged behind the Christians. Jewish artisans did not have the financial means to prepare a large inventory of merchandise and were thus forced to make do with a limited supply, while the Christian artists, some of whom were wealthy merchants, opened large and organized stores. Moreover, the Arab guides often led tour groups directly to the Arab stores, circumventing the Jewish stores entirely (Hershberg 1977; Shiryon 1943).

The dragoman

As we saw, Palestine in general and Jerusalem in particular were visited by a new type of sightseer beginning in the nineteenth century: the intellectual who came to learn about the land and did not suffice with a visit to the holy sites (Bar and Cohen-Hattab 2003; Shepherd 1987). These visitors were often helped by the local population, who translated the country's language for them, led them on its unfamiliar streets, and at times even provided armed protection from bandits on the roads. A new status quickly emerged: the "tour manager," who took upon himself the provision of riding and pack animals; guaranteed lodgings, food, and a security escort; planned and executed tours; and explained throughout the journey. These people were called "dragomans" in the European languages. The name "dragoman" was no more than a corruption of the Arabic term "tarjuman," or translator (Avitsur 1984). With the increased number of visitors in the region, dragomans organized in ports such as Beirut, Jaffa, or Alexandria, and there were able to meet visitors and offer their services (Browne 1853). Many of the Western visitors to Palestine at the end of the Ottoman era used the dragomans' services and documented their impressions in travel journals. One visitor to Palestine describes the dragomans in the Beirut port offering their services to his delegation in a humoristic tone:

> Morning after morning some gorgeously arrayed interpreter would present himself with a packet of testimonials from those whom he had led in charge through the country, supplemented by his persona, assurances that he was a very polyglot in language, a rival of Soyer in his cookery, a paragon of valour in danger, and the ally and brother of every Bedouin chieftain in the desert. Meanwhile his competitor for our purses would remain at the door, listening eagerly, and taking note of every weak point in his qualifications, which he was sure in turn to make the strong one in his own.
>
> (Tristram 1865)

The dragoman could be Christian or Muslim, native-born or from one of the immigrant groups who settled the land in the nineteenth century. Those traveling with a dragoman for a long period of time were advised to sign a written contract in order to precisely define his obligations to the group and note the agreed-upon payment (Baedeker 1912).

One famous dragoman in Palestine in the second half of the nineteenth century was Rolla Floyd, an American Christian who came to Palestine in 1866 and was one of the founders of the American colony in Jaffa. Floyd began to guide tours in the early 1870s. Due to his fluent English and his expertise in the history of the country he was a most sought-after dragoman amongst American groups—to the extent that they would reserve his services in advance through letters and telegrams. Floyd would usually prepare the equipment, horses, mules, and servants and organize trips of the highest quality. It comes as no surprise that he is often described in sources from the time as the best dragoman in the Holy Land: he knew the country and its customs thoroughly, spoke Arabic fluently, was well-versed in the Bible and quoted it in the correct locations, and, most important, was attentive to the needs and desires of the travelers under his care (Spafford-Vester 1950). In 1876 Floyd was officially appointed representative of Thomas Cook & Son in the East. In those years his reputation was at its peak and he guided many high-profile individuals, military officers, members of parliament, princes, and barons (Floyd 1981; Shepherd 1987).

According to the Baedeker guide, Jerusalem at the end of the Ottoman era had 14 dragomans, most of whom spoke English and at least one other foreign language (Baedeker 1876). Oversight on tour guiding in the city eventually came in the form of a series of courses given to translators in the early 1890s by the British research foundation the Palestine Exploration Fund (PEF), after it became clear that many dragomans were not well-versed in information about the land. In an effort to supervise the tour guiding the municipality even obligated the guides in the city to take a test on material having to do with Jerusalem; those who passed were certified (Ben-Arieh 1986b).

Conclusion

The second half of the nineteenth century was a time of tremendous change for Jerusalem. Political winds and improved transportation led to an increase in tourism; in turn, the increasing number of visitors to the city demanded services and lodgings, transforming the city itself.

The strategic foothold European countries hoped to gain with the demise of the Ottoman Empire, coupled with the unique nature of the city as sacred to members of three religions, made it a destination for thousands. Countries offered assistance and lodgings in Jerusalem to their citizens, eager to expand their physical control in the land.

By the end of the era, with the growing number of tourists and pilgrims, the city's appearance had altered dramatically. The newly paved Jerusalem–Jaffa road—and, later on, the Jaffa–Jerusalem railroad—led visitors to Jaffa Gate. Hostels, hotels, travel agencies began to crop up inside the Old City and outside its walls. The area in and around Jaffa Gate underwent improvements and cafés, stores, and museums opened. Electricity was gradually introduced to the ancient city. Jerusalem was growing at an unprecedented rate.

With all of the changes, the city's economy began to transform as well. The tourist industry flourished as tourists frequented cafés, restaurants, museums, and souvenir shops and paid for tour guides and guidebooks. Seeds of modern tourism were thus seen clearly in the Jerusalem of the end of the Ottoman era and continued to develop with British rule in the city at the end of the First World War.

Note

1 This last statement is true primarily for descriptions of the church in the nineteenth century. See Ben-Arieh 1984, 237–253. On the Christian ceremonies in the church and other sacred Christian sites in the city, see Luke 1932, 1–47; on the place of Palestine and Jerusalem in particular in Christian history and philosophy, see Wilken 1992.

References

Agstner, Rudolf. 1996. "The Austrian Lloyd Steam Navigation Company." In *Austrian Presence in the Holy Land in the 19th and early 20th Century: Proceedings of the Symposium in the Austrian Hospice in Jerusalem on March 1–2 1995*, edited by Marian Wrba, 136–157. Tel Aviv: Austrian Embassy.

Ariel, Yaakov and Ruth Kark. 1996. "Messianism, Holiness, Charisma, and Community: The American-Swedish Colony in Jerusalem, 1881–1933." *Church History* 65 (4): 641–657.

Avigad, Nahman. 1954. *Ancient Monuments in the Kidron Valley* [in Hebrew]. Jerusalem: Bialik Institute.

Avitsur, Shmuel. 1972. *Daily Life in Eretz Israel in the Nineteenth Century* [in Hebrew]. Tel Aviv: Am Hassefer.

Avitsur, Shmuel. 1984. "The First Guides in the Holy Land" [in Hebrew]. In *Zev Vilnay's Jubilee Volume*, edited by Ely Schiller, 413–422. Jerusalem: Ariel.

Azarya, Victor. 1987. "The Armenians in Jerusalem: A Quarter" [in Hebrew]. In *Zev Vilnay's Jubilee Volume*, edited by Ely Schiller, 45–49. Jerusalem: Ariel.

Baedeker, Karl. 1876. *Jerusalem and Its Surroundings: Handbook for Travellers*. London: Dulau.

Baedeker, Karl. 1912. *Palestine and Syria: Handbook for Travellers*. Leipzig: Karl Baedeker.

Bar, Doron and Kobi Cohen-Hattab. 2003. "A New Kind of Pilgrimage—The Modern Tourist Pilgrim of Nineteenth Century and Early Twentieth Century Palestine." *Middle Eastern Studies* 39 (2): 131–148.

Ben-Arieh, Yehoshua. 1984. *Jerusalem in the Nineteenth Century: The Old City*. Jerusalem and New York: Yad Izhak Ben-Zvi.

Ben-Arieh, Yehoshua. 1986a. *Jerusalem in the Nineteenth Century: The Emergence of the New City*. Jerusalem and New York: Yad Izhak Ben-Zvi.

Ben-Arieh, Yehoshua. 1986b. "Nineteenth-century Western Travel Literature to Eretz Israel: A Historical Source and Cultural Phenomenon" [in Hebrew]. *Cathedra* 40: 159–188.

Ben-Dov, Meir, Mordechai Naor, and Zeev Aner. 1983. *The Western Wall*. Tel Aviv: Ministry of Defense.

Brendon, Piers. 1991. *Thomas Cook: 150 Years of Popular Tourism*. London: Secker & Warburg.

Brinker, Dov Natan, ed. 1941. *Jerusalem Yearbook I: The Jewish Quarter* [in Hebrew]. Jerusalem: n.p.

38   *Pilgrimage and tourism in the late Ottoman period*

Browne, John Ross. 1853. *Yusef, or The Journey of the Franji: A Crusade in the East.* New York: Harper and Brothers.
Burns, Jabez. 1872. *Help-Book for Travellers to the East.* London: Cook's Tourist Office.
Carmel, Alex. 1981. "Russian Activity in Palestine during the Late Ottoman Period" [in Hebrew]. In *Jerusalem in the Modern Period,* edited by Eli Shaltiel, 81–116. Jerusalem: Yad Izhak Ben-Zvi, Ministry of Defense.
Carmel, Alex. 1986. "The Kaiser's Album, 1898" [in Hebrew]. *Cathedra* 39: 79–86.
Carmel, Alex and Ejal Jakob Eisler, eds. 1999. *Der Kaiser reist ins Heilige Land: Die Palästinareise Wilhelms II. 1898: Eine illustrierte Dokumentation.* Stuttgart: W. Kohlhammer.
Cohen-Hattab, Kobi and Yossi Katz. 2001. "The Attraction of Palestine: Tourism in the Years 1850–1948." *Journal of Historical Geography* 27 (2): 178–195.
Cohen-Reiss, Ephraim. 1967. *Memories of a Son of Jerusalem* [in Hebrew]. Jerusalem: Sifriyat Hayishuv.
Cook, Thomas. 1891. *Cook's Handbook for Palestine and Syria.* London: T. Cook.
Cook, Thomas. 1907. *Cook's Handbook for Palestine and Syria.* London: T. Cook.
Davis, Rochelle. 1999. "The Growth of the Western Communities 1917–1948." In *Jerusalem 1948: The Arab Neighborhoods and Their Fate in the War* edited by Salim Tamari, 32–67. Jerusalem: Institute of Jerusalem Studies, Badil Resource Center.
Dunning, Harry Westbrook. 1907. *To-day in Palestine.* New York: J. Pott & Company.
Eliav, Mordechai. 1991. "The Case of Shimon Rosenthal: Apostasy, Return to Judaism and Relapse" [in Hebrew]. *Cathedra* 61: 113–132.
Feifer, Maxine. 1985. *Tourism in History: From Imperial Rome to the Present.* New York: Stein and Day.
Finn, James. 1877. *Byeways in Palestine.* London: J. Nisbet.
Floyd, Rolla. 1981. *Letters from Palestine: 1868–1912.* Edited by Helen Palmer Parsons. Dexter, ME: s.n.
Frumkin, Gad. 1954. *The Way of a Judge in Jerusalem* [in Hebrew]. Tel Aviv: Dvir.
Gavish, Dov. 1984. "The American Colony and Its Photographers" [in Hebrew]. In *Zev Vilnay's Jubilee Volume,* edited by Ely Schiller, 127–144. Jerusalem: Ariel.
Gibson, Shimon. 2003. *Jerusalem in Original Photographs 1850–1920.* Winona Lake, Ind.: Eisenbrauns.
Gibson, Shimon and Rupert L. Chapman. 1995. "The Mediterranean Hotel in Nineteenth-Century Jerusalem." *Palestine Exploration Quarterly* 127: 93–105.
Glass, Joseph B. 1992. "Joseph Navon Bey's Contributions to the Development of Eretz Israel" [in Hebrew]. *Cathedra* 66: 87–110.
Glass, Joseph B. and Ruth Kark. 1991. *Sephardi Entrepreneurs in Eretz Israel—The Amzalak Family, 1816–1918.* Jerusalem: Magnes Press.
Goren, Haim. 1998. "Preparations in Jerusalem for the German Emperor's Visit" [in Hebrew]. In *For the Sake of Jerusalem,* edited by Haim Goren, 200–202. *Ariel* 130–131. Jerusalem: Ariel.
Grunwald, Kurt. 1978. "Origins of the Jaffa-Jerusalem Railway" [in Hebrew]. In *Chapters in the History of the Jewish Community in Jerusalem,* edited by Menachem Friedman, Ben Zion Yehoshua, and Yosef Tobi, II:255–265. Jerusalem: Yad Izhak Ben-Zvi.
Hershberg, Avraham Shmuel. 1977. *In the Land of the East* [in Hebrew]. Jerusalem: Yad Izhak Ben-Zvi, facs. edition.
Hopwood, Derek. 1969. *The Russian Presence in Syria and Palestine: Church and Politics in the Near East, 1843–1914.* Oxford: Clarendon Press.
Hughes, Hugh C. 1981. *Middle East Railways.* Harrow: Continental Railway Circle.

Kark, Ruth. 1984. *Jaffa—A City in Evolution, 1799–1917* [in Hebrew]. Jerusalem: Yad Izhak Ben-Zvi.

Kark, Ruth. 2001. "From Pilgrimage to Budding Tourism: The Role of Thomas Cook in the Rediscovery of the Holy Land in the Nineteenth Century." In *Travellers in the Levant: Voyagers and Visionaries*, edited by Malcolm Wagstaff and Sarah Searight, 155–174. London: Astene.

Kark, Ruth and Shimon Landman. 1981. "Muslim Neighborhoods outside the Jerusalem City Walls during the Ottoman Period" [in Hebrew]. In *Jerusalem in the Modern Period*, edited by Eli Shaltiel, 174–211. Jerusalem: Yad Izhak Ben-Zvi and Ministry of Defense.

Kroyanker, David. 1985. *Jerusalem Architecture—Periods and Styles: Arab Buildings outside the Old City Walls* [in Hebrew]. Jerusalem: Keter.

Kroyanker, David. 1987. *Jerusalem Architecture—Periods and Styles: European-Christian Buildings outside the Old City Walls* [in Hebrew]. Jerusalem: Keter.

Levontin, Zalman David. 1924. *To the Land of our Fathers* [in Hebrew]. Tel Aviv: Eytan and Shoshani.

Limor, Ora. 1978. "Christian Traditions of the Mount of Olives in Late Antiquity and the Early Middle Ages" [in Hebrew]. Jerusalem: Master's thesis, the Hebrew University of Jerusalem.

Luke, Harry Charles. 1932. *Ceremonies at the Holy Places*. London: Faith Press.

Luncz, Avraham Moshe. 1891. *Guide to Eretz Israel and Syria* [in Hebrew]. Jerusalem: A. M. Luncz.

Luncz, Avraham Moshe. 1916. *Eretz Israel Yearbook: Informative and Literary* [in Hebrew]. Jerusalem: A. M. Luncz.

Nance, Susan. 2007. "A Facilitated Access Model and Ottoman Empire Tourism." *Annals of Tourism Research* 34 (4): 1056–1077.

Nir, Yeshayahu. 1985. *The Bible and the Image: the History of Photography in the Holy Land, 1839–1899*. Philadelphia: University of Pennsylvania Press.

Onne, Eyal. 1980. *Photographic Heritage of the Holy Land, 1839–1914*. Manchester: Institute of Advanced Studies, Manchester Polytechnic.

Perez, Nissan N. 1988. *Focus East: Early Photography in the Near East (1839–1885)*. New York: H. N. Abrams.

Pick, Walter Pinhas. 1990. "Meissner Pasha and the Construction of Railways in Palestine and Neighboring Countries." In *Ottoman Palestine 1800–1914: Studies in Economic and Social History*, edited by Gad G. Gilbar, 179–218. Leiden: E. J. Brill.

Press, Yeshayahu. 1964. *A Hundred Years in Jerusalem: Memories of Eretz Israel* [in Hebrew]. Jerusalem: Reuven Mass.

Reiner, Elchanan. 1988. "Pilgrims and Pilgrimage to Eretz Yisrael, 1099–1517" [in Hebrew]. Jerusalem: PhD diss., the Hebrew University of Jerusalem.

Reiner, Elchanan. 1999. "'Since Jerusalem and Zion Stand Separately': The Jewish Quarter of Jerusalem in the Post-Crusade Period (13–15th Centuries)" [in Hebrew]. In *Studies in Geography and History in Honour of Yehoshua Ben-Arieh*, edited by Yossi Ben-Artzi, Israel Bartal, and Elchanan Reiner, 277–321. Jerusalem: Magnes Press, the Hebrew University of Jerusalem, the Israel Exploration Society.

Rubinstein, Danny, ed. 1992. *Light for Jerusalem: The Story of the Jerusalem Electric Corporation* [in Hebrew]. Jerusalem: Israel Electric Corporation.

Schölch, Alexander. 2006. *Palestine in Transformation 1856–1882: Studies in Social, Economic and Political Development*. Washington, DC: Institute for Palestine Studies.

Shepherd, Naomi. 1987. *The Zealous Intruders: The Western Rediscovery of Palestine*. London: Collins.

Shilony, Zvi. 1994. "The Activities of Comte de Piêllat in Palestine (1884–1925)" [in Hebrew]. *Cathedra* 72: 63–90.

Shiryon, Yitzchak. 1943. *Memories* [in Hebrew]. Jerusalem: the author's son.

Shoval, Noam. 1996. "Swedish Activities In and Around Jerusalem at the Beginning of the Twentieth Century" [in Hebrew]. *Cathedra* 81: 61–74.

Shoval, Noam and Kobi Cohen-Hattab. 2001. "Urban Hotel Development Patterns in the Face of Political Shifts." *Annals of Tourism Research* 28 (4): 908–925.

Smirek, Robert A. 1973. "The Beginning of Tourism to Palestine" [in Hebrew]. *The Second Million: Israel Tourist Industry, Past-Present-Future*, edited by Chaim H. Klein, 21–24. Tel Aviv: Amir.

Spafford-Vester, Bertha. 1950. *Our Jerusalem: An American Family in the Holy City, 1881–1949*. Garden City, NY: Doubleday.

Swinglehurst, Edmund. 1982. *Cook's Tours: The Story of Popular Travel*. Poole Dorset and New York: Blandford Press.

Tidhar, David. 1949. *Encyclopedia of the Pioneers and Builders of the Yishuv* [in Hebrew]. 19 vols. Tel Aviv: Sifriyat Rishonim.

Tourret, Richard. 1989. *Hedjaz Railway*. Abingdon, Oxon GB: Tourret.

Tristram, Henry Baker. 1865. *The Land of Israel, a Journal of Travels in Palestine Undertaken with Special Reference to its Physical Character*. London: Society for Promoting Christian Knowledge.

Twain, Mark. 1900. *The Innocents Abroad*. London: Collins Clear-Type Press.

Weinberg, Mordechai. Gershon. 1916. *Rabbi Eliezer Lipa Kaminetz* [in Hebrew]. Jerusalem: Frumkin.

Wilken, Robert L. 1992. *The Land Called Holy: Palestine in Christian History*. New Haven and London: Yale University Press.

Withey, Lynne. 1997. *Grand Tours and Cook's Tours: A History of Leisure Travel, 1750–1915*. New York: W. Morrow.

Yaari-Poleskin, Jacob and Eliezer Steinman. 1930. *Edmond de Rothschild (The Well-Known Benefactor)* [in Hebrew]. Tel Aviv: Hapoel Hatzair.

Yaffe, Binyamin. 1985. "Kaiser Wilhelm II's Visit to Palestine and Reactions in the British Press" [in Hebrew]. *Kivunim* 27: 43–51.

Yehoshua, Ya'akov. 1966. *Childhood in Old Jerusalem: Chapters of Lifestyle from Past Days* [in Hebrew]. 5 vols. Jerusalem: Reuven Mass.

Zifroni, Gavriel. 1977. "'Red' Russians and 'White' Russians in Jerusalem" [in Hebrew]. *Cathedra* 5: 162–195.

Zuta, Hayyim Aryeh and Eleazar Lipa Sukenik. 1920. *Our Land: A Guidebook to Eretz Israel and Neighbouring Countries* I [in Hebrew]. Jerusalem: The Zionist Commission.

3 When West meets East

Tourism in Jerusalem under British
rule (1917–1948)

December 11, 1917, was a typical autumn day for Jerusalem. However, the 200 meters General Edmund H. Allenby strode from Jaffa Gate to the internal citadel gate, where he gave a festive speech on the occasion of the conquest of Jerusalem from Ottoman control, represented the dawn of a new day for Jerusalem. From a peripheral city in the Ottoman Empire it would quickly become the country's capital once again. A line of British planners would arrive, helping devise Jerusalem's rapid urban development. Jerusalem would become Mandatory Palestine's center of politics and enlightenment, but would also hold a renewed function within the battles over its sacred spaces and over the pilgrim routes. In parallel, the foundations of tourism would expand to a scope and quality never before seen in the city.

In the coming pages, we examine the development of tourism in Jerusalem during the time of British rule. In the first section, we study the evolution of the city—the increase in tourist arrivals and the resulting changes in tourist infrastructure and city attractions. In the subsequent section, the use of tourism as a tool in the contentious reality that existed—with Jews and Arabs struggling for political recognition—is examined in depth.

Mandate-era Jerusalem: a new type of tourism

In the history of the Middle East, the years between 1917 and 1948 constituted a fateful era. On the ruins of the "sick man on the Bosphorus"—the crumbling Ottoman Empire—a new political map was shaped by the Allies, Great Britain and France. Four hundred consecutive years of Ottoman rule had ended and Palestine was seized and ruled by Britain, at the time a Western European industrial and imperialist superpower with a democratic-parliamentary regime.

The era of British reign was a revolutionary and intense one in the chronicles of the country and Jerusalem: the British delineated the political and administrative boundaries of the country, restored it from the physical ruins wrought by the First World War, and stimulated its economic development and modernization in many realms. The growth and change were unmistakable in the country's physical infrastructure and public services, and great progress was evident in the realms of commerce and the manufacture of a variety of consumer products—all of which made possible and influenced the development of tourism in Palestine.

Much of the work of the British centered around new transportation and communications infrastructure to and within the country. This was primarily expressed in the development of railway infrastructure; in the overhaul and maintenance of the existing roads and their adaptation for the needs of advanced motor transportation; in the building of a communications system that was reliable and current, including post, telegraph, and telephone; in the modification of ports to the changing needs; and in the development of airports. All of these activities aimed to create a more developed physical infrastructure which, though intended first and foremost to aid the British government's activities, was nonetheless enjoyed by the local residents and the visitors who entered the country's gates. In reality, tourism in Palestine in the period of British reign would not have developed had the British authorities not cultivated the transportation and communications infrastructure in the country.

The new tourism trends in British-ruled Palestine were clearly expressed in Jerusalem, and the mark of that period is still visible today. The British recognized the historical and international heritage of the city and its importance to members of the three monotheistic religions. They established Jerusalem as the capital of Palestine, leading to many changes in its status. The British were the first to prepare an urban plan, which was, among other things, intended to preserve the city's special character, to regulate its preservation, and to direct future development. The city began to see new cultural and leisure centers. Another milestone was the opening of large hotels, foremost the King David Hotel, the first international-standard hotel in the country. International companies opened branches in the city, and local private initiatives cropped up—the appearance of boarding houses, the development of food services, the establishment of travel agencies, and the creation of an industry of tour-guiding services were all signs of the times.

Tourist traffic to Jerusalem during the Mandate era

Inbound tourism

Official Mandate sources list the numbers of tourists arriving in the country during 1926–1945 alone; a division between Jewish and non-Jewish tourists exists only from 1933 on. Similarly, existing data contain no details on visitor traffic to the country by region or city. Yet Jerusalem's centrality to tourists in the country at that time is unquestionable. Thus our working assumption is that the vast majority of tourists in the country found their way to Jerusalem.

Sources indicate that tourist traffic to Jerusalem grew in the early 1920s and reports state that many groups of tourists roamed the city streets.[1] The year 1925 was the first to see a substantial swell in tourism, during which some tens of thousands of tourists—evidently more than 50,000 people—visited the country.[2]

The Mandate government's Department of Statistics' data regarding the entry of tourists to the country for the years 1926–1945 are presented in Figure 3.1:[3]

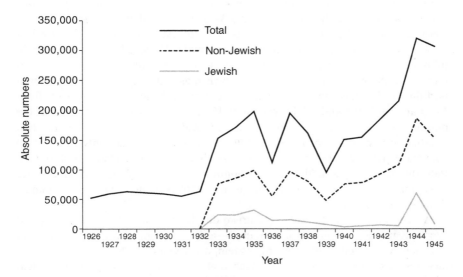

Figure 3.1 Inbound tourism to Palestine, 1926–1945.

The figure presents a moderate increase in tourism between 1926 and 1928, and an ensuing decrease, with 1931 the low point for tourism in the country in the Mandate era. These fluctuations, we may speculate, were connected to Palestine's internal conditions: before the 1929 riots the domestic situation was relatively calm, with an atmosphere that was conducive to a certain amount of growth in tourism traffic.[4] Conversely, the period after the riots and the international economic crisis of 1929—the Great Depression, which severely affected many countries directly and indirectly and led to the collapse of international markets—resulted in the slowing of tourist traffic to the country (Gross 1984). However, from the year 1932 and on a sharp increase was once again seen in the number of tourists.

Between 1932 and 1935, a surge was felt in the overall number of tourists arriving in Palestine. The first Maccabiah games, held in April 1932, and the Levant Fair, held that same year, had no small part in this. Many event participants went sightseeing around the country and, of course, in Jerusalem.[5] A peak was recorded in 1935, when nearly one hundred thousand tourists arrived in the country. This trend, it can be assumed, was also connected to the fact that these were years of growth, prosperity, and expanding economic activity for Palestine (Gilbert 1996, 129–139; Gross 1982a, 171–172; Gross 1982b, 139–140; Gurevich *et al.* 1944, 18; Horowitz 1948, 15–26).

However, subsequent years were less promising for tourism: in 1936 the number of tourists plummeted to nearly half of the 1935 arrivals. A recovery was felt in 1937[6] and this steep incline is plainly evident in the country's economy and balance of payments;[7] however, in the two subsequent years, until the end of the riots in the country (1936–1939, the years of the Arab Revolt) and the outbreak of the Second World War in 1939, there was once again a sharp decline in the number of tourists. The lowest point was 1939, with just 47,446 tourists entering the country (Horowitz 1948, 21).[8] The decline in inbound tourism in the years leading up to the Second World War was not only absolute but relative to outbound tourism as well—apparently in no small part due to the shaky internal security situation in those years. However, from 1940 and until the end of the war in 1945, there was a very steep rise in the number of entries to the country, which peaked in 1945 with more than 150,000 tourists (153,665).[9] Jewish tourism (noted in the data only from 1933) showed a peak in 1935 and a gradual decline thereafter; from 1938 and on Palestine's military situation, the economic conditions of Jews abroad, and the hazy political situation in most European countries made travel to the country difficult for most Jews.

A good portion of the inbound tourism during the years of the Second World War was in reality "tourism in fatigues"—allied soldiers who were stationed in the country, defined in state records as temporary visitors. These soldiers—military reinforcement based on the fear that Rommel's German armies, then advancing toward Palestine and Egypt, might invade—began arriving in the country at the beginning of the 1940s. The presence of these soldiers contributed a great deal to the country's economy in general and to the growth and prosperity of some of the tourist services in particular. In these years, some 100,000 soldiers served in the country on a regular basis, and tens of thousands of others came temporarily for training, courses, vacation, and recovery (Gelber 1995, 412–416; Nathan *et al.* 1946, 589–591; Samuel 1970, 190–194; Sherman 1997, 127–173).

During the war years domestic tourism also grew. The prohibition against leaving the country and the closing of its gates for military reasons reinforced the need to develop domestic tourism, and entertainment and leisure sites appeared around Palestine (Department of Statistics 1946, 45, table 18; Gross and Metzer 1999, 300–324).

Thus the inbound tourist traffic to the country during the British Mandate period had two principal waves: the peak of the first wave was recorded in the mid-1930s, as part of the economic prosperity in the country at the time. The outbreak of the events of 1936–1939 and the Second World War in 1939 led to a decrease in the scope of tourism in the country. In the years of the Second World War a second wave of tourists came to the country, a good portion of which was made up of allied soldiers.

A tally of the total number of visitors reveals a substantial increase of some hundreds of percent in the number of visitors to Palestine relative to the end of the Ottoman period. In the last decades of Ottoman rule in the country, a surge had been felt in pilgrim traffic. According to some estimates, their numbers in the first half of the nineteenth century reached several thousand a year, while in the second half of the century and in the early twentieth century the number reached 10,000 and even 20,000 pilgrims each year. The peak was, it would appear, in the final years before the First World War, when the number of pilgrims visiting the country was estimated as between 15,000 and 25,000 a year.[10]

In contrast, in the years under discussion (1926–1945) nearly 1,600,000 people visited the country, putting the annual average at nearly 80,000. Even taking into account that during the years that do not appear in the Department of Statistics' publications (the first years of the British Mandate until 1926 and the last three years of its reign), the number of visitors was no doubt lower than the annual average, the average number of visitors per year in the Mandate period was some tens of thousands greater than the average number of visitors at the end of the Ottoman period.

Tourism in Jerusalem: bed nights

The increase in tourism can be further studied by looking at average length of stay (in days) of different visitors to the country (between 1938 and 1945) with a breakdown by religion; the picture painted by these figures is presented in Table 3.1:[11]

The most noticeable trend is that all tourists' average duration of stay decreased over the years. This can be attributed, among other things, to the improvement in transportation during the British Mandate period, which enabled people to travel from place to place in a relatively comfortable and swift fashion. This trend had a direct effect on the various tourist services as well, as they were forced to contend with visitors' shortening duration of stay.

The data further indicate that the stay of Muslim visitors was the shortest—a fact connected, it would seem, to the places of origin of most Muslim visitors, who came from neighboring countries and returned to them shortly thereafter. The average Jewish duration of stay was the longest, most probably due to the relatively large distance they had to traverse in order to visit the country; when they arrived they stayed longer than the Muslim and Christian visitors before beginning their journey home. Christian tourists had an average duration of stay that was closer to the Muslim average, possibly connected to the country being, for some, only one stop in a wide-ranging journey to many countries in the region, a fact that shortened the length of their stay in Palestine. These hypotheses are supported by Department of Migration data regarding travelers

Table 3.1 Average duration of stay of tourists in Palestine, members of three religions

Year	Jews	Muslims	Christians	Total
1938	35.7	16.6	13.9	19.4
1939	34.6	15.3	19.1	20.8
1940	31.2	9.4	17.4	12.1
1941	26.0	8.9	20.5	11.7
1942	20.8	12.3	15.8	13.4
1943	19.4	8.4	12.5	9.6
1944	18.7	7.9	11.0	8.8
1945	19.4	7.5	11.2	8.6

between 1935 and 1945 who required transit visas. More than 166,000 such visitors entered the country, half of them Christian (84,111 people, approximately 50 percent), many of them (72,505 people, approximately 43 percent) Arab (most probably Muslim), and a small minority Jewish (9,561 people, or 6 percent).[12]

If we multiply the data on duration of stay by the number of tourists we can extrapolate the annual number of overnight stays. In contrast with the number of tourists, which in reality notes only the number of entries to the country, figures about overnight stays teach us about the tourists' stays in actuality. These figures can also better teach us about the tourism trends in the country in those years and about the corresponding development of tourist services.

Figure 3.2 demonstrates that it was actually the year 1938 that recorded the largest number of overnight stays in the period between that year and the end of the Second World War. Thus, despite the growth in number of tourist entries in the war years (as presented in Table 3.1), practically speaking there was no increase in the number of overnight stays, a fact that supports the claim that the majority of those entering the country during the time of the war were what was known as "tourism in fatigues" and not tourists in the accepted sense of the phrase.

A new city: sweeping changes in Jerusalem's urban geography

The increase in visitors during the Mandate period occurred in parallel with the changes in Jerusalem's urban geography. In this section, a selection of developments in the city is presented. Later in the chapter we take a look at the changes at Jerusalem's main attractions and the way in which they accorded with the

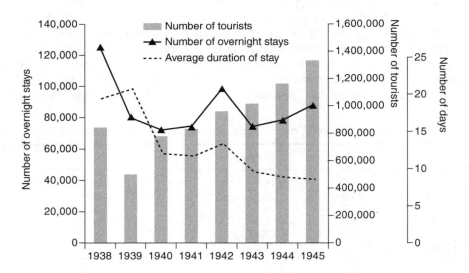

Figure 3.2 Number of bed nights of all tourists, 1938–1945.

characteristics of tourists visiting the city during the period. The emergent reality in Jerusalem's holy sites during the time of the Mandate was, of course, a function of the British regime and its attitude to the city's sacred and historical sites. This was expressed in the adoption of the status quo principle at holy sites, in the various plans introduced by the British, and in the activities of the government's Department of Antiquities.

The status quo was adopted, in effect, on the very day Jerusalem was conquered, December 11, 1917. On the plaza at the base of the David Citadel, General Allenby, commander of the military, expressed Britain's desire to preserve the status quo in the holy places; practically speaking, this meant freedom of worship in the places sacred to members of the three religions, as had been the case during the Ottoman Empire (Berkovitz 1978, 24–33; Cust 1930). This act helped form bonds of trust and cooperation between representatives of the communities on one hand and the central British rule and its affiliates on the other during most of its years of rule in the city.

New plans made by the British focused on the city's future development, establishing several principles that helped develop tourism and increase the city's appeal (Hyman 1992; Shapiro 1973). In the first years of British rule two comprehensive master plans and one preliminary detailed outline were composed: the first urban master plan by William McLean was published in July 1918; following that, a second plan was created by Patrick Geddes in 1919. In 1922, Geddes and Charles Ashbee composed the first outline.[13] In later years, two additional detailed outlines were composed by Clifford Holliday (1930) and Henry Kendall (1944) along the same lines.

In all of these plans, several of the principles that helped preserve, direct the development of, and organize the city's space in the years of British rule were expressed:

- The Old City was specified as the city's historical and architectonic focus but not its functional one—it was not destined for renewed building but rather for preservation.
- The development of the new city moved west along two main urban development axes, one toward the south and the other to the north-northwest.
- A transportation system was drafted based on the train's entry from the south; roads in five directions—Gaza, Jaffa, Nablus, Jericho, and Hebron—were integrated in the internal traffic of the city using radial and ringed links.
- Restrictions on permitted building height and materials were proposed, ultimately making it impossible to build in any material other than stone.
- A basic division of the city to residential areas and commercial areas, with a designated subdivision for business in the form of offices, workshops, and industry, were suggested.
- Other areas around the city were defined as green, open areas and were forbidden for building, primarily the ridge of the Mount of Olives to the east of the Old City, a green strip around the Old City walls, and the public parks in

residential areas. Ranges of greenery were planned along the road to Nebe Samuel in the north and along Jaffa Street. The Russian Compound and Mamilla park were also designated greenery areas, and parks were established near the Monastery of the Cross and around the Schneller Orphanage (Biger 1981, 21–22; Kendall 1948, 4–10).

The final two outlines, Holliday's and Kendall's, were the first to designate special areas for archaeological preservation with the supervision of the Department of Antiquities. This was the case primarily in the area of the City of David and the Tombs of the Sanhedrin (Shapiro 1973, 145, 147).

Over the course of British rule in Jerusalem the city grew and spread in all directions. In this brief period, some one hundred thousand residents joined the city, many new neighborhoods and public buildings were built in both new neighborhoods and old ones, the area of the city tripled in size and reached 63 square kilometers, and its urban landscape was formed. At that time Jerusalem was also named the country's capital, a function it had not filled since the fall of the first Crusader kingdom in 1187 (Biger 1989, 183–216; Eisenstadt 1998, 38–55).

At the initiative of the first high commissioner, Herbert Samuel, a governmental Department of Antiquities was founded in 1920.[14] The department was charged with the preservation of the sacred and historical sites in the city and its unique cultural spirit; a law of antiquities was passed in 1920, giving the department the authority to care for historical and archaeological sites around the country. The department also ran salvage excavations in advance of development and construction, took care of artifacts discovered in the excavations, and was involved in the establishment of a number of governmental archaeological museums around the country. The most prominent of these, known as the Palestine Archaeological Museum (or the Rockefeller Museum), was established in Jerusalem (Fawzi 2006; Luke and Keith-Roach 1922, 80–82). This range of activities contributed both directly and indirectly to Jerusalem's preservation, to its cultivation as a city with unique cultural characteristics, and in this way to its establishment as an international and local tourist city as one.

Jerusalem's attractions: changes during the British Mandate

In order to review the city's primary sites in light of the development of tourist infrastructure, we will focus on its three main religious foci—the Church of the Holy Sepulchre, the Temple Mount/Haram al-Sharif, and the Western Wall— through which we can examine the changes that took place in the central attractions in the city during British rule. To use the terms of modern tourism research, these three sites constitute the city's central tourism district, the areas in the city that are common to most visitors, visited by the various groups despite the differences in their attitudes to the same shared space. In the remainder of the city's sites segmented spaces were created—each of the sites not located in the "central tourism district" was visited by a different group of people with a set of unique characteristics (Bowman 1991; Shachar and Shoval 1999).

The British took great pains to ensure a tranquil atmosphere at holy sites. On weekdays police officers could be found at the sensitive religious places in order to ensure calm and public order. In securing the three main holy sites in the city, the police adopted a defined general policy: they attempted to send Arab officers to Haram al-Sharif, Christian officers to the Church of the Holy Sephulchre, and near the Western Wall they took care to maintain a mixed guard of Jewish and Arab officers.[15]

THE CHURCH OF THE HOLY SEPULCHRE

During the period of British rule, the Church of the Holy Sepulchre was one of the city's major attractions—for pilgrims, for tourists, and even for the many allied soldiers who visited the holy sites in the Old City and its surroundings.[16] No organized data exist on the number of tourists who visited the church at the time, but the site's importance is expressed in guidebooks, tourist maps, and the tourist itineraries offered by travel agents and agencies, in which a visit to the church held a prominent place; it is thus safe to assume that many of those who came to the city visited it.

The church's centrality for visitors is also expressed in the different preservation activities that took place over the years. The church was protected as part of the Ottoman status quo; consequently, with the antiquities law of 1920, responsibility for its preservation (like other historical buildings in the city) was transferred to the Department of Antiquities (Great Britain, Colonial Office 1925). The Department of Antiquities' assessed the church early on, expressing the need to take care of the church's façade decorated in the Crusader period—in particular the trimmings on the lintels above the entrance to the church[17]—which had experienced wear and tear over time.[18]

The Department of Antiquities' responsibility for preservation was put to a real and decisive test around the mid-1930s, when the church's structure began to crumble and there was a concern it would collapse completely. The fear for the well-being of the worshippers and visitors led the Department of Antiquities to summon William Harvey, a renowned British expert in preservation of old buildings, to thoroughly check the structure of the church and propose practical steps for stabilizing and refurbishing it.[19] Harvey arrived in the country in September 1933; in a detailed professional review, he determined that certain parts of the church could collapse at any moment and that immediate action was necessary.[20]

The building's physical state worsened until the Department of Antiquities chose to temporarily stabilize the church in 1935, using iron scaffolding that covered almost the entire façade and wood scaffolding in the internal part of the rotunda (Hoade 1946, 143). Furthermore, in early April 1938, prior to the Easter celebrations, the Department of Antiquities decided to close the building on the grounds that it was a danger to the public.[21] Visiting the church was thereafter only possible on holidays and even then only for a select few, primarily clergy.[22] Other visitors were forced to suffice with looking in from the outside at the church, still in scaffolding and frequently closed until the end of the Mandate period.

Aside from criticizing the scaffolding and the "disfigurement [of] the façade" (Matson 1946, 146), it was not uncommon for visitors to voice criticism of the internal appearance of the church. During this new period, in which a Western, European-oriented regime heralded a new spirit in the country, many tourists found the artistic taste that characterized the interior of the church and its displays jarring. Some described what they saw inside the church as it compared to Western aesthetics: a collection of displays without a guiding hand, most notably cheap displays alongside royal gifts, dark lighting in many unsightly lamps, and more (Conway 1923, 149; Farmer 1945, 64–84; Martelli 1938, 206–209; Weatherhead 1936, 234).

Some Mandate-era changes were also evident in the religious rites that took place in the church. According to descriptions, the sense of religious emotion and power that accompanied the rites in the Church of the Holy Sepulchre during the Mandate period was akin to the mood that had prevailed in earlier periods. The religious rites, which were the source of attraction and interest for many pilgrims and visitors, preserved their character for generations. However, in contrast with the past, the British paid closer attention to maintaining public order in the Church of the Holy Sepulchre, primarily on the holidays which included religious rituals (Farmer 1945, 182–184; Holliday 1997, 44–45; Morton 1935, 329–333). The British, advocating public order and etiquette and in the spirit of Allenby's declaration and the Mandate charter, saw it as their obligation to hold the rites according to clear standards. In religious ceremonies and events that took place in the city and around it, members of the three religions kept relative calm and coordinated with the police and army, who were put on alert, especially during Easter week (Lumby 1934, 118; Luke 1932, 17–47; Samuel 1970, 58–59).[23]

HARAM AL-SHARIF/THE TEMPLE MOUNT

For hundreds of years Jerusalem, like Palestine as a whole, was under Muslim rule, and thus the city's religious significance for its rulers was primarily Muslim. The holiest places for Muslims in Jerusalem were in the plaza of Haram al-Sharif (known to Jews as the Temple Mount)—the Dome of the Rock and the Al-Aqsa mosque, which were sites of pilgrimage for Muslims in the country and outside of it. These places were under Muslim control from the seventh century, when Muslims conquered the country (with the exception of the days of Crusader control of the city), until the British arrived. Only in the second half of the nineteenth century were visits to the site made possible for non-Muslims.[24]

Shortly after British military rule was established in Jerusalem, initial contact was made between the authorities and the Muslim Waqf. A professional relationship existed between the employees of the mandatory Department of Antiquities and the administration of the Waqf throughout the period of the British Mandate. Supervisors from the Department of Antiquities were given unlimited access to almost all places on the mount and they were permitted to measure, document, and conduct preservation and monitoring surveys even in the Dome of the Rock and the Al-Aqsa mosque.[25]

During the period of British rule, Haram al-Sharif and the Church of the Holy Sepulchre were considered the two most important sites in Jerusalem and the most highly recommended for visits in the city.[26] The Dome of the Rock and Al-Aqsa mosque were sources of wonder and awe for visitors, who praised the Dome of the Rock and saw in it one of the most impressive buildings in the world.[27] And indeed, until the events at the Western Wall in the late 1920s, a trend of liberalization was evident on the part of the Supreme Muslim Council toward the visits of non-Muslims in Islamic holy places, Haram al-Sharif in particular. In the absence of a detailed listing, we can state that according to general estimates, several hundred Muslim pilgrims arrived at the mount each year from neighboring Arab countries and from countries like Persia and India.[28] The mount also welcomed domestic visitors; several tens of thousands of Muslim visitors came to the mount each year from Jerusalem itself, the city's environs, or other regions in the country.[29]

The renewed interest in Haram al-Sharif in the early 1920s led the Supreme Muslim Council to reorganize the visiting procedures and hours (Kupferschmidt 1987, 237). The council printed a short guide in English in 1924 (*A Brief Guide to al-Haram al-Sarif*) and later published several more editions in a number of languages.[30] The guide states that the site is open from 7.30 in the morning every day but Friday. Visitors are asked to leave by 11.30 in order not to disturb midday prayers. Entry is paid and the fee is collected at the Chain Gate. The guide also notes that visitors must be aware that the site as a whole—and not just the buildings—is sacred for Islam and therefore its sanctity must be respected; in particular, one must refrain from smoking in the entire area and not enter with dogs. The end of the guide includes a map indicating the central sites on the mount. At certain times, the council allowed allied soldiers to enter the plaza free of charge. Photography was permitted in the outdoor plaza but not inside the buildings (Farmer 1945, 85).

THE WESTERN WALL

In keeping with the trend that began near the end of Ottoman rule, the interest of Jews, pilgrims, and visitors in the Western Wall as a symbol of Jewish culture continued to grow during the period of British rule, and this was emphasized in tour books published during the Mandate period (Elston 1929, 134; Hoade 1946, 234; Luke and Keith-Roach 1922, 95; ibid. 1930, 123; Luke 1924, 128–129; Lumby 1934, 138–139; Maisler and Yeivin 1940, 218–219; Matson 1946, 180–181; Vester 1920, 130–131; Zuta and Sukenik 1920, 85).

In the case of the Western Wall, as in the case of other religious sites, the involvement of the British in the goings-on at the Wall's plaza derived from its desire to preserve the rights of the different religions at holy sites as much as possible and to ensure free access and freedom of worship. [31]

In August 1929, a series of violent acts against the Jews began as a result of a conflict over the right to pray at the Wall; 133 Jews were killed by Arabs and many were injured or lost their possessions. In the years following the 1929 riots and in the spirit of the regulations set regarding the Western Wall in "His Majesty's Order in Council, 1931," law and order was maintained in the plaza, including on holidays (Urnstein 1968, 246).

Beginning with the installation of electricity at the Wall's police station in 1944, physical improvements were made to the plaza and its surroundings and part of the plaza was lit as well (Urnstein 1968, 339). Furthermore, a path was paved to the plaza from the southwest, in addition to the old path that arrived at the Wall from the northwest (Maisler and Yeivin 1940, 218). This path greatly improved the accessibility to the Wall for worshippers and visitors (Urnstein 1968, 243).

In the 1930s and 1940s, the number of visitors—foreign and domestic—to the Wall increased; the vast majority of the public visiting was, of course, Jewish worshippers, primarily around the holidays. From the events journal kept by the Western Wall supervisor on behalf of the Chief Rabbinate and the national institutions it appears that the most intensive days of prayers and visits at the Wall were the days of Passover. Each year, between three and four hundred thousand people visited the Wall, and during the holidays the number of visitors was between 30 and 50 percent of the yearly total (Urnstein 1968).

The greatest change in religious sites during British rule was their adaptation to suit increasing tourist demand. The British regime, a major agent pushing for the preservation and cultivation of these sites from its arrival in the city, was in no small part responsible for this. British policy endorsed continuity in the internal running of the sacred places as per the status quo, but at the same time saw a need to make changes and instill new norms in the city's primary sites in two main realms: (1) keeping public order in the sacred spaces and guaranteeing the rights of each community to hold religious ceremonies; and (2) preserving the municipal space while emphasizing religious and historical sites. The new norms that the British brought to the city created more appropriate conditions for the arrival of additional visitors and the development of modern tourism in Jerusalem. This set the stage for the new attractions that appeared, transforming the existing landscape.

New attractions in Jerusalem

Our discussion of the new attractions during the period of British rule focuses on culture and leisure centers. Of the new attractions at the time, two buildings stand out in their effect on the changing city: the Palestine Archaeology Museum (Rockefeller Museum) and the YMCA building. Both played a prominent role in the tourist infrastructure that developed in the city at that time.

THE PALESTINE ARCHAEOLOGY MUSEUM

One of the primary functions of the British Department of Antiquities was to supervise the archaeological activity in the country and establish a museum to preserve and display the various findings. In 1925, American millionaire John D. Rockefeller was persuaded by his friend, Orientalist and Egypt researcher James Henry Breasted, to donate the sum of two million dollars for the establishment of an archaeological museum in Jerusalem.[32] The Archaeological Museum was the Department of Antiquities' magnum opus in the country's museology, and was considered of vital importance in the preservation and display of antiques uncovered during the period of British rule. As one of the city's new attractions, its establishment had an important influence on Jerusalem's tourist status.

The conditions for Rockefeller's donation to the establishment of the museum were agreed upon in late 1927. The main features: the Mandate government would donate the land called Karm al-Sheikh located at the northeast corner of the city wall and extending over an area of eight acres for the building of the museum; the municipal incinerator nearby would be permanently moved; and the land near Karm al-Sheikh would be included in Jerusalem's municipal plan. The new museum's collections would include any material that could shed light on the history of humankind in the land of Palestine, and findings from nature would be included only insofar as they related to human activities in antiquity. Thus the museum would be an archaeological institution and not a nature museum. It was further agreed that the establishment of the museum and its administration in the future were the responsibility of the Mandate government, in consultation with an international steering council in which the government would place its trust. In return, Rockefeller agreed to raise a donation of two million dollars no later than January 1, 1931; the first million dollars were to be given for establishing the building and purchasing equipment and the second million for funding the ongoing activities of the museum and the Department of Antiquities.[33]

Following negotiations, the Mandate government purchased a little over eight acres of land from the al-Halili family for the price of 15,500 Palestine pounds.[34] High Commissioner Plumer created a special division within the Department of Public Works to deal solely with the construction of the building, funded by the Rockefeller Foundation. Architect Austen St. Barbe Harrison, the Mandatory government's chief architect at the Department of Public Works during the years 1923–1937, was asked to design the building.[35] Harrison toured Europe in order to closely examine its renowned museums and spent several months studying building practices in the Old City.[36] The cornerstone was laid on June 19, 1930, construction was completed at the end of 1937, and the museum was opened to the public on January 13, 1938 (Zusman and Reich 1987, 55–56).[37] The story of the museum's construction and a warm recommendation to visit it were included in nearly all of the city's guidebooks printed from then on (see, for example, Maisler and Yeivin 1940, 224–225; Matson 1946, 37–38; Vilnay 1946, 106–108).

The data on the number of visitors to the museum indicate that from its opening in 1938, when 600 people came on average each month, there was a general and gradual increase in the number of visitors, peaking in 1943 with more than 4,000 visitors each month. From 1944 and on, the number of visitors declined; in the final years of the Mandate, the numbers—though fragmentary—present a notable drop. Similarly, the data indicate that the number of visitors each day was low in the first two years, but from the beginning of the 1940s it was estimated at more than 100 people a day on average. The total number of visitors to the museum over the course of a decade stood at more than 284,000, with an average 2,368 visitors each month.[38]

As noted above, many of those who entered Palestine in the Second World War as tourists were in fact allied soldiers. It is therefore likely that a good if not great portion of the visitors to the Palestine Archaeology Museum in the war years were allied soldiers who came to the city alone or in groups, and that the museum was an important part of their touring route in Jerusalem.

The appearance of the museum in tourist maps and guidebooks, and the available data regarding the number of people visiting over the years, indicate that the museum took an increasingly important place in the tourist map in the city (Gilbert 1996, 137). The museum constituted a landmark—both in the role of archaeology in Jerusalem's tourist infrastructure generally and in museum culture in particular. The fact that archaeological findings were being viewed by a heterogeneous public that was willing to pay money for it taught the Department of Antiquities that archaeological sites and artifacts could be transformed into an economic lodestone.[39] During the period of the divided city (discussed in the next chapter), the museum continued to serve as an archaeological museum; the Jordanians even displayed the Dead Sea Scrolls discovered in the caves at Qumran there (Katz 2005, 132–135).

THE YMCA BUILDING

The impressive and stately building belonging to the Young Men's Christian Association became one of Jerusalem's central cultural centers in the Mandate period. The association, founded in London in 1844 with the aim of emphasizing the development of each person's spirit, soul, and body, established centers to further its goals in different places around the world.[40]

The Jerusalem branch of the association was first established in January 1878 in order to hold activities consistent with the goals of the association (YMCA 1933, 19–21; YMCA n.d., 2–3). The association worked out of rented buildings in the city and its members met several times during the Ottoman period, but information about its activities during those years is scarce (see YMCA 1933, 19–20; YMCA n.d., 2–3). The British conquest in 1917 provoked the association to act, giving it a chance to supply its services in the realms of guidance and hospitality to the many allied soldiers in the land, among other things. During the days of military rule, association members in Jerusalem led tours to historical and religious sites for more than 50,000 soldiers on vacation in the city. For some of the forces stationed west of the Holy Trinity Church in the Russian Compound, the association supplied tents and temporary cabins (YMCA 1933, 22). At the same time, the association published guidebooks for visitors.[41]

In the early 1920s, the association purchased a plot of land from the Greek Orthodox Church, roughly seven acres in size, at the upper part of the Nikephoria area along what is today King David Street. American architect Arthur Loomis Harmon, one of the Empire State Building's planners, was charged with designing the building. In July 1928 the cornerstone was laid in the presence of High Commissioner Plumer, and in April 1933 General Allenby inaugurated the building, emphasizing the newly established center's contribution to the relationship between Jews, Christians, and Muslims in the city.

The building was considered the most impressive and striking of YMCAs the world over. Its design and ornamental façade expressed the aspiration to make the building a social and cultural center for the city's three monotheistic religions (Avusher 1981, 172–173; YMCA 1933, 21–24).

The YMCA building's appearance in the city's landscape and the association's activities for all three religions in the city—primarily in the realms of culture, education, and sport—constituted a real contribution to the city's attractions and was one of the most prominent cultural innovations to take place in Jerusalem at the time.

From its establishment, the new building drew the attention of many groups. The association's education committee in the city was aware of this and saw fit to integrate within its lecture series a lecture on the special characteristics and symbolism of the new building.[42] For the guidebooks, inclusion of the building in the descriptions of the city was an imperative. The excitement about the building's style and ornamental components is palpable in the books; they also recommend a trip to the top of the observation tower from which one can see the city's spectacular view.[43] This was the first observation tower built in the western part of the city and was in itself an attraction for visitors.

In September 1930 the YMCA opened a course for members who wished to be trained as tour guides. During the course, 21 lectures were given on a variety of topics representing an assortment of fields that a tour guide at the time would need to know. The lectures were, among other things, in the field of tour-guiding methodology, archaeology, architecture, historical geography of Jerusalem in different periods, and museology. Particularly noteworthy were the lectures given by Mr. Salma on "What a Guide Must Know," Dr. Herzberg on "Identifying Ancient Buildings and Holy Places," Mr. Keith-Roach on "Being a Guide," Dr. Mayer on "Temple Mount Sites" and "the Israeli Museum of Archaeology," and Dr. Canaan on "Folklore in Sacred Places." A passing grade on the final exam earned the graduate YMCA certification as a tour guide. Twenty-three students took the course.[44]

Guest rooms were built on the second and third floors of the building, intended primarily for young Christian members of the association coming to the land to work for the association. However, tourists who were not association members were also allowed to use the hostel services if there were vacancies.

During the Second World War, the YMCA's activities in Jerusalem were tied mainly to the allied soldiers who served in the city or visited it. The association ran tours around the city for them, opened an information office in the building primarily intended to help them find places to stay, and prepared itself to deal with a growing stream of visitors who wished to go up the observation tower. For most of the time, the hostel rooms were at almost full capacity. Guests were primarily soldiers, and the association was forced to turn many away due to lack of space.[45]

The YMCA building was a social and cultural center for many of the soldiers; the billiard tables, bar, library, reading room, writing room, and game room were almost always full and supplied the soldiers with a homey atmosphere. Many musical evenings took place under the auspices of the YMCA.[46] In effect, the war years made the YMCA the most prominent cultural center in the western part of the city. This is well illustrated by the number of events held in the building and the number of organizations and institutions (apart from the YMCA) who used its facilities, primarily the large auditorium: in 1943 alone more than 100 organizations held 265 different events in the building—an average of 22 events a month.[47]

Yet near the end of 1945, with the decrease of forces in the country, a decline in the number of soldiers in the city and a simultaneous slowdown in association activities and hospitality were reported.[48] The explosion at the adjacent King David Hotel in July 1946 led to the restriction of the association's activities for a number of months, and from that point on use of the building for cultural purposes continually decreased until the end of the year when a 50 percent decrease in demand for the building and accommodations was reported.[49]

The increase of tourist services in Jerusalem: accommodations

As an outgrowth of the increased tourist flow to Jerusalem, related support services developed over the years. In the coming pages, we discuss the trends in the field of hospitality. This realm is the essential one for examining the changes in the city; as opposed to other developing services, such as food, hospitality is the only field dedicated to the tourist alone.

No significant changes took place in Jerusalem's traditional accommodations—monasteries and church hostels—during the Mandate period; for the most part they continued to work in the format of eras past (Duff 1938, 212; Morton 1935, 34). Accommodations during the Mandate period consisted of three different types of establishments: The first were large hotels with more than 100 rooms, of an international style and standard not seen before in the city. Prominent examples of these are the King David Hotel and the Palace Hotel. The second type were the mid-sized and small hotels—the small with only a few rooms, the mid-sized, a few dozen. The third type consisted of boarding houses; most had only a few rooms, the larger ones had a few dozen units.[50]

Large hotels

One of the first hotels to renew its activities after the British conquered the city was the Fast Hotel,[51] which was, as noted earlier, one of the first modern hotels built in Jerusalem outside of the walls, near the end of the nineteenth century. In the first days of military rule in the city, the hotel was run by the British army and primarily served different military commanders visiting the city.[52] In the early 1920s, Jewish hotelier George Barsky leased the hotel from the Armenian Church—the building's owner—and the hotel's name was changed to the Allenby Hotel.[53] The hotel was one of the most technologically advanced buildings in Jerusalem at the time, with private facilities in the rooms, flowing hot and cold water, central heating, and electricity; it was the only building in the city at the time with a telephone.[54] A café in the hotel served as a cultural center in Jerusalem in the early days of British rule. Its auditoriums housed lectures, parties, dances, and orchestral performances in the early 1920s.[55]

In order to examine Jerusalem's new large hotels during the era of British rule, we will look at two hotels established at the time: the King David Hotel and the Palace Hotel.

THE KING DAVID HOTEL

The founders of the King David Hotel were the Mosseris, a Jewish family originating in Cairo and Alexandria. The family owned a bank that held Egyptians Hotels Ltd.; the company owned a chain of hotels in Egypt, including the Shepherds and Continental Savoy in Cairo and the Mena House near the pyramids at Giza. A combination of Jewish sentiment and business sense led the Mosseri family to plan a first-class hotel in Jerusalem after the First World War. In 1921 they founded the Palestine Hotels Company, which was registered in Jerusalem in 1929. In order to fund the hotel's construction, the company sold shares primarily to Egyptian businessmen and to wealthy Jewish companies and individuals around the world.[56]

Five hundred meters west of the Old City, overlooking the city walls, the Mosseri family purchased more than four acres from the Greek Orthodox Church for 31,000 Palestine pounds. Swiss architect Emil Vogt planned the building in cooperation with local architect Benjamin Chaikin and interior designer and architect G. H. Hufschmid. The building, rectangular in shape, was built from local pink limestone and its façade was designed as an elegant entryway. It contained 200 rooms and 60 bathrooms. The Swiss architect was asked to design the internal spaces to reflect the cultural atmosphere of the period of King David, and Hufschmid used motifs and trimmings from the world of ancient cultures, primarily Assyrian, Hittite, and Phoenician, integrating the Arab-Muslim style as well.

Construction on the hotel began in July 1929, and in January 1931 the hotel opened its gates. The hotel's inauguration was an extraordinary event, replete with pomp and splendor. Some 500 guests came to the ceremony, including representatives of the different religious communities in the city, government officials, judges, bankers, and other public figures. The local press reported that:

Aside from the many invitees, amongst the prime ministers and residents, many guests from abroad, especially Egypt, were present: directors of hotel companies, bank directors, the director of the sleeper car company in Egypt, the director of the "Egyptian Bourse," the Austrian consul in Egypt, and others. The hotel was impressive with its elegance and refinement, the likes of which had not yet been seen in the country.[57]

Unfortunately, hard times in the country left their mark on tourism and hotels, and the owners had no choice but to close the gates in the first summer of its operation. Only in 1933, with the economic recovery, did the hotel begin to turn a profit, and its reputation grew.[58]

The hotel incorporated Middle Eastern and European cultures in a variety of ways. Food arrived at the hotel each evening on a special train that made its way daily from Cairo and back. A good portion of the employees and waiters were from Egypt and Sudan, dressed in jellabiyas (traditional Arab garments) and white gloves, with a red fez on their heads. The management was Swiss and an Italian chef ran the kitchen.[59]

The list of guests who stayed at the hotel over the years, which can be found in the hotel's guest book, is extraordinary, and bears witness to the hotel's centrality during Jerusalem's evolution to an international tourist city beginning in the early 1930s. From the start, the King David Hotel was considered the most prestigious hotel both in the city and in the country; as such, it hosted kings, queens, princes, statesmen, Zionist and Arab leaders, film stars, authors, artists, and more.[60]

Construction of the King David Hotel was a central landmark in the development of urban tourist infrastructure and in the hotel field: while other hotels had operated in the city before, this was the first time a prestigious and stately hotel was built, a hotel whose services were on the level of a first-class European hotel, part of an international chain.

The King David Hotel became the symbol of Jerusalem, a cosmopolitan meeting place that facilitated social connections between military and civilian ranks. Formal and informal gatherings between high-society Englishmen, Jews, and Arabs at the time often took place in the grand halls or around the hotel's famous bar, and balls were held in the hotel to the strains of the most popular and accomplished orchestras (Lazar 1990, 52, 108, 112, 117; Sherman 1997, 164–165).

THE PALACE HOTEL

The Palace Hotel, also one of the largest and most grandiose in Jerusalem during the Mandate period, was built by the Supreme Muslim Council at the end of the 1920s. In 1928, the council resolved to use donations remaining from the restoration of Haram al-Sharif to build an elaborate hotel on the order of the large hotels built in capital cities in the West and East (Kupferschmidt 1987, 136–137). The establishment of the hotel, which was the largest construction project undertaken by the Supreme Muslim Council during the Mandate period, illustrates, inter alia, the increase in Arab tourism to the city—primarily from neighboring Arab countries—and the importance the council attributed to the trend (Reiter 2003, 359–360).

The hotel was built on Mamilla Road, on the seam between the Old City and the western part of the new city, which underscores the increasing importance of the urban development in the range overlooking the Old City from the west, particularly the various tourist services.[61] The building was designed by a Turkish architect[62] who created a large corner building with four floors and an impressive façade decorated with stylish and luxurious stone details. The hotel contained 140 rooms, 45 of them equipped with facilities, as well as an elegant restaurant, a bar, three elevators, and central heating.[63]

The building's inauguration took place on December 22, 1929.[64] However, the hotel's bad luck was apparent soon after its opening, when it became clear that the Supreme Muslim Council was unable to operate and maintain the hotel; its construction costs had deviated from the original plan, totaling 73,500 Palestine pounds as opposed to the planned 56,000 (Reiter 2003, 360). The nearby King David Hotel also made things difficult for the Palace Hotel in its early days. Early in 1930, the Palace Hotel was leased to Jewish millionaire George Barsky, who, as we saw, already owned the Allenby Hotel at the time. Though the agreement between Barsky and the council set a long lease period,[65] it appears the building ceased to serve as a hotel in the mid-1930s and was leased to the British government as office space.[66]

One of the prominent characteristics of the large hotels built in Jerusalem during British rule was their geographic location: they were in high and central compounds in the western and northwestern parts of the city, near the wall of the Old City and its central tourist sites. Similarly, and unlike some of the large hostels that were established outside of the walls intended mainly for pilgrims (the Notre Dame hostel across from the New Gate, for example), the large hotels were established primarily for the use of upper-class tourists. From the mid-1930s and on, with the increase in tensions, some of the hotels contained offices of the British government, primarily due to their central locations and large dimensions. Furthermore, while many of the mid-sized and small hotels were rented spaces, the large hotels were built to be hotels and were more permanent.

The opening of several large hotels in Jerusalem in the early 1930s, the King David included, was considered a milestone, the beginning of high-level hospitality services relative to other places in the world (Stead 1931, 27).

Mid-sized and small hotels

The second type of accommodation, the mid-sized and small hotels, developed at the same time near the roads outside of the Old City walls. As stated, no organized data exists regarding the number of beds in the city's hotels at the time, but generally it can be said that these hotels contained an average of a few dozen rooms.[67]

In contrast with the large hotels primarily serving the wealthy foreign tourists, the mid-sized and small hotels served both inbound and domestic tourists comprising all religions and classes: military, merchants, lawyers, students, housewives, engineers, doctors, teachers, officials, and even farmers (Genach-owski 1993, 310–313). In these hotels, as in the large hotels, technological innovations were often introduced; many hotels, primarily the mid-sized ones, boasted a telephone, electric lighting, central heating, flowing hot and cold water, bathrooms and the like, which were not yet found in private homes.[68] Many of the mid-sized hotels had a large room or a conference hall that could hold receptions, balls, wedding, and public and private events.[69] These were often of a folksy, local nature relative to the prestigious events that took place in the city's large hotels.[70] Some mid-sized hotels belonged to local chains developed at the time and were owned by individuals or families.

One example is the hotel chain established around the country and owned by the Jewish Warshavsky family. The first of the family members to work in the hotel industry was Todros Warshavsky, born in Jerusalem in 1877 and one of the pioneer hoteliers in the city. After the Second World War, Warshavsky leased the *khan* (caravansary) at Sha'ar Hagai, located on the main road between Jeru-salem and Jaffa, moving there with his family. Light meals and care of animals were available (Halevi 1989, 331–332). In 1921, Todros established the family's first hotel in Jerusalem on St. Paul Street (today Shivtei Israel Street) and in 1927–1928 he established the Tel Aviv Hotel (later the Ron Hotel) at 44 Jaffa Street (Kroyanker 2005, 235–237).

Todros had six sons, four of whom—Israel, Saul, Abraham, and Morde-cai—worked in the hotel business. Israel established the Atlantic Hotel on the corner of Ben-Yehuda and Mordecai ben-Hillel streets in the 1930s. The hotel operated for 18 years and was completely destroyed in the February 22, 1948, explosion on Ben-Yehuda Street. Saul ran the Ron Hotel. Abraham and Mor-decai were in charge of the Palatin Hotel on 4 Agrippas Street in Jerusalem. Todros had purchased the land for the Palatin Hotel and began to build it in 1935, but the riots in the 1930s made the economic situation worse, and he was forced to sell the building to the Kokia family and rent the hotel from them (Zacharia 1985, 3–6).

The mid-sized and small hotels in Jerusalem included, of course, the Arab hotels; however, information about them is scarce. Sources show that these hotels were smaller on average than the Jewish ones in the same category. The Sa'ada Hotel, for example, was designed for 12 to 15 visitors and the Al-Lakhanda al-Jedida contained 40 beds.[71] One of the relatively large Arab hotels was the Petra Hotel in Jaffa Gate, at the entrance to David Street, which had 50 beds in 22 rooms.[72] Visitors to the Arab hotels in the city were usually Muslim, rural, small merchants from the cities and villages around Jerusalem; from farther points in the country such as Jaffa and Haifa; or from neighboring countries such as Syria and Transjordan.[73] The hotels owned by the Greek Orthodox Church, such as the Bayt al-Maqdis and the Al Lakhanda al-Jedida Hotel, both in the first alleyway to the left of the entrance from Jaffa Gate, had, according to reports, a higher standard of services and middle-class guests.[74]

Boarding houses

The boarding houses, the third type of accommodation that developed at the time outside of the Old City walls, were found primarily in the Jewish garden suburbs such as Rechavia, Beit Hakerem, and Talpiot (Biger 1977). Usually they had several rooms for rent; a few had several dozen rooms. The boarding houses were distinguished from the hotels in their limited size; moreover, their cultural atmosphere and the special intimacy that prevailed in them set them apart. In contrast with the hotels, the visitors were a heterogeneous group with varied purposes to their visits. Guests at boarding houses were unmistakably domestic— from the country's local Jewish population and even from Jerusalem itself. Those who stayed at the boarding houses came for relatively long periods of time: many came for vacation and rest, hoping to walk around the streets and parks; some came for business, social involvement, or political activity. Generally, these guests were not interested in the historical and religious sites in the city,[75] thus this type of hospitality was better suited to areas that were far from the city's traditional attractions.

Jerusalem's boarding houses can be best understood by examining the boarding houses in the Beit Hakerem neighborhood, in the city's west. Beit Hakerem was one of the Jewish garden suburbs founded in the early 1920s in Jerusalem. The neighborhood, like other garden suburbs, was planned by architect Richard Kaufmann. Kaufmann designed the neighborhood on a relatively large area. Each of the residential units was allocated a comparatively wide piece of land, on which an open area was designated for planting a garden and trees. Along the central roads in the neighborhood, trees were planned and space was devoted to public parks. From its establishment, the neighborhood's appearance was a central component of the life in it. A committee was established in the neighborhood, responsible for planting, public parks, and anything related to its verdant appearance. Within a few years, the neighborhood was bathed in greenery; the shade of the trees and the clear air that characterized it became its emblems and the main attractions for vacationers. From the beginning of the 1930s, when vacationers began to arrive, the neighborhood was on the tourist map in Palestine generally and in Jerusalem in particular.[76]

Two types of boarding house infrastructure developed in the neighborhood: a rented room in a home and a boarding house that rented rooms. Thus, for example, in March 1943 the neighborhood had 13 boarding houses and 55 homes that rented rooms.[77] In its 1944–1945 report, the neighborhood committee stated that vacationers stayed at its boarding houses and in rented rooms for approximately 40,000 days;[78] the 1945–1946 report registered 45,000 days.[79]

The neighborhood committee was also charged with marketing the neighborhood throughout the country as a place of rest. Using advertisements, publications, and articles in the press, the neighborhood was presented as the ideal place to spend an annual vacation. Moreover, the committee turned to the Carmel Film company to create a movie about the neighborhood, which was screened at cinemas around the country. The neighborhood committee printed a series of postcards of the view and of quiet corners in the neighborhood, which served as a means of marketing and an additional source of income.[80]

Part of the process of institutionalizing the vacation phenomenon in the neighborhood was the establishment of the Vacation and Neighborhood Improvement Committee in the early 1940s. Some of its activities included signage on the streets and boarding houses, taking care of cleaning, organizing cultural activities in the neighborhood such as concerts and lectures, collecting vacation tax, and preparing statistics about the vacationer traffic in the neighborhood for the purpose of taxation and supervising prices.[81] The vacation activity in Beit Hakerem led to the establishment of cafés and places of entertainment in the neighborhood as well. The Har Aviv House was well known for its courtyard café, which became a neighborhood cultural center with concerts, exhibits, lectures, dancing, and more.[82]

In the absence of organized data from which to create a precise cartographic picture of the development and distribution of accommodations, we present a picture of the hospitality and recreation services in the city in the first half of the year 1940 as surveyed by David Amiran. The map does not distinguish between the sizes of the accommodations, but the geographical dispersion that appears shows four prominent concentrations of hospitality services that developed in the city: Jaffa Gate and its immediate surroundings, Julian's Way, the triangle area (Ben-Yehuda Street, King George Street, and Jaffa Road), and the Jewish garden suburbs (see Figure 3.3).[83]

From the records of hotels and boarding houses in some of the address and phone books of the time a fairly clear picture about the development of accommodations in Jerusalem during the British rule period appears: From the beginning of the period a gradual growth in the number of hotels and boarding homes in the city is noticeable. The peak of this trend appears in the mid-1930s. In the 1920s, it was primarily the number of hotels that grew, while the number of boarding houses was relatively low. From the early 1930s a more massive increase in available accommodations took place: the number of hotels grew by 50 percent and the number of boarding houses grew threefold and more (Oriental Advertising Company 1920, 173–174; Pevzner 1926, C:71–72; Trade and Industry 1932, 278–248).

The end of the 1930s and the 1940s were characterized by a large decrease in the available accommodations in the city, primarily the number of hotels; at the end of that period the numbers were similar to the numbers in the mid-1920s. The number of boarding houses also dropped, though more moderately. It is possible that one of the reasons for this was the shaky military situation during the last years of Mandatory rule, which primarily affected the hotels. Boarding houses had several noticeable advantages: they were generally found in private homes, so the operating costs were far lower than those of hotels; thus they could survive the difficult years and at times still supplement the owners' livelihood. Another advantage came from their geographical location: they were found primarily in areas that were far from the center of the city, where the increased military activity took place. The difficult time for accommodations in the city

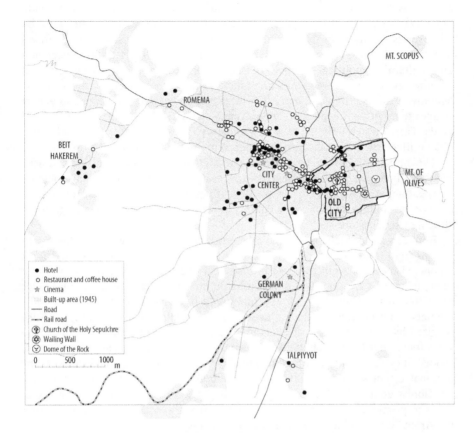

Figure 3.3 Hospitality and recreation services in Jerusalem, 1940.

was in the second half of the 1930s, on the heels of the outbreak of rioting during the Second World War, and until the end of the British Mandate in the country (Address Book 1935, 23–25; ibid. 1942, 26–27; Hale-Or 1948, 30).

Jerusalem, then, was transformed under the British Mandate: with modern infrastructure, contemporary cultural centers, tranquility at religious sites, and new accommodations, it was now more accessible and attractive for tourists from abroad. But beyond the change and renewal, there was also great conflict—and the locals' understanding of tourism was decidedly different from that of the tourists.

Tourism as a political tool in the Jewish–Arab struggle in Mandate-era Jerusalem

One of the primary considerations behind a tourist's decision to visit a certain area is his or her perception of that area. In other words, the image an area projects is one of its main attractions. This image, however, is neither materially objective nor set in stone. More often than not it is formed and reformed by whoever is involved in or in control of the country's tourist industry—travel agents, tour guides, press, and guidebooks. These, unwittingly or not, inject specific cultural or political perspectives into their country's various sites, which together create an overall, and indubitably subjective, image of the country. Moreover, tourism may be, and often is, exploited in order to create and export images that both correspond to and advance distinctive political and ideological goals. This was certainly the case in Mandatory Palestine, where Jews and Arabs alike utilized the tourist industry in order to promote their national ambitions.

The period of British rule saw a paradigmatic shift in Palestine's tourist industry. Increasingly Westernized, Mandatory Palestine was also an increasingly attractive place to visit. As we saw, if previously pilgrims had formed the bulk of the country's visitors, the country was now swamped by an ever-growing stream of secular tourists.[84]

Both Jews and Arabs wished to take advantage of this new influx, hoping to benefit from it not only economically but also politically. Local Arabs and Jews competed over the right to serve tourists and over the opportunity to promote their image of Palestine. But it was a battle in which the Arabs, having, under the Ottomans, acquired a virtually monopoly over the country's—albeit rudimentary—tourist industry, had a distinct edge over the Zionist movement. Still, inspired by a combination of economic motives and nationalist ambitions, the Jews fought hard to breach the Arabs' stranglehold over Palestine's tourist trade. Indeed, it can and will be argued that the Jewish effort to break the largely Arab-dominated tourist industry in Palestine was both driven and shaped by nationalist Zionist goals. The Jews consciously sought to exploit the tourist market in order to promote a Zionist view of Palestine while at the same time preventing the Arabs from peddling their image of the country.

The Arab strategy in political tourism

The flourishing tourist market under the British Mandate coincided with a new, more strident phase of the Arab–Jewish national conflict. Under British reign, two distinct and conflicting societies emerged—Jewish and Arab-Palestinian. British policy found itself in the middle of a struggle: on one side, the aspirations of the Zionist movement and Jewish settlement to build a national home for Jews in the land of Israel; on the other, the Arab efforts to prevent these aspirations from coming to fruition. In the 30 years of British rule, the country became the stage for political conflict and armed and violent clashes between Jews and Arabs.

As a result, tourism became an increasingly important battleground—economic but also political—with both the local Arabs and Jews intent upon cornering the local tourist market.[85] According to the Jerusalem-based Zionist Trade and Industry Department, from the moment tourists began arriving in Jerusalem the Arabs made detailed plans to prevent anyone but themselves from profiting economically. Arab tour guides, it noted, directed tourists only to non-Jewish stores, Jewish drivers did not receive work, and the Allenby Hotel—considered the best and largest hotel in the city—was boycotted by Arab tour guides. If this was not enough, the Arabs exploited the country's burgeoning tourist industry in order to spread anti-Semitic propaganda by distributing invidious anti-Jewish leaflets among their foreign charges.[86] Given the growing friction with their Arab neighbors and their pressing need to gain international support and leverage, it is no wonder that the Zionists were convinced of the necessity of trying to capture the country's tourist trade for themselves.

Jerusalem, a city of a mixed Arab-Jewish population, lay at the heart of the Arab–Jewish conflict. It was also, as the site of many of Palestine's holy places, one of the country's key tourist attractions. Not surprisingly, Jerusalem became the focus of the ideologically oriented national battle over Palestine's tourist industry.

Jewish sources in the early 1920s highlighted a number of facts concerning tourism in Jerusalem that were, in their eyes, extremely disturbing. First, there was the marked imbalance in the number of Jewish and Arab tour guides, with the latter greatly outnumbering the former. The Jewish daily *Haaretz* reported how "many Jewish tourists complain that there are no Jewish tour guides to lead them to the places they wish to see and for which purpose they came to Palestine."[87] Second, there was growing discord and hostility between Arab and Jewish tour guides. Third, and even more worrying for the Zionists, was, in the words of one source, that "gentile translators influence both Jewish and non-Jewish tourists visiting the country, by deliberately concealing Jewish historical sites and institutions from them, and by poisoning their minds with accusations and jealousy against our people."[88]

The Zionist Executive, the Zionist movement's governing body, aware that its cause was being gravely undermined by the Arab-controlled tourist industry, resolved to remedy the situation as quickly as possible. Discussing the matter for the first time in 1922, one of the movement's leaders pointed out that

> To date, tourists have come to the country and only the Arabs have benefited from them. This issue should interest the Zionist Executive from the political perspective as well, since the tourists are in the Arab-Christian sector where a variety of publications that speak out against us are distributed to them.[89]

He obviously impressed his listeners; according to the available—if limited—evidence, these years saw the beginning of a Zionist offensive on Palestine's tourist industry. The Zionist movement, defining tourism in political terms, consciously set out to exploit the tourist industry as part of its national political struggle. As such, it launched a coordinated attack on the country's oral, visual, and written tourist media. Guidebooks, tourist maps, advertisements, films, and tour guides were all used to shape and present the desired Zionist take on Palestine.[90]

The Zionist Information Bureau for Tourists

The "Zionist Information Bureau for Tourists," established by the World Zionist Organization on behalf of Palestine's Jewish population, opened its doors in 1925. Financed and run jointly by the Zionist Executive, the Jewish National Fund (Keren Kayemet), and the United Israel Appeal, the Bureau set itself three main objectives: first, to contact prospective tourists interested in coming to Palestine when abroad; second, to maintain contact with these tourists during their visit to Palestine, impressing upon them, firsthand, the diversity, magnitude, and importance of the Zionist enterprise; third, to introduce these tourists, upon their return home, to various local Zionist benefactors and charities (Zionist Federation 1925, 31–32).

As part of the Bureau's purview, its representatives would approach tourists either in the Qantara railway in Egypt or in one of Palestine's port cities—Haifa or Jaffa—and recommend Jewish hotels, tour guides, and Zionist itineraries.[91] Tourists were also given a concentrated but comprehensive introduction to the Zionist endeavor. The Bureau arranged meetings with local Jewish and Zionist activists. It organized trips to kibbutzim and agricultural communities, where the tourists could meet and mingle with Jewish settlers. Finally, Bureau agents would often accompany tourists on their travels throughout the country, making sure they obtained a Zionist perspective of the country.

Guidebooks, maps, and films

Hoping to harness more Diaspora Jews to the enterprise, the Zionists began to publish a variety of guidebooks designed specifically for Jewish tourists. These were written partially in order to fill a gap in the market. The introduction to one of the earliest Jewish guidebooks noted that

> Since our brothers in the Diaspora began to show an interest in settling our country, making aliyah [immigrating to Palestine] and traveling the country, the lack of a Hebrew book that would serve as a guide and show them the way during their travels in the land of the Hebrews has been felt. Books of this kind that do exist are in foreign languages and are written in the spirit of Christianity for Christian pilgrims, for whom Palestine is the Messiah's birthplace and the cradle of their religion. The Jewish traveler will not find the information he seeks in these books.[92]

But, as suggested in the above excerpt, these books were also written in order to impress upon Jewish tourists Palestine's Jewish heritage as well as the validity and viability of the Zionist endeavor. All this in the hope that they would either make a financial contribution to Zionist coffers or, better still, ultimately decide to settle in Palestine.

In 1922, the Zionist Trade and Industry Department published *Eretz-Israel for Jewish Tourists*. The book highlighted Palestine's distinctive Jewish affinities and its unique historical and religious association with the Jewish people. At the same time, the Jews' massive contribution to the building of modern-day Palestine was also described, and in enthusiastic detail. Naturally, old and new Jewish sites and institutions, particularly in Jerusalem, were all given pride of place in the book (Trade and Industry Department 1922).

The Zionist Information Bureau for Tourists also jumped on the publishing bandwagon, producing several guidebooks which similarly targeted Jewish tourists (Trade and Industry Department 1922). Apparently a lucrative business, with the growing number of tourists to Palestine, these "official" Zionist publications were soon joined by commercially published guidebooks boasting a Jewish orientation. Most of these books were written in Hebrew, though some were published in English and German.

But not only Jewish tourists were targeted. Over the years the Zionist Information Bureau published numerous guidebooks and educational pamphlets on Palestine, distributing them to travel agents in order to encourage Zionist-flavored tourism to Palestine.[93] From 1927 onwards, the Bureau began publishing an annual tour- and guidebook to Palestine. Initially printed in only German, English, and French, the book's first Hebrew edition was issued in 1937. The Hebrew guidebook's introduction divulged the philosophy behind this and other analogous publications.

Most guidebooks on Palestine, it observed, were

> limited to descriptions of the holy places and the most interesting historic and archaeological sites. They rarely mentioned the new Eretz Yisrael, in which the Jewish national homeland is taking shape. This guidebook, issued by the Zionist Information Bureau in Jerusalem's Julian Way, is intended to fill this void. This guidebook, now presented to the tourist for the first time in Hebrew, hopes to pave the way for the tourist to the newly developing Eretz Yisrael, to provide him with a comprehensive picture of Eretz Yisrael that is being built on the soil of this historic, ancient land.
>
> (Zionist Information Bureau for Tourists 1937, 9)

The chapter in the Bureau's book devoted to Jerusalem is of particular interest. In the mid-1930s editions, the Old City receives a mere two paragraphs, with the remainder of the chapter given over to an extensive survey of the new part of town. Jerusalem's new Jewish neighborhoods are discussed at length. The various Zionist institutions in the city are listed, as well as its many Jewish educational, health, and welfare organizations. Jerusalem's three cinemas are mentioned, together with its "concerts ... cafés and restaurants," all of which "play an important role the city's social life, as in Europe."[94]

While the new town certainly sounds appealing, the disproportionate space allotted to this part of the city is odd and somewhat disconcerting, given the Old City's undisputed historical importance. Yet this unequal division becomes understandable, even reasonable, once these guidebooks' aim—to promote the Zionist enterprise—is taken into account. Where better to do this than in

Jerusalem's flourishing new neighborhoods? No less important, this obvious imbalance, in that it both reflected and bolstered Jewish selfhood, also stemmed in part from the Zionist effort to consolidate a new Jewish Zionist identity.

Tourist maps were another tactic used by the Zionists in their assault on Palestine's tourist industry, and were drafted with much the same purpose in mind—to advance the Zionist endeavor. The maps of Palestine published by Zionist and other Jewish organizations were designed as more than simple tourist aids or to encourage tourists to visit and spend money in particular places. Emphasizing Jewish sites ancient and modern, they were a deliberate attempt to impose a specifically, even exclusively, Jewish Zionist identity on the country.[95] Highlighting the Jewish presence in the country, its cities, and its settlements, these Jewish-tinctured tourist maps are easily identified. This is particularly true as regards maps of Jerusalem, which depicted in great detail the city's new, primarily Jewish, neighborhoods, highlighting its various Jewish religious, cultural, and educational institutions, while at the same time relegating the Old City, often drawn in a rather schematic manner, to a relatively small section of the map (see Figure 3.4).[96]

Under the British Mandate, the Zionist movement made use of films to promote tourism and further the Zionist cause for the first time. A notable milestone in this respect was the film *To a New Life*, which premiered in Berlin in 1935. A model of celluloid propaganda, the film, while portraying Jerusalem as the center of the world's three great monotheistic religions, took care to accentuate the fact that Judaism's association with the Holy City antedated the other two by thousands of years. The film also offered various images of the city's holy sites, which quickly faded out only to be replaced with pictures of Jewish immigrants dancing on board a ship bound for Palestine. Indeed, after a perfunctory nod towards the Old City, the viewer was presented with a predominantly modern perspective of Jerusalem, featuring among other things the Strauss Medical Center, Jewish Agency buildings, and Hebrew University (Kohn 1991; Tryster 1995).

Tour guides

The cultivation of Jewish tour guides became a crucial element in the Zionists' campaign to break into Palestine's tourist industry and further the Jewish national enterprise. This was no surprise. The tour guide is a key element in the complex interaction between ideology and tourism.[97]

Cohen distinguishes between two types of tour guides: the geographical pathfinder and the spiritual guide or mentor. The former simply pilots tourists through unfamiliar environments or societies. The latter is more akin to "a specialist [who] serves as a 'guru' to the novice, adept or seeker, guiding him towards insight, enlightenment, or any other exalted spiritual state" (Cohen 1985, 8). In either case, the nature and quality of the tour guide's knowledge and method of imparting it is one of his or her most important traits. The choices they make in terms of what to emphasize, what to underplay, and what to ignore

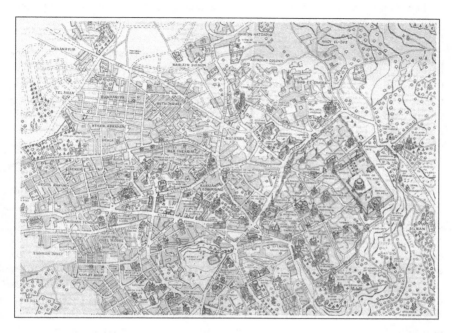

Figure 3.4 Part of Steimatzky's Jerusalem pictorial map 1941 (Steimatzky's Middle East
agency, Jerusalem, Tel Aviv, Haifa, Beirut, Damascus, Bagdad, Cairo,
Alexandria, 1942.).

entirely, together with their take on the sites shown and events experienced,
mean that tour guides often inject, consciously or unconsciously, an ideological
dimension into their commentary. Thanks to their virtual monopoly on information (within the tour group) tour guides can transmit a variety of messages to
their charges. And, while some tour guides have private agendas, more often
than not the ideological message underlying their exposition reflects either the
tourist establishment's or government authorities' policies. In other words, tour
guides are integral to any effort to impress upon visitors a particular image of the
country as well as specific social and political messages. This "power" wielded
by tour guides did not escape the Zionistic leadership.

   In areas of national conflict the tour guide becomes one of the national movement's primary spokespersons, used to promote its ideological goals. The more
intense the friction, the greater the reliance on tour guides, who, employed in an
increasingly sophisticated manner, become, in effect, soldiers in the national
struggle. This is precisely what happened in the case of Jewish tour guides in
Mandatory Palestine. Indeed, in the nationally motivated battle over the country's tourist industry, breaking into the Arab tour guide monopoly became one of
the Zionists' biggest challenges (Katz 1985).

The Zionist movement was well aware that information conveyed by tour guides was an important weapon in the national ideological struggle between the local Arab and Jewish communities. But, to its misfortune, Jewish tour guides were, to begin with, at a considerable disadvantage vis-à-vis their Arab counterparts. The latter enjoyed close, well-established links with the local representatives of all the major travel companies, including Thomas Cook and Clark. Not that it mattered; as these local representatives were mostly Arab they were not, in any case, inclined to farm out jobs to Jewish tour guides. And not just Jewish tour guides: Jewish drivers, souvenir shop owners, and proprietors of car rental companies all complained of being discriminated against, with local Arab representatives doing all they could to prevent Jews from working in the tourist trade.[98]

This state of affairs spurred the Zionist organization into action. In an effort to better the lot of Jewish tourist service providers, it contacted the head offices of the big international travel companies directly, asking them to steer their Jewish clients towards Jewish hotels, Jewish cafés, Jewish drivers, and, of course, Jewish tour guides. They asked Thomas Cook & Son specifically to ensure that all tour guides working on its behalf did not neglect Jewish sites when showing Jewish tourists around the country. In addition, the Zionist Executive in Palestine also urged its London counterpart to try and get Thomas Cook & Son to replace the current manager of its Jerusalem office, who it claimed was notorious for his lack of support for Jewish tourist service providers in the city.[99]

The Zionist Trade and Industry Department also decided to open a professional course for Jewish tour guides. The first course commenced in June 1922 and boasted 18 students.[100] Thus, the process of institutionalized tour guide training began in the early 1920s and not some time later as commonly assumed (Katz 1985, 64). Moreover, documents indicate that the Arab–Jewish conflict was one of the incentives behind the new venture. Tishbi, one of the members of the Zionist Executive, went so far as to state that he brought up the idea of holding such a course once he realized just "how dangerous the non-Jewish guides, who serve as tool of the enemies of the Yishuv, are."[101]

The course's syllabus, taught by several of the Jewish community's foremost experts on Palestine, included classes on local history, archaeology, and ethnography. Prospective tour guides were also schooled in rules of tourist etiquette and how to conduct themselves with visitors.[102] Those who successfully completed the original course, ten in number, were granted an official certificate and went on to found the Association of Jewish Tour Guides in Eretz Yisrael.[103]

The association, established in the summer of 1922, was the first Jewish tour guide union in Palestine formed on a professional basis. It welcomed anyone who had completed the Trade and Industry Department's course.[104] Among the association's goals, as listed in its constitution, were the development of tourism in Palestine, injecting a national Jewish spirit into all contact with tourists, and mutual assistance in business affairs.[105] Clearly the association's aim was not only to consolidate the tour guides' professional and economic statuses but also to promote the Jewish community's national and ideological goals. The Jewish tour guides, a combination of Cohen's geographic pathfinder and spiritual mentor, were to become a part of the concerted Zionist effort to impart a Jewish nationalist message to the country's incoming tourists.[106]

The British authorities step in

One of the biggest problems facing the Zionist Information Bureau in its early years was how to net the organized Christian tours, which accounted for a substantial portion of tourism in Palestine in general and Jerusalem in particular. The local Arab franchises of the big tourist companies, such as Thomas Cook and American Express, exercised a virtual monopoly over Christian tour groups. This obviously limited the Bureau's ability to supply work for its Jewish tour guides.[107] A report published by the Bureau in 1927, while admitting to some advances in the field, nevertheless painted a dismal picture of the Jewish tour guides' current situation:

> Of the tour guides trained by the Zionist Executive a few years ago, only seven are currently working. Besides these, other Jews work in this profession, some only during the [tourist] season…[in contrast,] there are one hundred Arab tour guides in Jerusalem, of which a fair number work only in the [tourist] season. The large travel companies work only with them, but also use Jews, although not the best ones.[108]

The British authorities, however, were aware of the difficulties facing Jewish tour guides. In 1927, the same year the Bureau published its bleak report, the administration issued "Tour Guide Ordinance, 1927." This, the first serious example of government intervention in the field of tourism, was not just a response to the discrimination suffered by Jewish tour guides. It was equally inspired by the mandatory authorities' realization that the battle between Arab and Jewish tour guides both reflected and fueled the growing political friction between the country's Arab and Jewish communities. Having identified the tour guide affair as a potential flash point exacerbating local national tensions, the British sought to defuse the situation using legislation.[109]

The new ordinance was meant to regulate Palestine's tour guide business. Henceforth, anyone who wanted to work as a professional (paid) tour guide had to receive a permit from the appropriate government authorities: the chief secretary in charge of tour guide licenses throughout Palestine and the regional governor responsible for licensing in his province. The High Commissioner's Office determined the conditions under which tour guide licenses were granted. The composition of license forms, the number of licenses to be issued, and the formulation of guidelines circumscribing the manner in which tour guides engaged in their profession also fell under the purview of the high commissioner. Furthermore, in order to ensure that only fully qualified tour guides received licenses, the ordinance required all tour guides who wished to shepherd visitors around the country's historical, archaeological, and religious sites to undergo a rigorous test set by the head of the

Department of Antiquities.[110] The ordinance also pronounced that henceforth the rates charged for guided tours were to be determined by the regional governor, making it illegal to charge higher than the established rate.[111]

The extent to which the British enforced these new regulations remains unclear. Nevertheless, the ordinance was a legislative milestone in both the history of tourism in Palestine and the Arab–Jewish conflict.

Tourism in the 1930s: continued tension

Government intervention notwithstanding, friction between local Arab and Jewish tour guides remained. Indeed, by the end of the 1920s, as the nationalist conflict between the two communities developed, Arab and Jewish tour guides increasingly locked horns as well. In early 1928, it was reported that Arab tour guides were preventing their Jewish counterparts from entering the Church of the Holy Sepulchre. To their great frustration, Jewish tour guides—despite having passed all the appropriate government tests (including one on the Holy Sepulchre)—found themselves able to escort tourists only as far as the entrance to the church's courtyard, where they were forced to hand over their charges to an Arab guide. Evidently, the Arab Christian and Muslim leadership, in blatant defiance of British legislation (which permitted all who had passed the tour guiding tests to guide in the church), plotted to ban Jewish tour guides from one of the more prominent Jerusalem landmarks.[112] Nor was it surprising that, with Jewish tour guides unable to offer access to Jerusalem's holy sites, most foreign tourist agencies turned to Arab tour guides instead.[113]

The 1929 riots led to an immediate and rapid deterioration in relations between Arab and Jewish tour guides, with the latter finding it almost impossible to squire their charges through Christian and Muslim holy sites. The Temple Mount/Haram al-Sharif was a case in point. Until 1929, Jewish tour guides were free to enter the site; after the riots, the Supreme Muslim Council banned all Jews. As the Temple Mount was a not-to-be-missed part of any tour of the city, foreign travel agents were naturally reluctant to hire Jewish tour guides.[114] Desperate, their livelihood threatened, Jewish tour guides turned to the British authorities, in the hope that they would order the Council to permit them to enter the sacred site. But the British, though sympathetic to the tour guides' plight, were loath to become involved in this political-religious imbroglio, thus exacerbating it further. Fearing that any change in the status quo as regards access to Haram al-Sharif/the Temple Mount would produce an Arab explosion, they refused to intervene, or even take sides. Entry to the site remained, as before, at the sole discretion of the Supreme Muslim Council.[115]

The Mandatory authorities' failure to help the Jewish tour guides forced the Zionist Information Bureau to take action itself. It initiated several meetings with local non-Jewish representatives of the big travel companies in the hopes of persuading them to employ Jewish tour guides.[116] Their efforts bore fruit. Relations between the Zionist organization and the travel companies improved, which, in turn, had a positive, if limited, effect on the predicament of Jewish tour guides.[117]

In the mid-1930s the growing number of tourists entering the country induced the Bureau to extend its activities abroad. In a public relations onslaught, it sent countless letters to travel agencies big and small throughout the world, asking them to encourage tourists to visit Palestine and to coordinate these trips with the Bureau. It even suggested that the companies appoint a clerk specifically for this purpose. Thomas Cook & Son, one of the world's biggest travel companies, was marked for special treatment. The Bureau held a number of meetings with the company's directors in London, during which the latter declared a genuine interest in promoting Jewish and gentile tourism to Palestine. Better still, they promised that in the future, company-sponsored tours would include not only the usual round of Christian and Muslim historical and religious sites, but also Jewish religious and historical sites, as well as Jewish settlements and other various points of interest representative of modern-day Palestine.[118] Nor was Thomas Cook the Bureau's only success story. Thanks to its overseas initiative, foreign travel agencies began to increasingly coordinate their activities in the country with the Bureau.

In order to accommodate this new encouraging volley of business, the Bureau engaged the services of Palestine and Egypt Lloyd Ltd. (PEL), an international travel agency and subsidiary of the Anglo-Palestine Bank (APK). The company, active since the early 1920s, had, over the years, worked closely with the Zionist movement and was responsible for organizing a considerable amount of Jewish tourism in the country.[119]

But despite the improvement in relations with foreign travel agencies, the political state of affairs in Palestine—in particular the 1936–1939 riots—further undermined the Jewish tour guides' position. With few jobs on offer, the number of Jewish guides dwindled, and those remaining often found themselves without work. The Zionist Executive did its best, but there was little it could do in the violent climate of the late 1930s.[120]

The impact of the Second World War on tourism in Jerusalem

The Second World War marked an important juncture in the Zionist movement's efforts to break into and guarantee its hold in the local tourist market. In effect, the Zionist movement used the changing conditions to its political advantage. Not that it seemed so at first, with the British ban on travel and immigration to Palestine. These various wartime restrictions obligated the Zionist Information Bureau, at least temporarily, to shift emphasis and concentrate almost exclusively on domestic tourism. In an effort to make the best of things, the Bureau labored to bolster domestic tourism, introducing local residents to the attractions of Palestine's various sites and tourist services. It did so, on one hand, in order to keep the Jewish tourist industry intact, and, on the other, in the hope that these new tourists, who normally went abroad for their holidays, would elect to spend their vacations in Palestine once travel was permitted again.[121]

With fear mounting that the front was advancing towards Palestine, the Zionist leadership announced that the Jews were ready to join the British war effort. As a result, thousands of local Palestinian Jews enlisted in the British armed forces. The new friendly relations between these Jewish and British soldiers had a direct and positive impact on the Zionist tourist industry, with the British soldiers increasingly curious about and eager to explore their comrades-in-arms' homeland.

Moreover, as the number of allied soldiers stationed in the country increased, so did the number of potential tourists. There was also the issue of what these troops were to do during their all-too-brief periods of leave. The Bureau, sensing an opportunity, quickly moved in, and in association with the Jewish Agency's Political Department provided leisure and recreation activities to thousands of allied troops. It was able to do so thanks to the marked improvement in the Jewish community's socioeconomic circumstances during the war. This and the concomitant improvement in Jewish tourist infrastructure allowed the Bureau to handle the growing number of soldier-tourists, offering them an increasingly wide range of choice services (Porath and Shavit 1982, 132–138).

The Bureau's concern for the soldiers' welfare was not just its way of contributing to the allied war effort. Its efforts on behalf of the troops also had specifically political overtones and objectives. It was hoped that the Allied powers, grateful for the Bureau's help in lightening the soldiers' burden, would prove more sympathetic to the Zionist cause. It was also hoped that by providing the allied soldiers with firsthand experience of the Zionist enterprise, by building up a positive picture of the Jewish settlement in Palestine in their minds, the soldiers would be influenced. Upon their return home, the Bureau hoped, these soldiers could act as ambassadors for the Zionist cause and influence public opinion—and so political opinion—in its favor.

During the war some 210,000 soldiers enjoyed the Bureau's services. They went on field trips organized by the Bureau, visiting various historic and religious sites as well as Jewish agricultural settlements and industrial enterprises. They were also given the chance to stay in the country's kibbutzim and moshavim[122] for three days of rest and recreation free of charge. Some 60,000 soldiers took advantage of this attractive offer. Clearly, with international tourism at a practical standstill, the Zionists saw no reason to abandon their politically oriented tourism policies; allied soldiers simply replaced the civilian tourists.[123]

The political nature of tourism, then, was quite evident in Palestine during the Mandate period. Though less is known about the actions taken by the Arab leadership to further its agenda through the tourism sector, the Jewish community in Palestine organized itself and used all tools at its disposal—professional contacts, new materials, tour guides, and more—to ensure that its vision was disseminated.

Conclusion

In the years discussed here, much like the years that preceded the commencement of modern tourism, the main attractions in Jerusalem (as in Palestine in general) were the historical and religious sites which had been in the city for generations. For the vast majority of visitors, these places were the chief reason for coming to the city in the days of British rule.

The great change in these attractions in the days of British rule was their adjustment to suit the growing demand of modern tourists. The British administration worked to preserve and cultivate these sites from its very arrival in the city; its policy touted continuity, in particular with regard to the status quo in internal administration of the sacred places. However, alongside this the British saw a need to effect changes and institute new norms in the city's well-known sites. It would appear, then, that the British activity on all levels in the field of public order, planning, and preservation created an atmosphere that was more suited to the development of holy and historical sites into sites of prayer and visiting. The suggested connection between the proliferation of visits in the city and the actions taken by the British cannot be proven empirically, however it is doubtful anyone would challenge the claim that these actions—and in particular, the British initiatives— made an important contribution to the increase of tourist attraction in the city.

The British Mandate era was a time of great change in Jerusalem. Alongside the improvements in transportation and infrastructure, many new buildings appeared. The Rockefeller Museum and the YMCA signaled a change in the city's cultural atmosphere, adding an aesthetic and modern element. The flourishing hotel industry was an important milestone in the development of the urban tourism infrastructure and teaches us perhaps better than anything about the tourism revolution that was the city's lot in the Mandate period. Hotels became one of the symbols of Jerusalem as a place of meeting for social and spiritual life. They became known as cultural centers in the developing city and held lectures, parties, dancing, and more.

Alongside the new building and hotels aimed at the tourist element, the service industry expanded as well—guidebooks, maps, and licensed tour guides were now commonplace. Thus the greatly increasing tourist component had a huge influence on the city's growing tourist industry—and its economy.

In the political arena, tourism was perceived as an area well worth investing in and fighting over, and not simply for economic reasons. While there is little doubt that both sides of the conflict saw tourism as an important source of revenue, its political benefits were considered equally if not more important. Indeed, with each side anxious to disseminate abroad its "true" interpretation of sites and events in Mandatory Palestine, the Arab–Jewish national ideological conflict undoubtedly gave added impetus to the Zionist efforts to break into the local tourist industry.

Though it is impossible to measure the degree to which tourism ultimately contributed to the fulfillment of Zionist aspirations, it is nevertheless evident that throughout the Mandatory period tourism was regarded, indeed wielded, by the Zionist movement as a political weapon. Nor, it must be said, did this process cease after the creation of State of Israel.[124]

In the next chapter we discuss the new tourist reality that prevailed in Jerusalem following the war that broke out in 1948, after the British left the country. This difficult reality—a city divided between two different political sovereignties—would exist in the city for nearly 20 years, from 1948 to 1967.

Notes

1 For example, "News from the Land of Israel" [in Hebrew], *Haolam*, March 28, 1924.
2 N. Mindel, Department of Licensing, Jaffa, to A. Hyamson, Department of Immigration, no location noted, July 18, 1925, 11, 1238, Tour/5, Israel State Archives, Jerusalem; Stead 1927, 23–24.
3 Department of Statistics 1946, 40–41. The data regarding the entry of tourists do not include tourists who stayed in the country illegally and were in fact not tourists to begin with.
4 For more on the relative calm in the country throughout most of the 1920s, see Porath 1974, 101–110, 158–168.
5 "Maccabiah Visitors Arrive in Jerusalem" [in Hebrew], *Haaretz*, March 27, 1932, p. 1.
6 The source of this sharp increase is, it would appear, the calm that prevailed in the country after the first wave of Arab protests that broke out in August 1936 and subsided in October of that year until the reawakening in summer of 1937. See Porath and Shavit 1982, 283–285.
7 Ettinger, "The Undercover Export," *Palestine Commercial Bulletin*, March 1938, 97–103.
8 Gurevich, Gertz, and Bachi note that 1936–1940 were, by their definition, years of "economic depression." See Gurevich, Gertz, and Bachi 1944, 9.
9 The economic recovery began primarily from 1941; the economic situation improved as a result of the industrial and agricultural development that helped the war effort. See Gurevich, Getz, and Bachi 1944, 19.
10 See Chapter 2 for more on the subject.
11 Department of Statistics 1946, xxx, table 31.
12 Department of Statistics 1946, xxx, table 32.
13 Ashbee was one of the leaders in the garden city movement, which developed in nineteenth-century England in response to industrial urbanization. See Ashbee 1917, 11–13; Ashbee 1923, 139–163. For Ashbee's biography, see Crawford 1985. For evaluation and a comprehensive discussion of Ashbee's work, see Hyman 1992, 357–414; Hysler-Rubin 2005, 81–102.
14 Great Britain, High Commissioner for Palestine, 1925, 8; for announcement, see "Antiquities in Palestine," *Palestine Weekly*, August 20, 1920, 489.
15 Old City officer in conversation with Urnstein 1968, 437; for testimony about the mixed guard at the Western Wall, see: Landa 1932, 43.
16 For an extensive description of the visits of British soldiers to the holy sites in Jerusalem shortly after its conquest, see "Holy Places of Jerusalem," *London Times*, March 29, 1918.
17 E. Keith-Roach, director of Jerusalem district, Jerusalem, to the chief secretariat, London, June 6, 1927, administrative files, Mandatory Archives, 45, ATQ, 113/1, Israel Antiquities Authority Archives, Jerusalem.
18 Director of the Department of Antiquities, Jerusalem, to the attorney general, district governor, and director of the Department of Public Works, June 13, 1925, administrative files, Mandatory Archives, 45, 113/1, Israel Antiquities Authority Archives, Jerusalem; R. Storrs, Jerusalem-Jaffa district, Jerusalem, to director of Department of Antiquities, Jerusalem, June 17, 1925, administrative files, Mandatory Archives, 45, 113/1, Israel Antiquities Authority Archives, Jerusalem.
19 Memorandum to E. Williams, curator of colonies, London, June 22, 1933, 2, G-108, 1796, Israel State Archive, Jerusalem.
20 Harvey's preliminary report, September 1933 (estimated), 2, G-108, 1796, Israel State Archives, Jerusalem. For Harvey's detailed reports, see administrative files, Mandatory Archives, 45, 113/3, 113/4, Israel Antiquities Authority Archives,

Jerusalem; for photographs of the state of the church prior to renovations and photographs of the various scaffoldings, see administrative files, Mandatory Archives, 86–87, Israel Antiquities Authority Archives, Jerusalem. Harvey's final report was also published as a book; see Harvey 1935.

21 Great Britain, Colonial Office 1938, 107. It should be noted that the closing of the church occurred only in part due to its physical state; it was also one of the actions intended to pressure the Christian communities to come to an agreement and fund the renovations. On this, see Cunliff-Lister, Colonies Office, London, to A. Wauchope, high commissioner, Jerusalem, November 16, 1934, administrative files, Mandatory Archives, 45, 113/8, Israel Antiquities Authority Archives, Jerusalem.

22 See "Both Easters in Jerusalem: Church of the Sepulchre under Repair," *London Times*, April 10, 1939.

23 Exceptions included the acts of violence that occurred during the Nebi Musa celebrations in Jerusalem in early April 1920. For background on their outbreak and a description of the evolution of the events from the Jewish perspective, see Dinur 1973, A, 2, 601–615; for a more critical evaluation of the events, see Porath 1974, 75–81.

24 Ben-Arieh 1984, 178–181. The Cook handbook printed at the end of the Ottoman period notes that the Ottoman government allowed the entry of tourists to the site only when accompanied by a consular representative and Turkish soldier. See Cook 1907, 80.

25 For more details on the Department of Antiquities' activities at the site during the Mandate, see Avni and Seligman 2001, 9–20.

26 For select examples, see: Hoade 1946, 219–234; Luke and Keith-Roach 1922, 91–95; Luke 1924, 97–125; Maisler and Yeivin 1940, 214–216, 219–221; and Vester 1920, 82–102, 103–131.

27 Descriptions of the experience of visiting the location appear in the accounts of many different visitors to Jerusalem in the period discussed and we will note two of them. Conway 1923, 149, notes that the Temple Mount stunned him primarily with its quiet and unexpected beauty. In his opinion, this is one of the world's architectural pearls, more beautiful than the Hagia Sophia in Istanbul. In Great Britain, High Commissioner for Palestine. Samuel 1925, 8, notes that "inside its walls can be found, singular in its genius, one of the most magnificent buildings in the entire world, Haram al-Sharif."

28 Kupferschmidt 1987, 133, and note 24 there. This low estimate is consistent with the data from the Department of Migration regarding the entry of Arabs for religious purposes in the years 1935–1965. In total, 3,156 Arab pilgrims entered during those years. See: Department of Migration 1946, xxviii, table 28.

29 This general statement is made in absence of quantitative data about the internal movement in the country, including the movement of pilgrims and tourists to Haram al-Sharif.

30 Additional editions in English were published in 1925, 1930, and 1935. In 1924, the guide was published in French. See: The Supreme Muslim Council 1924.

31 However, as part of the national struggle that developed in Palestine in those days the Western Wall plaza became a wrestling arena between Jews and Muslims. On the evolution of events in the 1920s that led to the 1929 riots see Storrs 1937, 633–635; Porath 1974, 213; Troyex 1931.

32 J. Breasted, The Oriental Institute, University of Chicago, to the high commissioner, Jerusalem, June 9, 1927, Colonial Office, 733, 142, 44581, Public Record Office, London. Main points regarding the stage of establishing the Rockefeller Museum can be found in Fawzi 2006; Zusman and Reich 1987, 53–56; see also the biography written about Breasted by his son: Breasted 1948, 376–388.

33 J. Rockefeller, New York, to Lord Plumer, Jerusalem, October 13, 1927, Colonial Office, 733, 142, 44581, Public Record Office, London; Lord Plumer, Jerusalem, to

J. Rockefeller, New York, November 6, 1927, Colonial Office, 733, 142, 44581, Public Record Office, London. See Ormsby-Gore, acting colonial secretary, London, to J. Rockefeller, New York, December 9, 1927, Colonial Office, 733, 142, 44581, Public Record Office, London, in which he expresses thanks on behalf of the British government and minister of colonies and sees the donation for the establishment of the museum as further testament to the country's historical and cultural importance. The terms agreed upon also appeared in "New Archaeological Museum in Jerusalem," *Official Gazette*, November 16, 1927.

34 Lord Plumer, Jerusalem, to Colonial Secretary Amery, London, April 4, 1928, Colonial Office, 733, 142, 44581, 146, 57053, Public Record Office, London. Plumer reports that the price for the eight-acre plot was initially 31,704 Palestine pounds but the government offered half of this amount, and the government's total offer stood at 15,500 Palestine pounds. The court confirmed the government's offer and the landowner eventually accepted it. For more on Karm al-Sheikh, see: Kark and Landman 1980, 196–198; 1981, 177–183.

35 Lord Plumer, Jerusalem, to colonial secretary, London, November 18, 1927, Colonial Office, 733, 142, 44581, Public Record Office, London; for a comprehensive essay on Harrison and his involvement in the development of the country in the Mandate period, see Fuchs 1992.

36 On the stages and features of planning the museum, one of the most important projects planned by Harrison in Palestine, see details in Fuchs 1992, 105–125.

37 Y. Shaw, "The Antiquities Ordinance, 1935," *Official Gazette*, December 9, 1937, supplement 2.

38 Administrative Supervisory Files, ATQ, PAM, Israel Antiquities Authority Archives, Jerusalem.

39 This approach is expressed in the words of the museum's director, Robert Hamilton. See Department of Antiquities, Jerusalem, to the secretary general of Jerusalem, September 4, 1945, 2, G-90–112, 992, Israel State Archives, Jerusalem.

40 On the chronicles of the association and its activities around the world, see Hopkins 1951; Latourette 1957.

41 Walker's guide had been published in 1919. Another guide was published by the association in 1942 with the increase in number of allied soldiers in the country. See Ennis 1942.

42 Waldo H. Heinrichs, association secretary, Jerusalem, to Fred W. Ramsey, YMCA International Committee, New York, September 16, 1932, International Division— Palestine, International YMCA Archives, Minneapolis.

43 See, for example, Maisler and Yeivin 1940, 229; Matson 1946, 29. The YMCA appears on tourist maps printed in the British period in the years after the building's construction.

44 Unsigned appendix to memorandum on the activities of the YMCA in Jerusalem, 1929–1930, April 26, 1930, International Division—Palestine, International YMCA Archives, Minneapolis.

45 A. L. Miller, YMCA Jerusalem, General Secretariat, 1940 Annual Report, January 27, 1941, International Division—Palestine, International YMCA Archives, Minneapolis; 1941 Annual Report, January 26, 1942, International Division—Palestine, International YMCA Archives, Minneapolis; 1942 Annual Report, June 25, 1943, International Division—Palestine, International YMCA Archives, Minneapolis; 1943 Annual Report, January 31, 1944, International YMCA Archives, Minneapolis; 1944 Annual Report, January 29, 1945, International Division—Palestine, International YMCA Archives, Minneapolis.

46 1942 Annual Report, June 25, 1943, International Division—Palestine, International YMCA Archives, Minneapolis.

47 1943 Annual Report, January 31, 1944, International Division—Palestine, International YMCA Archives, Minneapolis.

48 YMCA international division, communication protocols—Palestine. YMCA Jerusalem, General Secretariat, 1945 Annual Report, January 28, 1946, no author given, International Division—Palestine, International YMCA Archives, Minneapolis.

49 A. L. Miller, general secretariat, YMCA Jerusalem, 1946 annual report, January 27, 1947, International Division—Palestine, International YMCA Archives, Minneapolis.

50 For more on the features of accommodations in Jerusalem over the past 150 years, see Cohen-Hattab 2007; Cohen-Hattab 2010; Shoval and Cohen-Hattab 2001.

51 The hotel's activities in the first days after the city's occupation are related in Storrs's memoir, where he notes that upon arriving in Jerusalem on December 20, 1917, he went to stay at the Fast Hotel, which accepted officers at 25 qrush a day (full board). See Storrs 1937, 433.

52 A few months after the arrival of the British, the hotel was taken from the Fast family and the military made it a hotel for officers. See Goodsall 1925, 92.

53 Advertisement in *Haaretz* [in Hebrew], February 26, 1920. On the hotel's name, Storrs relates in his memoirs that the Jews demanded that the hotel be called the King Solomon Hotel and the Arabs the Sultan Suleiman—and each of the names would have caused the hotel to be boycotted by the other side. Thus Storrs ordered the hotel be named the Allenby Hotel. See Storrs 1937, 508.

54 Advertisement in *Doar Hayom* [in Hebrew], April 12, 1920; Oskotski 1921, 28.

55 Allenby Hotel, Jerusalem, to the Council of Jerusalem Jews, November 9, 1922, 398, Jerusalem Municipal Archives, Jerusalem; "Day to Day at the Allenby Hotel" [in Hebrew], *Doar Hayom*, December 21, 1920.

56 On the Mosseri family, the backdrop for the establishment of the hotel, its unique architectonic features, and its operation see Roman 2010, 11–25; Semberg 1993.

57 "In Jerusalem" [in Hebrew], *Davar*, January 20, 1931

58 "In Jerusalem" [in Hebrew], *Haaretz*, April 13, 1931; memorandum about the Palestine Hotels Company, unsigned and undated (possibly early 1930s), Colonial Office, 733, 225, 97324, Public Record Office, London.

59 "Building the Great Hotel" [in Hebrew], *Haaretz*, July 24, 1929; many additional details about the planning of the building, internal and external, can be found in Avraham Elmaliach, "One Hour in the King David Hotel" [in Hebrew], *Doar Hayom*, March 29, 1931. For engineering plans of the building see 8190, Jerusalem Municipal Archives, Jerusalem.

60 King David Hotel guest book (our thanks to the hotel's management for allowing us to view the guest book). In October 1938 the hotel became the Mandate's military and administrative center, chosen due to its central location and the ease of securing it. Less than a third of its rooms remained for commercial use. On July 22, 1946, the Etzel (the National Military Organization) managed to plant a large amount of explosives in the southern part of the building and destroyed it entirely. Ninety-one people were killed. Following the bombing, the hotel was closed to guests and all of its rooms given to the use of the British. At the end of 1948, the hotel was returned to the Palestine Hotels Company, restored, and reopened for the public. In 1956 the "Dan" hotel company, owned by Yekutiel Federman, bought the company's stocks; it has owned the hotel since. Roman 2010, 28–50.

61 This is true primarily with regard to hospitality services like the YMCA and King David Hotel or travel agencies.

62 Kupferschmidt 1987, 223, notes that the employment of a Turkish architect in the restoration of Haram al-Sharif and the planning of the Palace Hotel symbolizes one of the last formal connections between the Arab leadership in the country and the defunct Ottoman Empire.

63 For details on the architectonic uniqueness of the building, see Kroyanker 1985, 306–308. For more on the process of building the hotel see Katinka 1961, 257–263; the building's splendor at its inauguration in December 1929 is evident in pictures of

the main entry hall, dining room, hotel bar, and room with en-suite bathroom. See Kroyanker 1981, 70–72, 74.

64 Invitation to the Council of Jerusalem Jews on the opening of the hotel on December 22, 1929, 1320, 375, Jerusalem Municipal Archives, Jerusalem.

65 Memorandum of income and expenses of Barsky's hotels, January 1–5, 1929, undated, L51, 482, Central Zionist Archives, Jerusalem.

66 For some time after the hotel closed it seems the hotel restaurant continued to function as an independent restaurant while the hotel rooms were rented by the month. For more details on the history of the Palace building, see Kroyanker 1981, 61–65.

67 For example, the Rosenberg Hotel had 30 rooms in the mid-1920s (see "In Jerusalem" [in Hebrew], *Doar Hayom*, December 5, 1924) and the Amdursky Hotel on Julian's Way had 22 rooms with a total 35 beds in the second half of the 1920s. See Amdursky Hotel, Jerusalem, to the Council of Jerusalem Jews, November 9, 1922, Amdursky file, Jerusalem Municipal Archives, Jerusalem.

68 For two of the many examples from the press at the time: on the Continental Hotel, see advertisement in *Doar Hayom* [in Hebrew], November 4, 1925; on the Warshavsky Hotel see Oskotski 1921, 71.

69 For example, the Behr Hotel notes in an advertisement that it has "large halls the likes of which cannot be found in Jerusalem for weddings, balls, and family celebrations." See advertisement in *Haaretz* [in Hebrew], October 14, 1924.

70 For example, Izakson 1994, 59, states that the Jerusalem hotels of the 1920s were generally of a folksy nature.

71 Saada Hotel, undated, 105, 296c, Haganah History Archives, Tel Aviv; Al-Lakhanda al-Jedida Hotel, 14 July 1947, 105, 296c, Haganah History Archives, Tel Aviv.

72 Petra Hotel, June 29, 1947, 105, 296c, Haganah History Archives, Tel Aviv.

73 Zahara Palestine Hotel, July 20, 1947, 105, 296c, Haganah History Archives, Tel Aviv.

74 Bayt al-Maqdis Hotel, July 8, 1947, 105, 296c, Haganah History Archives, Tel Aviv; Al-Lakhandra al-Jedida Hotel, July 14, 1947, 105, 296c, Haganah History Archives, Tel Aviv.

75 So, for example, Avraham Hauser noted of his parents' boarding house (Hauser Pension, 7 Ben-Maimon Street) that his parents rented the house in 1935, and it contained two apartments—each with three rooms, with a total of twelve beds. The clientele was Jewish, mostly from the upper-middle class, including regular clients—so that the owner of the "Nur" match factory, for instance, came to the boarding house on the holidays. Guests at the boarding house included no small number of Jewish Agency officials coming to meetings in Jerusalem. The days of the Second World War were busy days, and the boarding house even hosted some Jews from Egypt who found refuge in the country following the German invasion. The boarding house had a sink in each room and a joint shower and facilities in each of the apartments. The house also boasted a phone and a dining room, where Hauser's parents slept when they were at full capacity. From: Hauser, personal communication.

76 Beit Hakerem Mutual Society Ltd., Beit Hakerem Report, 12, October 1, 1932–September 30, 1933, no page noted, 190, 2, Jerusalem Municipal Archives, Jerusalem.

77 Report of Committee for Neighborhood Improvement, income at the expense of vacation tax for the fiscal year April 1, 1942–March 31, 1943, 180, 1, Jerusalem Municipal Archives, Jerusalem.

78 Beit Hakerem Report, 23, April 1, 1944–March 31, 1945, p. 3, 190, 2, Jerusalem Municipal Archives, Jerusalem.

79 Beit Hakerem Report, 24, April 1, 1945–March 31, 1946, p. 5, 190, 2, Jerusalem Municipal Archives, Jerusalem.

80 The Beit Hakerem Committee for Neighborhood Publicity, Jerusalem, to Carmel Film, Tel Aviv, June 20, 1937, 180, 1, Jerusalem Municipal Archives, Jerusalem; in

the same year the chair of the committee, Yitzchak Yaakobi, held a special radio show called "Beit Hakerem's Fifteenth Year" which emphasized the vacation component of the neighborhood. See Landau-Mishor 2001, 39.

81 Protocol of meeting of the Neighborhood Publicity and Improvement Committee, June 25, 1939, 180, 1, Jerusalem Municipal Archives, Jerusalem; T. Wantik, chair of the Vacation and Neighborhood Improvement Committee, to members of the Vacation and Neighborhood Improvement Committee, February 9, 1945, 180, 2, Jerusalem Municipal Archives, Jerusalem; Kadari 1966, 84, 110–111.

82 For a description of the special atmosphere in the cafés in Beit Hakerem, see P. Azai, "Beit Hakerem" [in Hebrew], *Haaretz*, September 10, 1937; S. D. Gaon, "Beit Hakerem as a Place of Healing" [in Hebrew], *Davar*, July 26, 1939. For more on the distinctive vacation atmosphere in the neighborhood, see Haezrahi 1981, 173–175.

83 For an expansion on Amiran's 1940 urban geographic survey, which was the basis for the *Jerusalem Atlas* (1973), see Amiran 1984, 97–100.

84 This trend can be seen in Department of Migration 1946, 17–18. As noted, the growth of secular tourism in Palestine actually started at the end of the nineteenth century and the trend continued in the British period. See Bar and Cohen-Hattab 2003; Cohen-Hattab and Katz 2001.

85 On the economic and political importance of tourism in Palestine under the British Mandate, see Berger 1931; Cohen-Hattab 2001, 50–68; Cohen-Hattab and Katz 2001; Porath and Shavit 1982, 121–25; Shoval and Cohen-Hattab 2001, 908–925.

86 Trade and Industry Department, Jerusalem, to the executive of the Zionist organizations in America, New York, March 8, 1922, S-8, 1403, Central Zionist Archives, Jerusalem.

87 "Tourist Traffic" [in Hebrew], *Haaretz*, March 20, 1922.

88 Ben Zion Taragan, "More on the Tourists" [in Hebrew], *Doar Hayom*, January 3, 1923.

89 Meeting of the Zionist Executive in Eretz Yisrael, J. Sprintzak, March 6, 1922, 2b/ S100, Central Zionist Archives, Jerusalem.

90 Based on Butler's analysis of the tourist media's role in fashioning preferred ideological images. See Butler 1990.

91 Memorandum from Dr. W. Bloch, "The Role of the Zionist Tourism Information Bureau, and Turning into the Tourism Department of the National Institutions," Tel Aviv, September 28, 1944, KKL-5, 12957, Central Zionist Archives, Jerusalem.

92 Peres 1921, Introduction. Zuta and Sukenik in the introduction to their book *Our Land*, also published in the early 1920s, speak in a similar vein: "Our book is designed to serve as a guidebook to Eretz Yisrael for Jewish residents and tourists." See: Zuta and Sukenik 1920, Introduction. The high commissioner, in his introduction to the Hebrew edition of Luke and Keith-Roach's guidebook, observed that "the considerable interest that all Jews have in this country, those who live in it and those scattered all over the globe, requires the book to be translated into Hebrew." See: Luke and Keith-Roach 1924, Introduction.

93 W. Torenovsky, director of PEL Ltd., to A. Shamorek, director of the Trade and Industry Department., Jewish Agency, November 30, 1929, S-8, 215, Central Zionist Archives, Jerusalem; memorandum on "Tourism in Eretz Yisrael and its Problems," undated, unnamed author, S-25, 2659, Central Zionist Archives, Jerusalem; Zionist Information Bureau for Tourists to the Jewish Agency Executive, October 31, 1944, S-49, 649, Central Zionist Archives, Jerusalem; head office of the JNF to the national offices of the JNF, May 9, 1938, KKL-5, 9183, Central Zionist Archives, Jerusalem.

94 Zionist Information Bureau for Tourists in Eretz Yisrael 1933, 61; see also Katz 2000, 100.

95 Based on Del Casino and Hanna 2000.

96 One of the first examples of this kind of map can be found in Peres's guidebook, published in 1921. The map focuses on the city's western Jewish neighborhoods,

allotting very little space to its Muslim neighborhoods. In the 1930s and 1940s, Stei-matzky published several urban tourist maps highlighting the Jewish presence in the city (see Figure 3.4). Guidebooks issued by the Zionist Information Bureau also included maps that stressed the Jewish presence in the country in general and in Jerusalem in particular.

97 See for example: Cohen, Ifergan, and Cohen 2002; Dahles 2002; Holloway 1981.
98 N. G. Tisch (Tishbi), secretary of the Trade and Industry Department, Jerusalem, to Louis Lipski, chairman of the Zionist organizations in America, New York, August 16, 1922, S-8, 1403, Central Zionist Archives, Jerusalem. In his letter, Tishbi under-lines the fact that most local travel companies are anti-Jewish and constantly dis-criminate against Jewish workers. He mentions the numerous letters he has received, all complaining of Arab discrimination. In his opinion, the main problem is that Arabs own the local companies. See Geffen 1979; "News from the Land of Israel" [in Hebrew], *Haolam*, May 4, 1923. See also Jewish wagon-drivers (six in all), Jeru-salem, to the Zionist Executive in Palestine, Trade and Industry Department, Jerusa-lem, March 5, 1922, S-8, 1403, Central Zionist Archives, Jerusalem; Bezalel Baltinester, owner of a company trading in olive-wood products, shells, and prod-ucts of the Holy Land, Jerusalem, to the Zionist Executive in Palestine, Trade and Industry Department, Jerusalem, March 5, 1922, S-8, 1403, Central Zionist Archives, Jerusalem.
99 Zionist Executive, Jerusalem, to L. J. Stein, the Zionist Executive, London, Decem-ber 21, 1922, S-8, 1403, Central Zionist Archives, Jerusalem. For further informa-tion on Thomas Cook's attitude towards Jewish tourism in the first half of the 1920s, see Berkowitz 1997, 129–131.
100 "The Jewish School of Guides, Jerusalem," *Commercial Bulletin*, January 7, 1923.
101 Summary of a meeting on the subject of tourism, Trade and Industry Department of the Zionist Executive, Jerusalem, March 20, 1923, 1403, 1, Central Zionist Archives, Jerusalem. See also: N. Tisch (Tishbi), manager of the Trade and Industry Depart-ment, Zionist Executive, Jerusalem, to A. Rupin, March 9, 1922, S-8, 20, 8, Central Zionist Archives, Jerusalem.
102 The course's syllabus included: Dr. Braver, Writing about Eretz Yisrael; Dr. Klauzner, History of Eretz Yisrael; J. Peres, Historical Topography of Eretz Yisrael; Dr. Meir, Archaeology of Eretz Yisrael; Y. Ben-Zvi, Ethnography of the People Living in Eretz Yisrael; Mr. Fingalevsky, The Country's Most Important Flora; Dr. Mazieh, Looking after Your Health En Route; Mr. Kesselman, General Conduct with Reference to Tourists; Mr. Sukenik, Excursions. See: Tour Guide Certificate, Zionist Executive's Trade and Industry Department to Mr. Harry Chanoch. See: Chanoch 1988, illustration no. 23.
103 "The Tour Guide Course Examination" [in Hebrew], *Haaretz*, October 26, 1922; memorandum of the Association of Jewish Tour Guides in Palestine, 6 Heshvan 5683, S-8, 1403/1, Central Zionist Archives, Jerusalem.
104 *Palestine Weekly*, December 15, 1922.
105 Committee of the Association of Jewish Tour Guides in Palestine, *Journal of Tour Guides* no. 1, Kislev, 5683, S-8, 1403/1, Central Zionist Archives, Jerusalem.
106 N. Pinsker, in the name of the Association of Jewish Tour Guides, Jerusalem, pam-phlet for tourists coming to Eretz Yisrael, undated, 1403, Central Zionist Archives, Jerusalem.
107 M. Grunhut, director of the Zionist Information Bureau, Jerusalem, press conference on the issue of tourism, June 12, 1931, KKL-5, 3654/2, Central Zionist Archives, Jerusalem.
108 Dr. Levinson, Zionist Information Bureau for Tourists, Sivan 5687, report on the recently ended season, 824, Central Zionist Archives, Jerusalem. The situation described in the report remained more or less the same throughout the early 1930s. A local Jewish newspaper reported on groups of tourists from America, most of

whom were Jewish, but "since the tour guides and the drivers are for the most part Arabs (only 6 percent of the tourist guides are Jewish), they do not get to see much of Jewish Palestine." See: "Tourist Season" [in Hebrew], *Doar Hayom*, January 28, 1930. This corresponds with information supplied by the Arab Chamber of Commerce in Jerusalem during the mid-1930s, according to which there were 109 Arab tour guides in the city. See: Arab Chamber of Commerce 1937–1938, 227–229.

109 "An Ordinance Regarding the Granting of Licenses to Tour Guides and Their Supervision" [in Hebrew], *Official Gazette*, April 1, 1927.
110 E. T. Richmond, "The Tour Guide Ordinance, 1927" [in Hebrew], *Official Gazette*, November 1, 1927.
111 "Publication and Validity of the Tour Guide Ordinance, 1927," *Official Gazette*, July 1, 1927; for a positive assessment of government activity in this field and suggestions for improvement, see: *Palestine and Near East Economic Magazine*, 7, 1927, 216–217. Our thanks to Joshua Chanoch for giving us access to his father's archive, which contained Harry Chanoch's tour guiding license issued in accordance with the 1927 ordinance.
112 Z. Levinson, Jerusalem, to Commander Kisch, Jerusalem, February 14, 1928, KKL-5, 2493, Central Zionist Archives, Jerusalem; Z. Levinson, Jerusalem, to G. Agronsky, Jerusalem, May 1, 1928, KKL-5, 2493, Central Zionist Archives, Jerusalem.
113 "In the Tourists' Information Bureau" [in Hebrew], *Doar Hayom*, February 10, 1928.
114 Jewish Tour Guides, Jerusalem, to H. Sacker, the Zionist Executive, Jerusalem, December 3, 1929, S-25, 2710, Central Zionist Archives, Jerusalem.
115 M. Grunhut, summary of an interview with Keith-Roach, December 10, 1930, S-49, 278, Central Zionist Archives, Jerusalem. According to Vilnay, from 1930 onwards the Supreme Muslim Council banned Jews from entering the Temple Mount mosques and it was only after special lobbying that a permit was granted, for a price. See: Vilnay 1946, 30.
116 M. Grunhut, Zionist Information Bureau for Tourists in Palestine, Jerusalem, to the Committee of the Information Bureau, Jerusalem, January 27, 1930, KKL-5, 3654, Central Zionist Archives, Jerusalem; press conference on the question of tourism, June 12, 1931, KKL-5, 3654/2, Central Zionist Archives, Jerusalem.
117 Memorandum from M. Grunhut, director of the Zionist Information Bureau, July 31, 1932, S-30, 1549, Central Zionist Archives, Jerusalem. The document states that over the last three years relations have improved with the tour company managers in the city.
118 Memorandum of a conversation that took place in London between M. Grunhut, director of the Zionist Information Bureau, and G. Linton, and representatives of Thomas Cook, October 12 and 17, 1932, S-49, 278, Central Zionist Archives, Jerusalem.
119 Advertisement [in Hebrew], *Doar Hayom*, January 1, 1926. An announcement by Palestine Lloyd Ltd., on the occasion of its foundation, emphasized "the need to open transportation and tourist traffic to Palestine." The new company, which had "branches in Palestine and Egypt," promised to "work closely and vigorously with the Zionist Executive on the more essential issues of tourism in Palestine." PEL was responsible for the organization of Zionist conventions abroad and handled all official travel arrangements for members of the Jewish Agency Executive and the Zionist General Council. See W. Bloch, memorandum on the subject of the Zionist Information Bureau for Tourists in E-I, PEL and the Tourism Department of the Jewish Agency, June 6, 1937, S-54, 100, Central Zionist Archives, Jerusalem. For more information on Lloyd's activity during the British Mandate, see: Klein 1973, 25–32; memorandum submitted by PEL to the Jewish Agency, unsigned and undated (probably from 1935), S-640, Central Zionist Archives, Jerusalem.

120 R. Ginsberg, general manager, PEL Ltd., Jerusalem, to Dr. W. Sentor, the Jewish
      Agency for Israel, Jerusalem, December 17, 1936, S-640, Central Zionist Archives,
      Jerusalem; conversation between clerks at the Zionist establishment and the director
      of Thomas Cook, May 4, 1937, S-25, 2704, Central Zionist Archives, Jerusalem; W.
      Bloch, report on work of the Information Bureau for the period between April 1,
      1935, and March 31, 1937, Tel Aviv, June 15, 1937, KKL-5, 7705, Central Zionist
      Archives, Jerusalem.
121 Summary of a discussion on tourism by the representatives of the relevant institu-
      tions, February 1, 1937, KKL-5, 7703, Central Zionist Archives, Jerusalem; minutes
      of a meeting to discuss the organization of tourism in Palestine, January 7, 1938,
      KKL-5, 9183, Central Zionist Archives, Jerusalem; circular from the Jewish Agen-
      cy's tourism department, no. 3550/248/2115, April 25, 1938, KKL-5, 9183, Central
      Zionist Archives, Jerusalem.
122 The kibbutz and moshav were two types of agricultural communities that developed
      in the new world of the Jewish settlement beginning in the early twentieth century.
      The first kibbutz, Degania, was established on the shores of the Sea of Galilee in
      1909 and the first moshav, Nahallal, in the Jezreel Valley in 1921.
123 Review of the activities of the Political Department in dealing with the army, Jerusa-
      lem, July 31, 1940, S-25, 6728, Central Zionist Archives, Jerusalem; J. Hochstein,
      Zionist Information Bureau, Jerusalem, to J. Golan, Jewish Agency's Political
      Department, Jerusalem, February 13, 1942, S-25, 6738, Central Zionist Archives,
      Jerusalem; W. Bloch, report on activities of Zionist Tourism Information Bureau in
      Palestine for 5720, October 27, 1942, S-23, 115, Central Zionist Archives, Jerusa-
      lem; memorandum from Dr. W. Bloch, "The Role of the Zionist Information Bureau
      for Tourists and turning into the Tourist Department of the National Institutions,"
      Tel Aviv, September 28, 1944, KKL-5, 12957, Central Zionist Archives, Jerusalem;
      Zionist Information Bureau for Tourists, "Extract of Its Activities during the Period
      1939–1945," May 6, 1946, KKL-5, 14281, Central Zionist Archives, Jerusalem. For
      a general summary of the Jewish community activities vis-à-vis the British army
      during the war period, see Gelber 1995. Israel Hochstein (Zuriel), who joined the
      Jerusalem office of the Bureau in 1938 and was its manager between 1939 and 1940,
      described in detail the Bureau's activities before the war, and particularly its prose-
      lytizing efforts among overseas tourists. He also offered an account of its activities
      during the war when the aim was to "turn the Bureau into a club for allied soldiers,
      to interest these soldiers in Zionist activity in the country and to organize excursions
      to kibbutzim and moshavim" (Israel Hochstein [Zuriel], personal communication).
      Chanan Michaeli, who worked in the Tourism Bureau between 1944 and 1947, char-
      acterized the war years as a period of intensive activity targeting primarily allied
      troops. It was, he noted, "advertised that one could visit a kibbutz through the
      Bureau" (Michaeli, personal communication).
124 Competition between Arab and Israeli tour guides, to give but one example, con-
      tinued well into the late twentieth century. See: Bowman 1992. For an overview on
      the struggle between Israel and Arabs over the last 50 years concerning tourism
      activity, see: Mansfeld 1996.

References

Address Book. 1935, 1942. *Book of Commerce and Industry in the Land of Israel* [in
      Hebrew]. Tel Aviv: n.p.
All of Israel [in Hebrew]. 1932. Tel Aviv: Trade and Industry.
Amiran, David. 1984. "The Cartographic Survey of Jerusalem, 1940—A Contribution to
      the Methodology of Mapping in Urban Geography" [in Hebrew]. *Eretz-Israel* 17,
      97–100.

Arab Chamber of Commerce. 1937–1938. *Trade and Industry Guide* [in Arabic]. Jerusalem: Arab Chamber of Commerce.

Ashbee, Charles Robert. 1917. *Where the Great City Stands: A Study in the New Civic.* London: Essex House Press.

Ashbee, Charles Robert. 1923. *A Palestine Notebook 1918–1923.* London: Doubleday, Page and Company.

Avni, Gideon and Jon Seligman. 2001. *The Temple Mount 1917–2001: Documentation, Research, and Inspection of Antiquities.* Jerusalem: Israel Antiquities Authority.

Avusher, R. 1981. "YMCA Jerusalem" [in Hebrew]. In *Leisure and Recreation Culture in Israel*, edited by Uri Lipzin, 172–174. Tel Aviv: Goma.

Bar, Doron and Kobi Cohen-Hattab. 2003. "A New Kind of Pilgrimage—The Modern Tourist Pilgrim of Nineteenth Century and Early Twentieth Century Palestine." *Middle Eastern Studies* 39 (2): 131–148.

Ben-Arieh, Yehoshua. 1984. *Jerusalem in the Nineteenth Century: The Old City.* Jerusalem and New York: Yad Izhak Ben-Zvi.

Berger, J. 1931. "Tourist Development in Palestine." *Palestine & Near East Economic Magazine* 18: 345–350.

Berkovitz, Shmuel. 1978. *The Legal Status of the Holy Places in Israel* [in Hebrew]. Jerusalem: PhD diss., The Hebrew University of Jerusalem.

Berkowitz, Michael. 1997. *Western Jewry and the Zionist Project 1914–1933.* Cambridge: Cambridge University Press.

Biger, Gideon. 1977. "'Garden Suburbs' in Jerusalem—Planning and Development under Early British Rule, 1917–1925" [in Hebrew]. *Cathedra* 6: 108–131.

Biger, Gideon. 1981. *Urban Planning and Enforcement of Building Codes—Jerusalem under the British Mandate and Today* [in Hebrew]. Jerusalem: The Jerusalem Institute for Israel Studies.

Biger, Gideon. 1989. "Building and Construction in Jerusalem under British Rule, 1917–1948" [in Hebrew]. In *Jerusalem in Zionist Vision and Realization*, edited by Hagit Lavsky, 183–215. Jerusalem: The Zalman Shazar Center for Jewish History and the Center for the Zionism and the Yishuv at the Hebrew University of Jerusalem.

Bowman, Glenn. 1991. "Christian Ideology and the Image of a Holy Land: The Place of Jerusalem Pilgrimage in the Various Christianities." In *Contesting the Sacred: The Anthropology of Christian Pilgrimage*, edited by John Eade and Michael J. Sallnow, 98–121. London and New York: Routledge.

Bowman, Glenn. 1992. "The Politics of Tour Guiding: Israeli and Palestinian Guides in Israel and the Occupied Territories." In *Tourism and the Less Developed Countries*, edited by David Harrison, 121–134. London: Belhaven Press.

Breasted, Charles. 1948. *Pioneer to the Past: The Story of James Henry Breasted, Archaeologist.* New York: C. Scribner's Sons.

Butler, Richard. W. 1990. "The Influence of the Media in Shaping International Tourist Patterns." *Tourism Recreation Research* 15 (2): 46–53.

Chanoch, Linor. 1988. *My Grandfather—Harry Chanoch* [in Hebrew]. Jerusalem: Workshop for writing final papers, Hebrew Gymnasium.

Cohen, Erik. 1985. "The Tourist Guide: The Origins, Structure and Dynamics of a Role." *Annals of Tourism Research* 12 (1): 5–29.

Cohen, Erik, Maurice Ifergan, and Eynath Cohen. 2002. "A New Paradigm in Guiding: The Madrich as a Role Model." *Annals of Tourism Research* 29 (4): 919–932.

Cohen-Hattab, Kobi. 2001. "The Development of Tourism Infrastructure in Jerusalem During the British Rule, 1917–1948" [in Hebrew]. Jerusalem: PhD diss., the Hebrew University of Jerusalem.

Cohen-Hattab, Kobi. 2007. "The Development of the Hotel Industry and Tourist Accommodation in Mandatory Jerusalem" [in Hebrew]. *Eretz-Israel* 28: 404–411.

Cohen-Hattab, Kobi. 2010. "Pilgrimage and Tourism: Organization and Infrastructure" [in Hebrew]. In *The History of Jerusalem: The Late Ottoman Period (1800–1917)*, edited by Israel Bartal and Haim Goren, 197–210. Jerusalem: Yad Izhak Ben-Zvi.

Cohen-Hattab, Kobi and Yossi Katz. 2001. "The Attraction of Palestine: Tourism in the Years 1850–1948." *Journal of Historical Geography* 27 (2): 178–195.

Conway, William Martin. 1923. *Palestine and Morocco*. London: E. Arnold and Co.

Cook, Thoman. 1907. *Cook's Handbook for Palestine and Syria*. London: T. Cook.

Crawford, Alan. 1985. *Ashbee: Architect, Designer, and Romantic Socialist*. New Haven: Yale University Press.

Cust, Lionel George Arthur. 1930. *The Status Quo in the Holy Places*. London: H.M.S.O.

Dahles, Heidi. 2002. "The Politics of Tour Guiding: Image Management in Indonesia." *Annals of Tourism Research* 29 (3): 783–800.

Del Casino, Jr., Vincent V. and Stephen P. Hanna. 2000. "Representation and Identities in Tourism Map Space." *Progress in Human Geography* 24 (1): 23–46.

Department of Migration. 1946. *The Statistics of Migration and Naturalization for the Year 1945*. Jerusalem: Department of Migration.

Department of Statistics. 1946. *Statistical Abstract of Palestine 1944–1945*. Palestine: Department of Statistics.

Dinur, Ben-Zion., ed. 1973. *History of the Hagana* [in Hebrew]. Tel-Aviv: Am-Oved.

Duff, Douglas V. 1938. *Palestine Unveiled*. London and Glasgow: Blackie and Son.

Eisenstadt, David. 1998. *The Evolution of Jerusalem's Municipal Boundaries, 1863–1967* [in Hebrew]. Ramat-Gan: Master's thesis, Bar-Ilan University.

Elston, Roy. 1929. *The Traveller's Handbook for Palestine and Syria*. London: Simpkin Marshall.

Ennis, Alfred Reginald. 1942. *Round about Palestine*. Jerusalem: Young Men's Christian Association of Great Britain with H.M. Forces in the Middle East.

Farmer, Leslie. 1945. *We Saw the Holy City*. London: Epworth Press.

Fawzi, Ibrahim. 2006. *West Meets East: The Story of the Rockefeller Museum*. Jerusalem: Israel Museum.

Fuchs, Ron. 1992. *Austen St. Barbe Harrion: A British Architect in the Holy Land* [in Hebrew]. Haifa: PhD diss., the Technion—Israel Institute of Technology.

Geffen, David. 1979. "'A Visit to the Land of the Patriarchs'—The Diary of William Topkis, 1923" [in Hebrew]. *Cathedra* 13: 71–94.

Gelber, Yoav. 1995. "The Community as a Host Society" [in Hebrew]. In *The History of the Jewish Community in Eretz-Israel since 1882: The Period of the British Mandate*, edited by Moshe Lissak, 412–416. Jerusalem: The Israel Academy of Sciences and Humanities.

Genachowski, Dov. 1993. *More Stories of Jerusalem* [in Hebrew]. Jerusalem: Carta.

Gilbert, Martin. 1996. *Jerusalem in the Twentieth Century*. London: Chatto & Windus.

Goodsall, Robert Harold. 1925. *Palestine Memories 1917–1918–1925*. Canterbury: Cross and Jackman.

Great Britain, Colonial Office. 1925. *Report by His Britannic Majesty's Government on the Administration under Mandate of Palestine and Transjordan for the Year 1924*. col. no. 12. London: Colonial Office.

Great Britain, Colonial Office. 1938. *Report by His Britannic Majesty's Government to the Council of the League of Nations on the Administration Palestine and Transjordan for the Year 1938*. col. no. 166. London: Colonial Office.

Great Britain, High Commissioner for Palestine. 1925. *Palestine—Report of the High Commissioner on the Administration of Palestine, 1920–1925.* London: His Majesty's Stationery Office.

Gross, Nachum. 1982a. "The Economic Policy of the Government of Palestine during the Mandate Period" [in Hebrew]. *Cathedra* 24: 153–180.

Gross, Nachum. 1982b. "The Economic Policy of the Government of Palestine during the Mandate Period (continued)" [in Hebrew]. *Cathedra* 25: 135–168.

Gross, Nachum. 1984. "The Jewish Economy in Palestine during the Interim Years: 1928–1932" [in Hebrew]. *Zionism* 9: 207–220.

Gross, Nachum and Jacob Metzer. 1999. "Palestine in World War II: Some Economic Aspects" [in Hebrew]. In *Not by Spirit Alone: Studies in the Economic History of Modern Palestine and Israel,* edited by Nachum Gross, 300–324. Jerusalem: The Hebrew University of Jerusalem Magnes Press and Yad Izhak Ben-Zvi.

Gurevich, David, Aaron Gertz, and Roberto Bachi. 1944. *The Jewish Population of Palestine: Immigration, Demographic Structure and Natural Growth* [in Hebrew]. Jerusalem: The Department of Statistics of the Jewish Agency for Palestine.

Haezrahi, Yehuda. 1981. *City of Stone and Sky* [in Hebrew]. Tel Aviv: Ministry of Defense.

Hale-Or, Y. 1948. *Guide to Jerusalem* [in Hebrew]. Jerusalem: n.p.

Halevi, Shoshana. 1989. *Affairs at the Beginning of the Yishuv's History* [in Hebrew]. Jerusalem: n.p.

Harvey, William. 1935. *Church of the Holy Sepulchre Jerusalem Structural Survey: Final Report.* London: Oxford University Press and H. Milford.

Hoade, Eugene. 1946. *Guide to the Holy Land.* Jerusalem: Franciscan Press.

Holliday, Eunice. 1997. *Letters from Jerusalem during the Palestine Mandate.* London and New York: Radcliffe Press.

Holloway, J. Christopher. 1981. "The Guided Tour: A Sociological Approach." *Annals of Tourism Research* 8 (3): 377–402.

Hopkins, Charles Howard. 1951. *History of the Y.M.C.A in North America.* New York: Association Press.

Horowitz, David. 1948. *The Developing Israeli Economy* [in Hebrew]. Jerusalem: Bialik.

Hyman, Benjamin. 1992. "Between Heaven and Hearth: British Town Planning in Jerusalem." Submitted to the workshop on *Jerusalem in the Mind of Western World,* II, 1917–1948, Jerusalem.

Hysler-Rubin, Noah. 2005. "Planning the Artistic City: Charles Robert Ashbee in Jerusalem" [in Hebrew]. *Cathedra* 117: 81–102.

Izakson, Eliahu. 1994. *A View from the Bridge Generation* [in Hebrew]. Tel Aviv: Or Publishing.

Kark, Ruth and Shimon Landman. 1980. "Kasr al-Sheikh: A Castle in Jerusalem [in Hebrew]. *Teva Va'aretz* 22 (5): 196–198.

Kark, Ruth and Shimon Landman. 1981. "Muslim Neighborhoods outside the Jerusalem City Walls during the Ottoman Period" [in Hebrew]. In *Jerusalem in the Modern Period,* edited by Eli Shaltiel, 174–211. Jerusalem: Yad Izhak Ben-Zvi and Ministry of Defense.

Katinka, Baruch. 1961. *From Then to Now* [in Hebrew]. Jerusalem: Kiryat Sefer.

Katz, Kimberly. 2005. *Jordanian Jerusalem: Holy Places and National Spaces.* Gainsville: University Press of Florida.

Katz, Shaul. 1985. "The Israeli-Teacher Guide: The Emergence and Perpetuation of a Role." *Annals of Tourism Research* 12 (1): 49–72.

Katz, Yossi. 2000. "Zionism and the 'Marketing' of Eretz Israel: Zionist Tourism Guidebooks during the British Mandate Period" [in Hebrew]. *Cathedra* 97: 85–116.

Kendall, Henry. 1948. *Jerusalem—The City Plan: Preservation and Development During the British Mandate, 1918–1948*. London: H.M.S.O.

Klein, Chaim H., ed. 1973. *The Second Million: Israel Tourist Industry, Past-Present-Future* [in Hebrew]. Tel Aviv: Amir.

Kohn, Ayelet. 1991. "The Cinema in Eretz Israel in the 1930s: A Reflection of the Ideas of an Era" [in Hebrew]. *Cathedra* 61: 141–155.

Kroyanker, David. 1981. *Palace Hotel* [in Hebrew]. Jerusalem: The City Planning Division.

Kroyanker, David. 1985. *Jerusalem Architecture—Periods and Styles: Arab Buildings outside the Old City Walls* [in Hebrew]. Jerusalem: Keter.

Kroyanker, David. 2005. *Jaffa Road: Biography of a Street—Story of a City* [in Hebrew]. Jerusalem: Keter.

Kupferschmidt, Uri M. 1987. *The Supreme Muslim Council: Islam under the British Mandate for Palestine*. Leiden: Brill.

Landa, Myer. Jack. 1932. *Palestine As It Is*. London: E. Goldston.

Landau-Mishor, Yael. 2001. *Yitzchak Ya'akobi—Pioneer and Teacher* [in Hebrew]. Jerusalem: Old Board Association, Beit Hakerem.

Latourette, Kenneth S. 1957. *World Service: A History of the Foreign Work and World Service of the Young Men's Associations of the United States and Canada*. New York: Association Press.

Lazar, Hadara. 1990. *In and Out of Palestine* [in Hebrew]. Jerusalem: Keter.

Luke, Harry Charles. 1924. *The Traveller's Handbook for Palestine & Syria*. London: Simpkin, Marshall, Hamilton, Kent & Co.

Luke, Harry Charles. 1932. *Ceremonies at the Holy Places*. London: Faith Press.

Luke, Harry Charles and E. Keith-Roach. 1922. *The Handbook of Palestine*. London: Macmillan.

Luke, Harry Charles and E. Keith-Roach. 1924. *The Traveller's Handbook for Palestine and Syria*. London: Simpkin, Marshall, Hamilton, Kent & Co.

Lumby, Christopher. 1934. *The Traveller's Handbook to Palestine, Syria & Iraq.* London: Simpkin Marshall.

Maisler, Benjamin and Samuel Yeivin. 1940. *Palestine Guide for Navy, Army and Air Force*. Tel-Aviv: Olympia.

Mansfeld, Yoel. 1996. "Wars, Tourism and the 'Middle East' Factor." In *Tourism, Crime and International Security Issues*, edited by Abraham Pizam and Yoel Mansfeld, 265–278. New York: John Wiley.

Martelli, George. 1938. *Whose Sea? A Mediterranean Journey*. London: Chatto and Windus.

Matson, Olaf G. 1946. *The Palestine Guide*. Jerusalem: Joshua Simon.

Morton, Henry Vollam. 1935. *In the Steps of the Master*. London: Rich and Cowan.

Nathan, Robert Roy, Oscar Gass, and Daniel Creamer. 1946. *Palestine: Problem and Promise—An Economic Study*. Washington, DC: Public Affairs Press.

Oriental Advertising Company. 1920. *The Palestine Directory*. Cairo: Oriental Advertising Company.

Oskotski, Abraham. 1921. *The Whole of Jerusalem for the Year 1921* [in Hebrew]. Jerusalem: A. Oskotski.

Peres, Yeshayahu. 1921. *Travel Book—Eretz Israel and Southern Syria* [in Hebrew]. Jerusalem, Berlin and Vienna: Binyamin Hertz.

Pevzner, Yeshayahu, ed. 1926. *All of Israel* [in Hebrew]. Tel Aviv: Trade and Industry Department.

Porath, Yehoshua. 1974. *The Emergence of the Palestinian-Arab National Movement, 1918–1929*. London: Frank Cass.

Porath, Yehoshua and Yaacov Shavit. 1982. *The History of Eretz Israel: The British Mandate and the Jewish National Home*. Jerusalem: Keter.

Reiter, Yitzhak. 2003. "The *Waqf* in Changing Circumstances: The Economic Management and Political Role of the *Waqf* in Mandatory Jerusalem" [in Hebrew]. In *Economy and Society in Mandatory Palestine, 1918–1948*, edited by Avi Bareli and Nahum Karlinsky, 349–365. Sde Boker: Sde Boker Research Center.

Roman, Yadin. 2010. *The King David, 1930–2010* [in Hebrew]. Jerusalem: Dan Hotels Company.

Samuel, Edwin. 1970. *A Lifetime in Jerusalem: The Memoirs of the Second Viscount Samuel*. Jerusalem: Transaction Publishers.

Semberg, Fiona, ed. 1993. *The Story of the King David Hotel*. Jerusalem: The King David Hotel.

Shachar, Arie and Noam Shoval. 1999. "Tourism in Jerusalem: A Place to Pray." In *The Tourist City*, edited by Dennis R. Judd and Susan S. Fainstein, 192–200. New Haven: Yale University Press.

Shapiro, Shachar. 1973. "Planning of Jerusalem—The First Generation (1918–1968)." In *Urban Geography of Jerusalem: A Companion to the Atlas of Jerusalem*, edited by David Amiran *et al.*, 139–147. Berlin and New York: W. de Gruyter.

Sherman, Ari Joshua. 1997. *Mandate Days: British Lives in Palestine 1918–1948*. London: Thames and Hudson.

Shoval, Noam and Kobi Cohen-Hattab. 2001. "Urban Hotel Development Patterns in the Face of Political Shifts." *Annals of Tourism Research* 28 (4): 908–925.

Stead, K. W. 1931. *Economic Condition in Palestine*. London: H.M.S.O.

Storrs, Ronald. 1937. *The Memoirs of Sir Ronald Storrs*. New York: Putnam.

Supreme Muslim Council. 1924. *A Brief Guide to Al-Haram Al-Sarif*. Jerusalem: Supreme Muslim Council.

Trade and Industry Department, Palestine Zionist Executive. 1922. *Eretz Israel for Jewish Tourists*. Jerusalem: Trade and Industry Department.

Troyex, Y. 1931. *The Western Wall Trial: Report of the International Wall Commission* [in Hebrew]. Tel Aviv: Tel Aviv Publication.

Tryster, Hillel. 1995. *Israel before Israel—Silent Cinema in the Holy Land*. Jerusalem: Steven Spielberg Jewish Film Archive.

Urnstein, Isaac Avigdor. 1968. *Diary of the Wailing Wall* [in Hebrew]. Jerusalem: Urnstein House.

Vester, Fr. and Co. (Pub). 1920. *A Guide-Book to Jerusalem and Environs*. Jerusalem: F. Vester.

Vilnay, Zev. 1946. *Eretz-Israel Guide* [in Hebrew]. Tel-Aviv: Tour.

Weatherhead, Leslie D. 1936. *It Happened in Palestine*. London: Hodder and Stoughton.

YMCA. n.d. *The Jerusalem International YMCA*. n.p.

YMCA. 1933. *The Jerusalem Young Men's Christian Association*. Jerusalem: YMCA.

Zacharia, Shabtai. 1985. *Veteran Hotels and Hoteliers in Jerusalem* [in Hebrew]. Jerusalem: Ha'aguda Al Mishmar Yerushalayim.

Zionist Federation. 1925. *Report of the Zionist Federation Executive to the 14th Zionist Congress*. London: Zionist Federation.

Zionist Information Bureau for Tourists in Palestine. 1933. *Guide to New Palestine*. Jerusalem: Zionist Information Bureau for Tourists in Palestine.

Zusman, A. and Runy Reich. 1987. "The History of the Rockefeller Museum" [in Hebrew]. In *Zev Vilnay's Jubilee Volume* II, edited by Ely Schiller, 83–91. Jerusalem: Ariel.

Zuta, Hayyim Aryeh and Eleazar Lipa Sukenik. 1920. *Our Land: A Guidebook to Eretz Israel and Neighbouring Countries* I [in Hebrew]. Jerusalem: The Zionist Commission.

Archives and Collections

Central Zionist Archives, Jerusalem.
Haganah History Archives, Tel Aviv.
International YMCA Archives, Minneapolis.
Israel Antiquities Authority Archives, Jerusalem.
Israel State Archives, Jerusalem.
Jerusalem Municipal Archives, Jerusalem.
Public Record Office, London.

4   The divided city

The development of tourism in East and West Jerusalem (1948–1967)

On November 30, 1948, one year after the United Nations' resolution to divide the British Mandate territory of Palestine, a meeting was held in an abandoned house in the no-man's land between West and East Jerusalem, in the Musrara neighborhood near Damascus Gate. Present were Lieutenant-Colonel Moshe Dayan, commander of the Jerusalem district from the Israeli side, and Lieutenant-Colonel Abdullah el-Tell from the Jordanian side. Thus did the war that had erupted following the UN resolution officially end in Jerusalem. The officers spread a 1:20,000-scale map of Jerusalem on the dust-covered floor and each drew his military positions in grease pencil. Two lines were sketched on the map: Moshe Dayan drew the line of Israeli positions in red pencil and Abdullah el-Tell drew the Jordanian positions in green. The nature of a grease pencil is that its line is three to four millimeters wide—or 60 to 80 meters in reality, given the scale of the map. At the time, the pencil lines were not entirely clear, as they were writing on the floor; with time, the colored line markings expanded due to heat, and some blurred. The two signees could not have imagined that this map would become the binding document upon which Jerusalem's demarcation lines would be based for 19 years. With time, the lines themselves would expand to cover houses and even entire roads (Narkiss 1975, 24–46; Ramon 1987, 9–11).

The war that broke out in the country immediately following the UN resolution to partition the land on November 29, 1947—called "The War of Independence" by the Israelis and the "Nakba," or catastrophe, by the Palestinians—escalated with the exit of the British on May 14, 1948. It became a comprehensive confrontation between the newly established Jewish state and its Arab neighbors and had a serious impact on Jerusalem's economy and the size of its population. Grave battles were waged on the streets and the city was under siege for a period of time, with no regular supply of water or food. The military situation disabled a good portion of the factories, commercial centers were paralyzed, and many parts of the city were severely damaged.

In the armistice agreement signed between Israel and Jordan in Rhodes on April 3, 1949, the armistice lines set were identical to the lines defined in the November 30, 1948, agreement, and the map drawn in the abandoned building in Musrara, with its red and green lines, was adopted by the sides as the armistice map. In the coming years, this map would stir up many problems.

The ceasefire agreement established a new geographic and political reality with the end of the war: Jerusalem was divided by a border that stretched from its east, in which the holy sites for all three religions (with the exception of Mount Zion) were under Jordanian rule; its western section, from then on, was under Israeli control.

As a divided city, with a political border splitting its two sections, Jerusalem could not serve as a site of pilgrimage as it had in days past. For the first time in the history of modern Jerusalem a clear geographical and political boundary was created between the historical city and the new city. At the hub of the city there was an urban borderline; along it, a no-man's land extended between the city's two sections (Narkiss 1975, 11–55; Yizrael 1986, 17–26). Much of this area was destroyed, and remained in ruins throughout the years of the city's partition. This urban reality calls to mind the situation in Berlin after the Second World War, more so following the establishment of the Berlin Wall at the hub of the city (Strom 2001).

The impact on residents' sources of income was also related to the exit of the British from the city on the eve of the declaration of the state, as the British refused to cooperate with the United Nations with regard to the "partition" decision. In fact, there was no communication between the departing British government and the settlement leadership, no official transfer of the central government mechanism. The Israeli government, which replaced the British, was established first in Tel Aviv, and thus took from Jerusalem one of its main sources of income as the capital of British rule in Palestine (Huminer 1997, 75–107; Roman 1989, 217–234).

Moreover, as a result of the city's partition, western Jerusalem no longer served as a crossroads between the coastal plain and Transjordan, and between the country's south and north, but was left the very end of a dead end. Its status as a locus of services for its surroundings greatly diminished as a result of the destruction of most of the Arab villages from the strip that connected the city to the coastal plain. The border that split the two parts of the city and dissected its hub, too, was considered a "hostile border," which negatively affected the quality of life in the city and gave it the image of a dangerous place (Ganchovsky 1994, 116–188; Schweid 1994, 115–132). Indeed, the daily reality in the city was perilous, and sniper fire from soldiers manning posts along the urban line killed residents on both sides on a number of occasions.

Tourism in East Jerusalem was not greatly affected by the partition; in fact, most of the tourism to Jerusalem focused on this part of the city. The location of the religious and historical sites in the city's east meant that it was a draw; the tourist sector became East Jerusalem's primary source of employment. Moreover, a good portion of the tourism-based income throughout the West Bank[1] came from East Jerusalem.

The Israeli government declared West Jerusalem the capital of the State of Israel in December 1949.[2] However, the situation in the city was far from simple. Aside from the lack of holy sites, which undermined the city's importance as a pilgrim and tourist center, West Jerusalem faced two other problems, which weakened it in the face of the challenges anticipated in any capital city: (1) from outside, Israel's declaration of West Jerusalem as the capital of the state was unilateral and not officially recognized by the world's states, and the city's international status remained disputed (Golani 1992; Shalom 1993, 75–97); (2) internally, in the Mandate era the Jewish settlement's demographic and economic center of gravity had moved to the center of the country and Jerusalem had been weakened greatly in the state's first days (Gonen 2003, 439–488; Huminer 1997, 75–107; Roman 1989, 217–234).

As a result, tourism was one of the most noticeable economic realms in which West Jerusalem was affected by the new political situation. In the period of the divided city, when most of the city's attractions that were of historical interest were on the Jordanian side, West Jerusalem was no longer a significant locus of pilgrimage. The Jordanians in effect violated Article VIII of the armistice agreement signed between Israel and Jordan, under which the Jews were to be given free access to both the Western Wall and the Mount of Olives. The Jordanians prevented access of even Jewish non-Israelis to the Western Wall and all of the holy sites around Jerusalem throughout the period of partition. Israeli Muslims were also forbidden to enter the holy Islamic sites held by the Jordanians. Israeli Christians were permitted to cross the border and visit holy sites once a year, on Christmas (Gold 2007, 153–155).[3]

Recognizing the changing tides, Israel focused on a new type of site: the secular, national institute. The period of partition was one of new building and growth in West Jerusalem as the nascent state developed its political institutions and centers. While tourists continued to flock to the ancient sites in East Jerusalem, Jewish West Jerusalem was busy building the centers and institutions that would ultimately become its new secular tourist sites. Alongside these activities, West Jerusalem also uncovered a number of new ancient findings which drew in tourists.

In the coming chapter, we take a closer look at the development of the tourist industry in the years of partition. In the first section we discuss the eastern city, which became the central attraction for tourists and pilgrims; in the second section of the chapter the western part of the city is examined. East Jerusalem remained a tourist center and continued to evolve with its tourism; the western city, in the absence of the tourism industry it had relied on for so long, looked for other ways to stabilize its economy and cement its image as the state's capital. We will see that while little building took place in the eastern city, the western city was a changed place by the end of partition in 1967.

The majority of the attention in the chapter is naturally devoted to the geopolitical and urban development that occurred in the western part of the city for two reasons.

First, the pilgrimage and tourism activities in the eastern part of the city were in no small part a continuation of the existing situation in the years before the partition. In contrast, in the western part of the city the activity was largely a renewal of the urban landscape ex nihilo and the establishment of the young Jewish state's capital as a center for tourism and "national pilgrimage" like any capital (Hall 2002; Maitland and Ritchie 2009).

The second reason lies in the plethora of available sources on change and renewal in the western city on one hand and, on the other, the paucity and insufficiency of sources relating to the eastern part of the city.

East Jerusalem: tourism and change

The detailed 1944 urban outline drawn up by British planner Henry Kendall served as a legal document in East Jerusalem under Jordanian rule until June 1967. This plan forbade any building on the western slopes of Mount Scopus or the Mount of Olives and left the slopes of the Kidron River as open areas (see Figure 4.1). The pressure to permit building in these areas was blocked primarily by counter-pressure from churches and other Christian agents, and due to the fact that the head planner of Mandatory Jerusalem, Kendall, continued to lead the city's planning team during the Jordanian period as well. In addition, wide areas to the north of Sheikh Jarrah and to the border of Shuafat (today's Givat Hamivtar and French Hill) were held by dozens of owners; in many cases reaching a consensus between owners as to the land's development was impossible (Benvenisti 1976, 88–89). Yet over the years certain changes were inserted in the Kendall plan, primarily a reduction of open spaces in other areas, an expansion of construction quotients in residential areas, and an increase in size of commercial zones. Alongside this outline Jordan prepared two new plans.[4]

In 1963, East Jerusalem's municipality requested a general plan for the city from the American company International Brown Engineers. The plan did not become a binding legal document, but was rather a general conceptual proposal that included an attempt to clarify the city's problems and to suggest approaches to a solution. The document contained numerous recommendations for improving the city, including a suggestion to considerably increase the space zoned for planning in East Jerusalem and to plan it as one functional unit. In this space, the company recommended cultivation of the area to the west of the Mount of Olives and Mount Scopus ridge as open landscape, in which industries, cemeteries, agriculture, forests, and rural settlement would be permitted. The western flank of the Mount of Olives would remain in its current form, that is to say, an area of religious buildings. The channel of the Kidron River to the south of Silwan would be an area for sewage facilities and waste disposal. The remainder of the space was for urban development, with most of the land designated for residences. Sheikh Jarrah and the western flank of Mount Scopus were proposed as dense residential areas. Two moderately dense residential areas would extend from the historical city along Jericho Way and Ramallah Way, and the remainder of the land was reserved for low-density residences. The area to the north of the walls of the Old City to Josephat Valley was a proposed urban center.

Not long after the Brown company's plan was submitted, Kendall prepared a plan called "Jerusalem (Jordan) and Region Planning Proposals." It served as a guiding document, and urban construction plans with legal authority were based on it. This plan, whose conceptual roots lay in the Brown plan, extended over a broader area, was more clearly arranged, and detailed the various urban function areas set out in the conceptual plan.

East Jerusalem as a tourist destination during partition

From 1948 to 1967, the Jordanian government encouraged visits on the part of individual and groups of non-Jews, pilgrims and tourists, to the sacred and historical sites in the eastern city. The government even initiated national and religious events

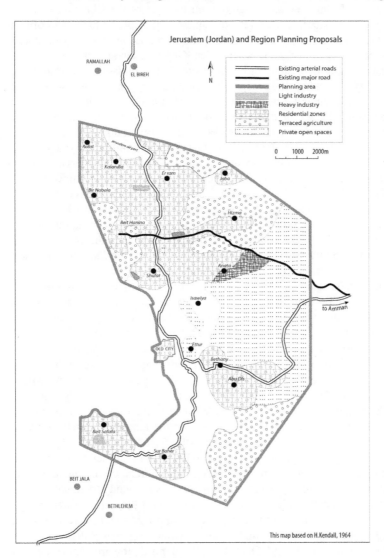

Figure 4.1 Jerusalem (Jordan) and region planning proposals, 1964.

that took place under its auspices and attracted many visitors. The activities of the Jordanian regime in the eastern city were designed to establish its hold on their part of the city and to make the name Jordan synonymous with the Holy Land—preserver of the holy places and defender of their heritage—in the consciousness of the Arab world and the world in general (Katz 2005, 118–136). One of the pinnacles of this campaign was Pope Paul VI's visit to East Jerusalem in 1964, sponsored by King Hussein, in which the pope went to holy places declared by the Jordanians to be national sites. The Jordanian government saw the arrival of the pope at the Christian sites under Muslim rule as recognition on the part of the Christian world of their reign in these places, and expressed it insistently in publications and official speeches. One manifestation of this was the series of stamps produced by the Jordanian government in honor of the visit, in which King Hussein and the pope are pictured against a backdrop of some of the holy sites in the Jordanian kingdom (Katz 2005, 124–129).[5] In taking these steps, the Jordanian king hoped to establish his status as Jordanian ruler and protector of the holy sites at the same time.

A comparison between the data on visitors to Jordan and Israel shows that the number of tourists in Jordan in those years was significantly greater than the number of tourists to Israel at the time—in fact, for nearly all of the years of partition it was more than double. No figures exist regarding the tourists visiting East Jerusalem alone, only the general number of entries to Jordan; however, we can assume that the vast majority of visitors visited East Jerusalem. These numbers show, for example, that 250,000 tourists visited Jordan in 1960 while in Israel there were only 118,000 visitors. The peak of tourism in Jordan during the partition era was in 1965, when nearly 750,000 people visited the country, while Israel saw only 296,000 tourists (Hashemite Kingdom of Jordan 1962, Number 13, 14; ibid., 1964, Number 15, 50).

From mid-1960s data on the economy in the eastern city, it is clear that tourism was the main source for much of the employment, with at least one quarter of those employed in East Jerusalem connected directly or indirectly to tourism. For instance, in 1966 an estimated 85 percent of the West Bank's income from tourism came from East Jerusalem (Hashemite Kingdom of Jordan 1965, Number 16, 50; Kimhi *et al.* 1976, 77). However, there are no figures on the overall number of tourists that year in the western part of the city. As will be seen later on, of the 291,000 tourists who came to Israel in 1966 there is a question about how many of them who visited West Jerusalem stayed overnight, and their number is no doubt considerably lower than the number of overnight tourists in Jordanian Jerusalem (Benvenisti 1976, 105; Roman 1967, 16–21).

The large number of tourists streaming into the eastern city led to a noticeable increase in tourist services, prominent among them hotels, travel agencies, tour guides, and taxis. A distinct concentration of hotels was found outside of Damascus Gate in the "East Jerusalem triangle" (on par with the commercial triangle created in the Mandate time in the city's western part that included Jaffa Road, King George Street, and Ben-Yehuda Street) which included Sultan Suleiman Street, Salah a-Din Street, and Damascus Road north toward Ramallah (see Figure 4.2; Shoval and Cohen-Hattab 2001, 908–925).

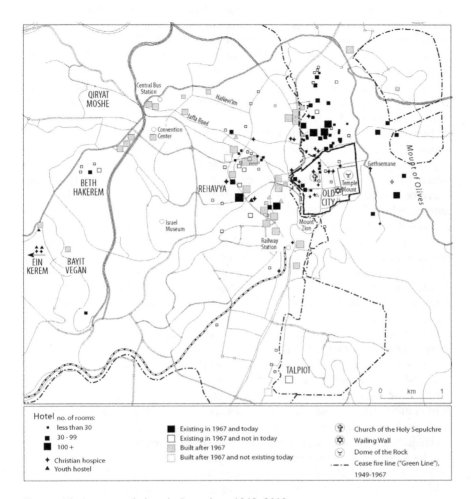

Figure 4.2 Accommodations in Jerusalem, 1948–2012.

In a comparative study conducted examining the number of hotels in 1964 in West Bank cities and on the eastern bank of the Jordan River it was found that most of the hotels—33 hotels of a total 56 (59 percent)—were in East Jerusalem. For the sake of comparison, Amman and Ramallah had five hotels each and the rest of Jordan's cities contained between one and three. Various tourist indices also found rather significant gaps between Jerusalem and other cities under Jordanian rule at the time: East Jerusalem had 150 official tour guides of the total 170 tour guides in the country and 33 of the total 52 travel agencies (Hopkins 1969, 20).

Parallel to the global rise in tourist traffic at the time,[6] the peak of activity in tourist services in East Jerusalem was in 1965 and 1966, when there were a little over 1,900 guest rooms in 51 hotels and 34 boarding houses and hostels, 73 travel agencies of various kinds, 183 souvenir stores, and a total of 4,200 people employed in the tourist industry (Gosenfeld 1973, 278–282). On the eve of the Six-Day War, the foremost attractions in the Old City were the Church of the Holy Sepulchre (visited by 97 percent of tourists), the Western Wall (87 percent), and the Temple Mount/Haram al-Sharif (77 percent), and outside of the Old City in East Jerusalem 90 percent of the tourists visited the church at Gethsemane (Gosenfeld 1973, 24).

Economically speaking, the eastern city relied almost entirely on the tourism sector. The sector's sensitivity to political and military tensions meant that the city's economy was precarious: any tension that brought to a reduction in the stream of visitors would necessarily cause an economic crisis. The city's imbalanced economic structure was no coincidence; it was the work of the Hashemite regime, which limited the development of Jerusalem to ensure that it did not damage the status of Amman as capital of the Hashemite kingdom. In effect, as Hashemite rule grew stronger in Jerusalem, the political status of Arab Jerusalem lessened. Palestine's Arabs challenged the authority of the Hashemite monarchy on their issues—especially regarding King Abdullah's willingness to sign a ceasefire agreement and reach a settlement with Israel. The strengthening of Jerusalem as a political center of the West Bank would advance Palestinian power; thus the regime worked consistently and with full force to establish the status of Amman as the single political and economic center of the kingdom (Benvenisti 1976, 50–57, 104–107).

Yet it would be a mistake to conclude that during the period of Jordanian rule the Hashemite Kingdom cut itself off from Jerusalem. As described above, Jordan saw Jerusalem as an important holy city, and aimed to invest in the Haram al-Sharif area and establish its sovereignty over the place. In this framework the Jordanian government even took responsibility for the ongoing maintenance of the Al-Aqsa mosque and the Dome of the Rock, including restoring the dome itself, which needed special treatment due to the ravages of time. From the second half of the 1950s, King Hussein related to Jerusalem as the spiritual capital of Jordan, even if he did not give that any practical meaning (Gold 2007, 159–160; Katz 2005, 88).

Tourist services in the eastern city

As noted, sources on tourist activity in the eastern city during the partition era are quite scarce. This is particularly noticeable in terms of tourist services, which were in great part characterized by economic activity in the private sector that was not required to keep detailed records. One of the most prominent hotels built in the eastern city during the time of partition was the Intercontinental, built on the Mount of Olives and planned by American architect William Tabler. The hotel was built in the early 1960s in a symmetrical form characteristic of many of the American hotels built at the time. It had a low horizontal shape, with seven arches on its façade and wings of rooms on both sides (Kroyanker 1991, 335).

The land (nearly eight acres in size) was owned by the Jordanian government, which had established a company named Holy Land Hotels Company that issued 120,000 shares at a worth of 600,000 dinars. The hotel contained 200 rooms and planned to enlarge to 300 rooms.[7] The government made contact with the Intercontinental Company, a global management company, to manage the hotel. The hotel was considered one of the most prestigious in East Jerusalem, and it hosted many of the eminent visitors who came to the city during the period of partition.

The eastern part of the city, then, maintained and even expanded its tourist sector during the years of partition; its fortune in holding the vast majority of tourist attractions meant that tourism was, for the most part, a continuation of years past. The western city, however, was bound for years of change. A Jerusalem without holy spaces would demand innovation and renewal.

West Jerusalem: capital of the new state

While the Hashemite monarchy had an ambivalent attitude to Jerusalem's political status, the State of Israel's approach to West Jerusalem was to a great extent the opposite: in December 1949 the Israeli government pronounced the western section of Jerusalem the capital of the State of Israel (Katz 2003, 133–166). This act had political, social, economic, and tourist implications, as we will soon see. In the first years after the establishment of the state, Israel's government took steps to establish Jewish hold in the western city. The types of activities employed in the western city to brand it the young state's capital can be classified in two categories.

The first type of measures, steps taken from "above," were acts with a symbolic-governmental nature. The authorities formed three symbolic physical centers:

- the "Holocaust and Rebirth" center—through the burial of Herzl's bones on the Mount of Remembrance and its establishment as a national cemetery (Azaryahu 2002, 22–35) and the establishment of the Yad Vashem Holocaust museum nearby (Brog 2006);
- the "national" center—the construction of a National Quarter with government offices (Katz and Paz 2004, 232–259), the Knesset (or parliament; Hattis Rolef 2000, 131–170; 2002, 171–180), and Binyanei Ha'uma ("the Buildings of the Nation"); and
- an "education and culture" center—building of the Hebrew University on Givat Ram and the Israel Museum, which after the reunification of the city became the museum center.

All of these were steps taken by the western city's governmental institutions, designed to create ex nihilo institutions, at least physically, and to give West Jerusalem the image of a capital with government institutions, state monuments, and new national buildings. These steps had real significance over time, when West Jerusalem drew countless visitors to the city. Jerusalem's transformation into Israel's capital led to the intensive construction of functional and symbolic institutions, which both served the needs of the state and became themselves sites for tourist visits.

Other steps in the western part of the city came from "below," and they generally had a more folksy and emotional nature, naturally touching the everyday lives of residents. In the early years after the establishment of the state, these activities took a few paths: a number of tour routes were formed around the western part of the city, pilgrimage traditions to alternative sites (like Mount Herzl) appeared, pilgrimages on festivals were restored (primarily to Mount Zion), and several archaeological sites in the western part of the city were identified, with some undergoing re-excavation (Cohen-Hattab 2007, 189–217).

Within the initiatives directed from "above," one of the major endeavors in cultivating the western part of the city was the construction of Binyanei Ha'uma (the "Buildings of the Nation," a convention center we will look at more closely later on), whose planners hoped it would serve as an attraction for residents and visitors to the city. The idea was to expose the public to the renewed national enterprise through conventions and national and cultural events. With the state's ten-year anniversary, the "First Decade" exhibition was held at Binyanei Ha'uma, summarizing the Zionist enterprise in the country until that point, an exhibition that served national-educational purposes for the country's residents regarding the meaning of life in the State of Israel (Limor 2002; Selzer 2006). While the building was a government endeavor, it was not designated a national institute, but rather given a cultural purpose: it was intended to host congresses and theatrical and musical performances.

New construction in West Jerusalem

Mount Herzl

Mount Herzl is named for Theodore Herzl, visionary of the Jewish state. Herzl passed away on July 3, 1904, and was buried in the family plot in the Vienna cemetery. In his will, Herzl requested that the Jewish nation transfer his remains to the land of Israel. This was executed only after the establishment of the state; on August 17, 1949, Herzl was reinterred on the uppermost point of the highest peak in West Jerusalem. The ceremonial burial was the first step in the transformation of Mount Herzl to a site with crucial national significance, a symbolic site of Zionist heritage (Naor-Wiernik and Bar 2012, 107–136).

The decision to bury Herzl in West Jerusalem had far-reaching implications: a cemetery was created at the site, and three themes in the different parts of the mountain created a Zionist memorial space functioning as a national pantheon. First, Zionist leaders from the period before the establishment of the state, first and foremost Herzl, were buried there. This part of the mountain represents the Zionist awakening and the struggle for Jewish independence in the period before the establishment of the State of Israel. The second theme represented on the mountain is manifest in the military cemetery: the contribution of the Hebrew settlement in the war against Nazi Germany and the commemoration of the struggle for the State of Israel's rebirth. The third subject is the nation's leaders; the mount constitutes the burial place of presidents, prime ministers, and Knesset speakers, representing Israeli sovereignty (Azaryahu 2002, 22–35; 2005, 369–383).

Beyond its contribution to West Jerusalem's symbolic landscape, Mount Herzl began to serve as a central ceremonial site for the Israeli sovereignty's rituals in the national capital. The first event held there took place in early December 1949, mere months after Herzl's burial. A large protest was held in West Jerusalem against the UN's intention to disengage Jerusalem from Israeli sovereignty. The climax of the protest was an "oath of allegiance" to Jerusalem at the site of Herzl's grave; the location itself was a proclamation of commitment to the Zionist vision embodied by Herzl.

An essential national tradition also developed at the site: the ceremony opening the celebrations on Israel's Independence Day, held for the first time on the eve of Independence Day in 1950 (Azaryahu 2005, 378). In fact, from the establishment of the state Mount Herzl became a site of interest for many of the city's visitors. Their presence swelled as the symbolic significance of the mountain continued to grow—it became a locus for Israeli national memory in Jerusalem in particular and for the State of Israel in general (Azaryahu 1995, 55–62).

Yad Vashem

In close proximity to Mount Herzl, an additional symbolic center began to develop in the 1950s: Yad Vashem, the national commemoration museum for the Holocaust and heroism. Many saw the juxtaposition of Mount Herzl and Yad Vashem as an expression of the national narrative about the establishment of the state; the term "from Holocaust to Rebirth"—from the devastation of the nation in Europe to Jewish sovereignty in Israel—aptly articulated this vision. The proximity symbolized the connection between Holocaust and rebirth, with the Jews' struggle against the Nazis closely linked to the War of Independence (Feldman 2007).

Yad Vashem was established pursuant to the "Holocaust and Heroism Remembrance Law—Yad Vashem 1953," which resolved to establish the museum in West Jerusalem. The law determined that

> the role of Yad Vashem is to collect the memories of all of the members of the Jewish people who fell and gave their lives, fought, and revolted against the Nazi enemy and its helpers in the homeland, and to erect a name and monument for them, the communities, and the organizations and institutions that were destroyed because they belonged to the Jewish people.[8]

Two of Yad Vashem's main sites were built in the decade leading up to the Six-Day War (1967): in 1961, the Hall of Remembrance, the first of the commemorative buildings, was constructed at Yad Vashem;[9] roughly one year later the Avenue of the Righteous among the Nations was inaugurated (Brog 1996, 14–17; Silberklang 2003, 6–7). In the years following the war, other buildings and monuments would be added, establishing Yad Vashem as the principal memorial site for commemoration of the Holocaust—both nationally and internationally.[10] With its inauguration, Yad Vashem would itself become a central attraction in West Jerusalem for countless visitors to the city, Jewish and non-Jewish alike.

Despite Levi Eshkol's words, the placement of the Mount of Remembrance near Mount Herzl and the military cemetery was not a result of planning by Jerusalem's city leaders or the government; rather, it was an idea first formulated by Mordechai Shenhavi, originator of the Holocaust commemoration idea (Brog 2006, 112–113). In 1952, alongside the initiative for parliamentary legislation to determine the national nature of Holocaust commemoration, Shenhavi began to enlist support for his new idea: linking Yad Vashem and Mount Herzl. "This ridge, organically connected to Mount Herzl and the military cemetery, will become a valuable asset to the capital Jerusalem, and attract masses of visitors from Israel and abroad."[11] One year after the Knesset approved the law, on July 29, 1954, the cornerstone was laid for the Yad Vashem buildings in Jerusalem—the administration and archive buildings. President Yitzhak Ben-Zvi noted among other things that

> the place on which we stand is holy ground—the land of the Mount of Remembrance next to the mountain that bears the name of the visionary of the state of the Jews. And the mountain is worthy of this proximity.
>
> (Brog 2006, 165)

The symbolic meaning of the transition from Holocaust to rebirth was underscored in the connecting path between Yad Vashem and Mount Herzl, inaugurated in 2003. The path expresses an idea deeply embedded in Israel's national calendar in the transition from Holocaust Remembrance Day to Memorial Day for Israel's Fallen Soldiers to Independence Day. At the end of the path on Mount Herzl stands the "last scion" monument, which honors Holocaust survivors who immigrated to the country only to fall in battle in the War of Independence, those who were the final scions of their families, destroyed in the Holocaust (Brog 2003, 65–99; Levine 2006, 38–43).[12]

The National Center and the Education and Culture Center

Within the deepening recognition of Jerusalem as capital, it was resolved that a governmental quarter would be built, which would symbolize Israel's political sovereignty. Givat Ram, at the center of West Jerusalem's urban area, was chosen. Alfred Mansfeld and Munio Weinraub, the first architects of Yad Vashem, were selected to design the complex. Three sections were planned: a campus of the government and various authorities; an educational center, with the Hebrew University at its center; and a cultural area, with the Israel Museum

at its center. The governmental complex was distanced from Jerusalem's historical nucleus, both so that it would not compete with or overshadow the Old
City's holy places and out of military considerations, which required keeping
government institutions out of the line of Jordanian cannon fire. The first building on the ridge was Binyanei Ha'uma, inaugurated in 1951; next, in 1954, construction of the Hebrew University's new campus began (it was inaugurated in
1958); afterwards, the Israel Museum was inaugurated (1965); finally, the
Knesset building was built, inaugurated in 1966 (Azaryahu 2005; Brog 2006,
112–113).

Binyanei Ha'uma: vision and purpose

The central national enterprise built in West Jerusalem in the first years after the
birth of the state, with activities intended for a wide audience, was Binyanei
Ha'uma (the Buildings of the Nation). As we will see, its establishment reflected
two complementary concepts: the symbolism afforded by the city's Jewish heritage and history and the new national content cast into it. The establishment of a
center for conferences and national and cultural activity, through which the
public would be exposed to the national enterprise, could, it was hoped, create a
central attraction in West Jerusalem for residents and assorted visitors to the
city.

At the end of the war in 1948, with the partition of the city, Dr. Itzhak Nebenzahl, director of the Jerusalem Development Department, presented his vision
for the western city. In the absence of natural attractions, Nebenzahl said:

> Today we must create new loci of attraction if we wish to keep the tourist
> occupied for several days. This is the decisive importance of the great enter-
> prise which the Jerusalem Development Department began, that is the estab-
> lishment of a large building for congresses, assemblies, and exhibitions,
> with an amphitheater for celebrations on an international standard. This
> enterprise will enable Jerusalem to be the center of cultural activity for the
> Jewish nation as a whole, and thus to attract tens of thousands of guests for
> prolonged visits to the city each year.[13]

Daniel Auster, mayor of Jerusalem at the time, also saw the establishment of
Binyanei Ha'uma as the most important cultural enterprise founded in Israel. He
emphasized the economic aspect of its establishment:

> This undertaking, Binyanei Ha'uma, will be the center of culture and
> tourism for the nation of Israel, and one of the most important cultural and
> tourist centers in the entire world. The enterprise will attract tens of thou-
> sands of guests and tourists: from Israel, from the Diaspora, and from the
> corners of the world. Construction will cost some one million lira, but mil-
> lions of lira, some in foreign currency, will flow annually to Jerusalem and
> to Israel generally. Binyanei Ha'uma is liable to change Jerusalem's

economic system from its very foundations. The existence of this project will give a strong push to the investment of private equity in the hospitality, industry, craft, labor, transportation, and various service sectors as well, and even to the agriculture in the immediate vicinity of Jerusalem.[14]

The originator and the spirit behind the establishment of Binyanei Ha'uma was Alexander Ezer (Yevzerov), who was appointed director of the Jewish Agency's Finance Department in 1949.[15] In that capacity, and based on his great experience organizing exhibitions for Israeli products and Orient fairs in Tel Aviv in the 1920s and 1930s, Ezer suggested the construction of a building that would be a center for West Jerusalem's economic, social, and cultural life.[16]

The establishment of Binyanei Ha'uma was part of Ezer's broader vision. Its essence was the exchange of the accepted definition "Jerusalem—The Holy City for Three Religions," suited for East Jerusalem and holy places, for a definition more befitting West Jerusalem, exclusive to Judaism and the State of Israel: "Jerusalem—A Spiritual Center for World Jewry." Ezer's suggestion made it possible to dedicate West Jerusalem spiritually for Jewry alone, to create Jewish continuity in the western part of the city, and to expand its place in the global Jewish consciousness rather than just the Israeli. Through Binyanei Ha'uma, he felt, Jewish Jerusalem could capture a place for itself as a spiritual and national center; the concept of a spiritual center for world Jewry would acquire concrete meaning if they could present the compositions of world Jewry in the fields of culture, art, and society in the city on a regular basis. For this, all central Jewish institutions, parties, and organizations, wherever they were located, must take part in making West Jerusalem a spiritual center for Judaism and actively fill in that content.[17]

In the spirit of this idea, three goals were set for the building. The primary goal was to create a place in which the Zionist Congress could hold its assemblies—not in the Diaspora but in Jerusalem. Global Jewish congresses and other international congresses would be held there. The building would express the eternal connection of the nation of Israel and the world Zionist movement with Jerusalem in the most tangible manner possible. Its establishment would realize the Zionist movement's dream of creating a cultural and artistic center in the city. The second goal was to enable West Jerusalem to hold plays, concerts, and other cultural activities for the wider public in a modern building suited for the times. The third goal was to build a large assembly building that would make it possible to hold exhibitions on Jewish and international subjects in the city.[18] It thus appears that Binyanei Ha'uma was designed to be one of the main tools in making West Jerusalem a global Jewish cultural center. It would help the city, the visionaries felt, to fill a symbolic role in the eyes of the nation and the entire world, a role Jerusalem had filled in the lives of Jews around the world for centuries.

The originators of the endeavor, headed by Alexander Ezer, must have seen in their mind's eye the exhibitions and fairs held in the country beginning in the 1920s. They attracted hundreds of thousands of visitors over the years and

constituted one of the most important expressions of growing interest on the part
of tourists in the country during the days of British rule. These events, such as
the Orient fairs, presented products from the country and had the participation of
companies from overseas. Such events held a central place in marketing the
Jewish sector in the land and building its unique image, and attested to the economic development in the state becoming a center of trade with the world's
countries.[19]

The conditions of the tender for construction of Binyanei Ha'uma make clear
the building's intended symbolic role in the new national and cultural identity of
the western city. This is especially evident in the description of its imposing
presence in the urban space:

> These blocks of buildings will constitute the nucleus of a civilian and public
> center in Jerusalem that will serve the city, the country, and world Jewry.
> Taking into consideration the building's character, function, and surroundings,
> the complete solution will be manifest not only in a logical and functional
> organization of all different elements that the building is composed of but also
> the design of a true and attractive architectonic image of the building and the
> governmental national sentiment that lies in it ... this will be a natural center
> of the expanding city ... and will dominate the entire setting as a prominent
> architectonic center, to which the gaze is drawn from all sides.
>
> (Quoted in Kroyanker 1991, 92)

The tender to plan the building was won by architect Zeev Rechter, considered
one of the country's leaders in modern architecture.[20] On his considerations in
integrating modernity with the continuity of the Jewish heritage in the building's
design, Rechter stated:

> From the day I began to build in the land of Israel, I reached the understand-
> ing that we need modern buildings, buildings that tell the coming genera-
> tions about the creative spirit of Jews in our generation and the new society
> they are building in this part of the world. Thus Binyanei Ha'uma will be
> beautiful and expansive. But the line will be as simple as possible and the
> material—pink Jerusalem stone. I would like for this to be a sanctuary for
> Jewry.[21]

Indeed, Rechter wanted Binyanei Ha'uma to express Jewish continuity and creativity and to even be a type of haven for Jewry. But he also emphasized that
despite its dimensions it would project an atmosphere of freedom, adding to the
new sense of national creativity in the state's early years. A person should feel
free and comfortable in the building, he felt, as only in that type of environment
could talent be fully expressed. In effect, Rechter saw in his mind's eye a building that communicated the integration of tradition and innovation, political independence and Jewish heritage flawlessly—all in new Jerusalem, capital of the
developing Jewish country.[22]

On the day that Binyanei Ha'uma's charter was signed (January 25, 1950), Ben-Gurion also spoke of the national importance of the establishment of the building in Jerusalem, and saw in it the symbolic continuity of the western city:

> Jerusalem is not only the capital of the state, but was and will be the capital of the Jewish nation. Jerusalem under Israel's sovereignty will serve as the center of the spirit, science, Bible, friends of goodness and justice of all Jews in the world. The capital of the State of Israel will host in it, by virtue of the place it holds in Jewish and global history, Jewish and global assemblies as well, and will be a global center for justice and peace in the world.[23]

Similar words were written in the introduction to the building's charter: Binyanei Ha'uma would be a "shrine for the nation in all of its creative paths, a place of assembly for our achievements material and spiritual, and an archive and ornament for the treasures of national rebirth."

The building would later become part of the planned district outlined by planners of the western city: on Givat Ram and the university hill across Rupin Road the governmental center would be built; on the other side of the hill a center for culture and the mind would be constructed.[24] As fate would have it, ancient relics of the Roman tenth legion were discovered at the site of Binyanei Ha'uma during the digging of foundations.[25] Alexander Ezer and others saw in this, of course, great symbolism: "on the place whence the destroyers of the Temple came, a central building for the rebirth of the nation will rise."[26]

During the severe economic crisis of the early 1950s the building encountered financial difficulties; sufficient funds to ensure the project's completion were lacking at the beginning of work. Yet only half a year after the construction's commencement, in 1951, the Jewish Agency plenary administration determined that the next Zionist Congress would be held in Israel, in the summer of 1951. It would need to be held in Binyanei Ha'uma, despite the fact that construction was only partially complete, in the spirit of the goals that accompanied the decision to establish the building.[27] Indeed, in August 1951 the 23rd Zionist Congress—the first to be held in the State of Israel—was held there, but the congress took place in an unfinished building, in a section prepared provisionally for that purpose (Ben-Arieh and Wager 1994, 100).

The budgetary problems continued to accompany construction in subsequent years. The next major events in the building—the "Conquest of the Desert" exhibition in 1953 and the 24th Zionist Congress in 1956—were also held in an unfinished building. Toward 1958 construction was somewhat accelerated for the sake of the state's "First Decade" exhibition, but the building was only completed in the early 1960s. From then until the inauguration of the Jerusalem Theater in 1971, Binyanei Ha'uma served as the capital's primary hall for events, and most of the concerts, shows (including two Eurovision competitions), and large political and social conventions in the city were held there.

The first noticeable test for the realization of the dream of holding international conventions at Binyanei Ha'uma was the "Conquest of the Desert" exhibition held in September and October of 1953. This was the first international exhibition held in the country since the establishment of the State of Israel. In the background stood, as stated, the desire to develop Jerusalem as a city of conventions and to create in it enterprises of culture, art, sport, and popular folklore, suited to the state and the new national spirit. As a city not known for industry and lacking famous historical sites, exhibitions and conventions were, for the administration of Binyanei Ha'uma, of utmost economic and national importance.[28] The goal in holding the exhibition in Jerusalem and on the subject of conquering the desert was to demonstrate the achievements of various countries in their struggle against the desert; present innovative methods in various fields of agriculture; transform the city into an international meeting place for commercial delegations; encourage the development of commerce between Israel and other countries; aid agricultural and industrial development in the Middle East; and spur the economic development of Israel and other countries by settling deserts.[29]

Companies from Europe and America, alongside many Israeli companies, participated in the exhibition. They displayed products in three large pavilions: agriculture, construction, and transportation. Special pavilions were erected for the industrial workers' union, Hapoel Hamizrachi (religious labor Zionist movement), and the Histadrut (trade union association), as well as for some separate companies such as the "Shell" oil company. The large auditorium hosted performances, concerts, and other events: a conference on the development of the Negev region, a Maccabiah day, a day for the Teachers' Union, a conference promoting science, a youth day, a village day, and a State of Israel day. Some 300 movies were screened, showing how deserts were tamed in other countries. The Israel pavilion included a joint display of the government offices and settlement institutions (the Jewish Agency, the Jewish National Fund, and Palestine Jewish Colonization Association). Solutions in the fields of forestation and swamp drainage were presented on four topics—land, water, agricultural settlement, and man conquering the desert, focusing on medical care, welfare, culture, and education.[30]

At the end of the exhibition, the chairman of the board reported that over the 19 days of the exhibition, it was visited by some 600,000 people from abroad, from around the country, and from Jerusalem itself. This was, in his opinion, "a singular opportunity for tens of thousands of people amongst us who did not know or recognize the enterprise of settlement and the building of the country to see, to understand, and to learn about events in the country." In his estimation, the exhibition increased the city's turnover by at least one million liras, an effect felt in the cafés, hotels, entertainment venues, stores, and transportation.[31]

A description given by one of the visitors at the exhibit illustrates the great excitement it stirred up:

The nation streamed in the tens of thousands in all possible vehicles to Binyanei Ha'uma. They crowded onto buses full to suffocation. They squeezed into train cars with no air to breathe. Whoever had a penny in his pocket did not lament ten liras for various types of "specials" [taxis]. People did not grumble over fancy prices in restaurants or hotels. People heard that at the exhibition there was something to elevate the spirit in these crazy days.[32]

The description of the journey to the exhibition and the visit that "elevated the spirit" can to a great extent be compared to a pilgrimage or visit at a holy place. The exhibition being located in Jerusalem, and the desire to establish the city's status as capital in that period, naturally intensify this image. People of all classes, the rank and file, streamed to the city, crowded into overstuffed buses, or spent what they could to take a taxi came to the exhibition. Like a pilgrimage, it seems the difficulties of the journey intensified the meeting with the sacred space and the experiences that took place there.

The second large exhibition held in Binyanei Ha'uma was the "First Decade" exhibition, which opened in Jerusalem on June 5, 1958 and closed on August 21 of the same year. The government chose to hold the exhibition and it served as one link in the chain of decade celebrations that lasted a year (Selzer 2006). Its declared goals were to summarize the events of the state's first decade and give residents information on the happenings in the state in those years, to inspire identification on the part of the observer and to tie him or her not only to the daily reality but also to the state's past and present, and to serve as a justification for the establishment of the state through emphasizing the suffering and sacrifices—and thus to fill a national educational role about the meaning of life in the State of Israel.[33]

What were the reasons behind holding the exhibition in Jerusalem rather than Tel Aviv or Haifa? Arguments about the role the government ascribed to the exhibition in the processes of nation formation and constructing national identity were voiced alongside economic claims. So, for example, there were those who felt that holding a large exhibition in Jerusalem would add more weight and validity to Jerusalem as capital of the country, or that the exhibition would revive sleepy Jerusalem and serve as an important economic agent in the city. Furthermore, in Jerusalem the conditions necessary for this type of exhibit were already in existence; in other cities it would have incurred great expense.[34]

With the close of the exhibition, the press reported that the number of visitors reached 600,000 (of which 154,000 were children), as opposed to the 850,000 originally expected. The decade book claimed that the number of visitors reached half a million (Limor 2002, 10). Either way, less than one third of the country's total residents at the time came to the event.[35]

Indeed, the government and the board of the exhibition had designed it for residents and tourists as one, and took pains to ensure that it had the character of an informative and educational enterprise and would be of interest to the visitors.[36] In her research on the "First Decade" exhibition, Galyah Limor notes that the subjects that stood out at the exhibit were Zionist and secular in nature, and focused on the young State of Israel. Yet Limor emphasizes that the placement of the exhibition in Jerusalem lent it a special status, and the historical and religious past of the city added substance that was beyond the present. The "First Decade" exhibition was the largest event to take place in the years of Jerusalem's partition. It reflects an attempt to highlight the state's national endeavors—especially in West Jerusalem, cut off from its religious legacy—but also to tie the city's modern Zionist heritage to its religious and historical heritage.[37]

However, holding the exhibitions at Binyanei Ha'uma exposed no small number of difficulties in encouraging tourism to the capital and transforming it into a center for visitors. The first exhibition, "Conquest of the Desert," was not a genuine success in attracting international tourism. The portion made up of tourists at the exhibit (of the total 600,000 visitors), was, it turns out, small, and only a slight increase was recorded in the number of tourists to Israel in September 1953 relative to the same period in 1952. It appears that one of the main reasons for this was that the exhibition was publicized overseas too short a time prior to its opening.[38] An additional issue marring the exhibition was the refusal of global powers and most other countries to officially participate in an Israeli exhibition held in Jerusalem, which, as stated, they did not recognize as the state's capital.[39]

No small amount of criticism was voiced regarding the "First Decade" exhibition, primarily by the press at the time.[40] Prior to the exhibition Binyanei Ha'uma was refurbished and two of the walls covered, but the other two stood bare. The press stated one day after the opening that "only half of the shame is covered now." One of the sharper critics of the exhibit in the weekly *Haolam Hazeh* wrote a scathing critique of the exhibit under the heading "The Catastrophe Exhibition."[41] He claimed, among other things, that in advance of the exhibition some of the building's sections were incomplete, some wings were entirely unprepared for the opening, the exhibition itself was boring and loaded with pictures that were similar to one another, and that it contained vacuous slogans and a tedious amount of numbers.[42]

Moreover, if one of the deciding factors in holding the "First Decade" exhibition in Binyanei Ha'uma was the claim that the exhibition funds would make it possible to complete the building, this did not turn out to be the case. Owing to the high costs of both exhibitions, it was decided that no further exhibitions would be held there until spaces around the building and the building itself were fully prepared. In effect, the vision of Binyanei Ha'uma as a center for international assemblies was not fully realized until it joined the International Association of Convention Centers, based in Lausanne, Switzerland. Only in 1964, some 15 years after the cornerstone was laid, did the association's delegation visit Binyanei Ha'uma, and as a result of its conclusions Binyanei Ha'uma was accepted as the only meeting place in the country that was a member of the international association.[43] In the mid-1990s, with advances in the political process between Israel and its neighbors and the Palestinians, and with the constant rise in tourism, widespread investments were made to turn Binyanei Ha'uma into a modern international conference center, and its name was changed to the International Convention Center (ICC).

Mirroring the old: new national centers

The new spaces created in West Jerusalem replaced the old sites in more ways than one. They were more than tourist attractions and governmental institutions; in many ways they reflected the ancient sites that had been lost to Jordan.

First, the compound comprising the Knesset building, the Israel Museum, and the new campus of the Hebrew University formed the new national center of Israel, in essence a mirror image of the ancient Jewish elements of Jerusalem, counterbalancing the Old City. Thus, a new center, secular in nature, symbolizing political power, historical roots, and modern science and learning, came to replace the Old City, the center of which was the epitome of religious beliefs and values. It therefore comes as no surprise that, at present, the Israel Museum and the Knesset are major tourist attractions in Jerusalem (Cohen-Hattab 2007; Shoval 2009).

The other compound of Jewish national symbolism, the memorials at Mount Herzl and Yad Vashem, make up a sacred space of the highest order in a civic religion; both are regarded as the most important symbols in the painful road to Jewish national revival. The entire Herzl compound is, then, new Jerusalem's mirror image of the Mount of Olives Cemetery just opposite the eastern walls of the Old City.

West Jerusalem: urban plan

The development of West Jerusalem after the war derived directly from the new reality created in the city, with the separation of Israeli Jerusalem from its religious and historical center. A number of plans drawn up influenced the city's development, and—as we will see—this was related to tourist sites and services in the various parts of the new city (Amiran 1986, 9–70; Efrat 1967, 73–108).

From the end of the Mandate until 1967, four plans were drawn up for Jerusalem—two for the western city and two, as we saw earlier, for the eastern city under Jordanian rule. The first Israeli plan for West Jerusalem was prepared in 1949 by Heinz Rau, an architect from the Planning Division, at the time affiliated with the Prime Minister's Office. The plan dealt with the entire city, without taking into account the partition at the end of the war; however, it also broadened the city's borders westward considerably. The fundamental principles of the plan influenced the plans that followed it and the city's development until today (Kendall 1948; Shapiro 1973, 139–147).

The basic assumption of Rau's plan was that the city center must be moved westward to the area where Binyanei Ha'uma was eventually built. A number of reasons were given: the city's development was taking place in the west and the majority of the population would reside far to the west of the current industrial triangle (Jaffa Road, Ben-Yehuda Street, and King George Street) in the future. Thus it would be easier and more efficient if the center was moved to a place that was more central for the population. Making the center closer to the city's entrance from the west would ease the traffic in the city's arteries; the existing hub was old and would be difficult to renew and adapt to new needs, and thus it was considered preferable to minimize the activity in it, opening a state-of-the-art center nearby instead. Givat Ram, west of the old built area, was intended to be the government precinct.

However, as Rau's plan was only conceptual and not binding in nature, the government chose to prepare a new, legally binding plan for the city. In 1954, the District Planning Office of the Ministry of Interior's planning division began the process. The new plan included the main points of the Rau plan, and was approved in a 1959 legal document. Its main thrust was the expansion of the Jewish population's spread to the west and the strengthening of existing neighborhoods (Benvenisti 1976, 82–92; Efrat 1976, 49–62; Hashimshoni, Schweid, and Hashimshoni 1974, 78; Kroyanker 1991, 20–21).

The central idea guiding both plans was, then, the recognition that the Old City and commercial triangle that emerged from it could no longer serve as the urban hub in planning. A cultural and government center would be established in the heart of the new western city and urban planning would focus around it. The construction of the Knesset, the university, Binyanei Ha'uma, and the Israel Museum was not only a response to the functional needs that were born with the determination that West Jerusalem was the capital of Israel, but also a desire to reinforce its status and express visually, in a prominent and dignified manner, the city's new place as a capital with fitting institutions of government, culture, and symbolism (Efrat 1973, 9–20; Schweid 1994, 115–132).

Tourism in the state of Israel and Jerusalem during partition

Given the lack of precise figures regarding the entry of tourists to West Jerusalem, the upcoming analysis relies on the existing data on the entry of tourists to Israel, under the assumption that a portion of them visited West Jerusalem as part of their visit. This should be emphasized, and must be distinguished from eras discussed in earlier chapters and from the period following the Six-Day War that will be discussed later; in the period of partition, West Jerusalem was not on the tourist map as it had been before and certainly not in the way it would be later on.

Tourist traffic: trends

From its establishment, tourist traffic to the State of Israel gradually increased: in 1948, 4,500 tourists were recorded entering the country, in 1949, the people entering the country numbered 22,000, and during the early 1950s, the number was on average 35,000 a year. At ten years of age (1958), a peak increase of approximately 60 percent was recorded in the number of visitors relative to the previous year: 68,100 in one year. In 1960, over 100,000 tourists came to Israel for the first time (117,662). The trend of growth continued: in 1963, over 200,000 tourists (218,460) visited Israel, and in 1966, on the eve of the Six-Day War, more than 300,000 (328,077) visited (see Figure 4.3). It should be noted that throughout the whole period there were no significant changes in the tourists' duration of stay, so this growth reflects an increase in the number of tourist bed nights as well (Central Bureau of Statistics 1968, 88, table D/1).

The transfer of responsibility for west Jerusalem's tourism

The burgeoning State of Israel faced serious existential problems—both militarily, as a result of the hostility of the neighboring Arab countries, and socially and economically, mostly as a result of the large waves of immigration that arrived during the 1950s. The political establishment viewed tourism as an instrument to encourage immigration of Jewish tourists from the U.S. and Western Europe who initially came to visit Israel; in fact, the field of tourism was entrusted to the Ministry of Immigrant Absorption in the state's early years. Later on, with the crystallization of the understanding that tourism also held potential of global marketing using tourists, part of the responsibility was transferred to the Ministry of Foreign Affairs, while elements related to economic development of tourism were transferred to the Prime Minister's Office (Prime Minister's Office 1957). During the 1960s the volume of tourists grew, primarily thanks to significantly reduced prices on international flights and early organized popular tourism that had begun in the 1950s (Klein 1973; Schwartz 2004, 51–71). This awakening stemmed, of course, from the economic growth in Europe and North America in the decades following the Second World War, which allowed more and more people to travel to places that were relatively distant from their homes.

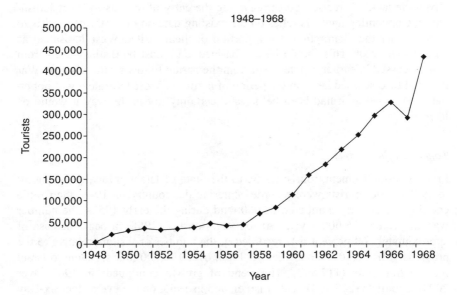

Figure 4.3 Inbound tourism to Israel, 1948–1968.

The quantitative increase of tourists from the state's decade mark and in the 1960s, at a rate of up to 60 percent a year, ultimately led to the recognition that tourism should be given the proper attention. As a result, the Israeli government resolved on December 22, 1964, to establish a Ministry of Tourism, which was opened in January 1965 (Prime Minister's Office 1966, 345; Kimhi, Hyman and Gabriele 1976, 77) and led by Akiva Govrin, who became the first minister of tourism (Natan 1973, 77).

Efforts to augment tourism

Though there are no official figures regarding the number of visitors to West Jerusalem in the years of partition, other sources reveal that visits to the city in those days, by domestic and inbound tourists alike, could not be taken for granted. In December 1948, the Government Information Bureau for Tourists (formerly the Zionist Information Bureau for Tourists) was reopened, and with the onset of the tourist season it distributed material on West Jerusalem—for regular tourists (Jewish and non-Jewish) and for guests with central roles in Jewish institutions in the Diaspora—for the first time.[44] The Bureau attempted to deal with one of West Jerusalem's biggest problems at the time: its substandard image amongst visitors and residents of the country and its unstable security situation. At the end of 1949, the office reported on the difficult state of tourism in the city:

> The opinion that there is nothing to see in Jerusalem today and a lack of security on the road to Jerusalem, etc., has spread around the country, and this has negatively affected the tourists as well; they either do not come at all or suffice with a quick visit of a few hours, whose economic value is minimal.[45]

In light of the situation, the Bureau took upon itself to create plans for excursions and to prove that West Jerusalem also had things to see and visit. The list of tour routes suggested by the Bureau around the western part of the city in the years following partition illustrates the first attempts to shape West Jerusalem as an attraction for visitors, and included four main tour routes (see Figure 4.4).

1   A pedestrian tour of the northern part of the city in the Me'ah She'arim, Beit Yisrael, and Bukharan neighborhoods, and a lookout from one of the houses onto the city's northern parts in the direction of Hebrew University and Mount Scopus.
2   A bus or car tour in the western parts of the city, the Rommema, Kiryat Moshe, Beit Hakerem, and Beyit Vegan neighborhoods, Herzl's grave, and Ein Kerem.
3   A tour of the national institutional buildings and the Bezalel Museum.
4   A bus or car tour in the city's southern areas, including Ramat Rachel and the neighborhoods of Talpiot, the German Colony, the Greek Colony, Katamon, Talbieh, Yemin Moshe, and the City Center.

On Tuesdays and Saturdays a special tour was offered to David's Tomb and Mount Zion, from which the eastern part of the city—the Old City in general and the Temple Mount/Haram al-Sharif plaza more specifically—could be seen.[46] To a great degree, Mount Zion filled the religious vacuum created in the western city once there was no longer access to the sites in the Old City and the eastern city. Over the years, Mount Zion, and David's Tomb in particular, became a central location and a prominent symbol for pilgrimage to West Jerusalem (Bar 2004, 233–251). Mount Zion, of course was the only religious site remaining under Israeli control; many traditions were tied to the site and visitors streamed to it. The roof of the building over David's Tomb, and the Room of the Last Supper next to it, served as the nearest observation points to East Jerusalem and the holy places—primarily the Western Wall and Mount of Olives—which were under Jordanian control and not accessible. An additional pilgrimage connected to David's Tomb was the Holocaust Cellar, erected near David's Tomb; many Jews would visit it and even pray there (Bar 2005, 16–38).

Tourist itineraries in the western city in the early years after partition also highlight the efforts made to shape West Jerusalem as a national-cultural center and an attraction for visitors, with ostensibly no dependence on the religious and historical places in the city.

In 1950, the recovery from the war and return to life as usual was seen in the western part of the city. In the summer of that year, many tourists came to Jerusalem and the accommodations, restaurants, and cafés were at full capacity. Various travel agencies—Israeli and international—reopened branches, and areas in the western city that had closed for security reasons during the Mandate, such as the Russian Compound and its environs, were opened for visits. It was further reported that Herzl's grave attracted many visitors from Israel and from abroad.[47] However, the tough economic reality in the country in the early 1950s had an unsurprising influence on Jerusalem's tourism industry. In an evaluation by the Commission of Inquiry for Jerusalem on the State of Tourism in the Western City in 1953, approximately five years after the establishment of the state, it was reported that

> Tourists are only seen in Jerusalem for a few hours, and travel agencies bringing them to the city return them for the most part on the same day. Domestic tourism was also greatly hit by the economic crisis in the country. Owners in the hospitality sector have complained…as they improved and expanded their businesses for naught, as there are no tourists visiting this season and their businesses are half-empty.[48]

One of the central problems that West Jerusalem faced in tourism services was the low number of tourist bed nights. So for example in 1953 government agencies reported that tourist traffic was felt at Mandelbaum Gate, where many groups crossed the border from East Jerusalem to West Jerusalem, but only a very small number of these stayed overnight in the western city. This was true both for groups organized by Jewish travel agencies and for those organized by clergy. Most of the groups that crossed to Israel at Mandelbaum Gate in the morning did not stay overnight in Jerusalem but rather continued in the afternoon to stay in another place like Tel Aviv, Haifa, or Nazareth.[49]

In the summer of 1954, border incidents and unrest were reported; these were apparently factors in the cancellation of a number of planned events in the capital, such as the Purim holiday celebrations and the Independence Day parade. This new reality hurt a number of service branches in the city, the tourist services in particular.[50]

The following years did not show much of an improvement in the state of tourism in West Jerusalem. Despite the fact that it was the capital of Israel and despite the fact that the government institutions were located there, Jerusalem did not top the list of visits in Israel, especially relative to Tel Aviv, which was considered the economic, cultural, and social center of life in the country. As is clear from the tourist bed-night figures in Israel, in 1961 Jerusalem made up 18 percent of the total tourist bed nights, in 1962 it decreased to 15 percent, and it continued to fall to 13 percent in 1963. In contrast, in Haifa these years recorded a stable trend of 12 percent of the country's total tourist bed nights and Tel Aviv saw more than 40 percent of the total tourist bed nights on average for those years.[51]

West Jerusalem's part in the national economy in those years was negligible as well. In 1963, for example, the national income from tourism reached roughly $53 million, or approximately 2.5 percent of the country's total income for that year.[52] Yet Jerusalem's portion of that was 5 percent of the tourism income, standing at only $2–3 million, or 0.08 percent of the country's income at the time (Rolbant 1964, 307).

The developing tourist industry in West Jerusalem

Revival and restoration of historical monuments in the western city

From its inception, Zionism was occupied with the return to the Jewish homeland, hoping to connect the people to the landscape. New Jewish nationalism could be built on this soil, land all Diaspora Jews could connect to earlier eras of Jewish presence in the country. The scientific field used to establish and prove the Jewish link to the country was archaeology. Addressing the biblical or Hasmonean eras, for example, there was a clear attempt to reconnect the new immigrants to the ancient past; the long periods during which there was no noticeable Jewish presence in the land were omitted (Davis 2004; Feige 2002, 22–35 and sources there; Shapira 2005, 1–36; Silberman and Small 1997).[53] After the state's establishment, primarily in light of the mounting conflict between Jews and Arabs in the country, archaeology still, and increasingly, served as one of the central tools in guaranteeing roots and reinforcing the Jewish connection to land of Israel.[54] These types of activities took place in West Jerusalem in the first years after the establishment of the state, and in parallel to the pilgrimages to Mount Herzl and Mount Zion and the shaping of tour routes in the western city, attempts were made—primarily out of national and economic motivation—to find historical sites and to revive the remains of the past found in the western parts of the city.[55]

One West Jerusalem organization that began operations in this vein was the "Jerusalem Development Department," founded by the Jewish Agency.[56] The department was aware of the great benefit the plurality of attractions in the western parts of the city had: the recognition of West Jerusalem as capital would be established in a direct manner, its singularity as a cultural center would increase, and the number of tourists and duration of their stay would grow. All of these also had, of course, economic ramifications. In cooperation with the director of planning in the Prime Minister's Office, the Ministry of Religions, the Department of Antiquities, and the municipality, the Jerusalem Development Department was responsible for the improved appearance of the historical monuments in the western city.[57]

The Department of Antiquities identified a number of historical sites in western Jerusalem that should be improved for the benefit of the visitors.[58] The first of these was the Tombs of the Sanhedrin, ancient and fascinating tombs that it seemed could be prepared for visits with a relatively small investment.[59] Burial sites have long been places of pilgrimage. In modern times, lone graves and cemeteries have become preferred sites for non-religious visitors as well, as representative of one of the important and authentic expressions of local heritage, among other things. Thus they often fill a national role.[60]

The "Sanhedrin" was the council of elders and supreme court in Israel during the time of the Second Temple. The Tombs of the Sanhedrin is the name given to a group of caves hewn in stone at the end of the Second Temple period in northwest Jerusalem. The most famous tomb is found at the northern tip of the site, distinguished by an impressive entry plaza, extraordinary architectonic building, and a large number of burial chambers—approximately 70. This number led to a later belief that the members of the great Sanhedrin, numbering 71 people, were buried there, and thus the nearby neighborhood was named "Sanhedria." The special importance accorded to the Sanhedrin tombs stemmed from the fact that it is one of the oldest Jewish burial sites and one of the important remnants of Jewish activity found in the western part of the city.[61]

The Department of Antiquities, the Ministry of Religions, the Jerusalem Development Department, and the municipality took care of cleaning the caves and preparing them for visitors. The Jerusalem Development Department was tasked with coordinating the work and increasing the budget devoted to it, the work was be executed by the municipality, and the scientific oversight was the responsibility of the Department of Antiquities.[62] An additional—economic—reason was given for the preparation of the caves: the employment of a number of workers.[63] A map of the graves was even printed in a guidebook for visitors published by the Ministry of Education and Culture and the Department of Antiquities in the mid-1950s (Ministry of Education and Culture and the Department of Antiquities 1956).

In the early years, other historical and archaeological sites in West Jerusalem were listed as feasible sites, once prepared:[64] Herod's Family Tomb,[65] the

Mamilla reservoir and the ancient Muslim cemetery nearby,[66] the stone column in the Russian Compound,[67] the remains of a church and monastery in Abu Tor (the Hill of Evil Counsel),[68] and the remains of settlement in the Sheikh Badr neighborhood (see Figure 4.4).[69] This activity saw some results, as expressed in the report of the Interoffice Committee for the Improvement of Historical Sites in late 1950:

> A tourist visiting Jerusalem one year ago found nearly no ancient remnants in Jewish Jerusalem, save a visit to Mount Zion. Now, after the minimal activity (necessary due to budgetary issues) of the Department of Antiquities, a very interesting place to visit has been added—the Tombs of the Sanhedrin in which the cleaning and organizing has only just begun.... The cemetery in Mamilla added another interesting site for a visit, the Hill of Evil Counsel, remains at Givat Ram, Herod's Family Tomb...may force the tourist to devote a few days to his visit in Jerusalem and its environs...the showcase value of the [city's] antiques has barely been exploited until now.[70]

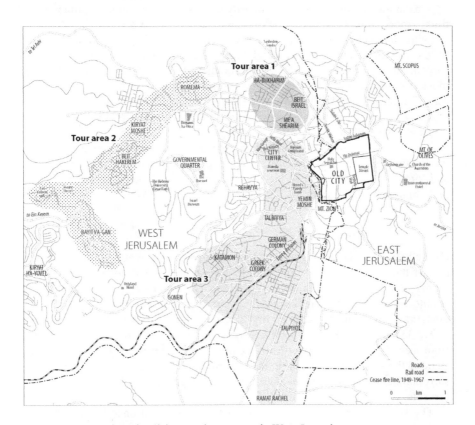

Figure 4.4 Attractions for visitors and tour areas in West Jerusalem.

The changes in West Jerusalem were not limited to attractions and holy sites. During the period of partition, West Jerusalem's tourist services also grew and shifted to meet changing needs.

West Jerusalem hotels

As we saw in the previous chapter, during the time of British rule a fairly developed infrastructure of tourism services was created in Jerusalem, particularly in its western section. After the 1948 war, a good number of the hotels and boarding houses that had run during the Mandate era were damaged to the extent that they could not house visitors. Other accommodations had been occupied during the war by the Israeli army, which did not hurry to evacuate even after the battles had ended, delaying repairs.[71] As described, the state of tourism during Israel's early years was not good, and this directly affected the development of accommodations. In the era of the partitioned city, a small number of hotels were built in the western part of the city.

In the 1960s, though, a certain awakening was felt in the city's tourism industry—as in the country at large—primarily thanks to the reduction in international flight prices and the beginnings of mass tourism. In order to supply for the growing demand, a number of hotels were built, including the Diplomat Hotel on the outskirts of the Arnona neighborhood, on the border between Israel and Jordan. Smaller hotels with 100 to 200 rooms were built in the center of the city; most prominently the Kings Hotel, the Presidents Hotel, the Orgil Hotel, and the Tirat Bat Sheva Hotel. The Holyland Hotel was built in the late 1950s in Jerusalem's west, on the outskirts of the city and the margins of the Bayit Vegan neighborhood (Baram 1981, 93–94; Kroyanker 1991, 19, 332–346). Over the years the scope of tourism in Jerusalem grew and some of the smaller hotels, like the Presidents Hotel and the Orgil Hotel, were unable to cope with the demand and forced to cease activity in the eighties, as they could not withstand the relatively high operating expenses (Kroyanker 1991, 332–334).

THE HOLYLAND HOTEL

Of the hotels, the Holyland was the first and most prominent built in the western part of the city after its partition and to a great extent it is considered the forerunner of modern hotels in West Jerusalem. The hotel was planned in 1952 by architect Zoltan Shimshon Harmat, built between the years 1955 and 1958, and inaugurated prior to the state's "first decade" celebrations in 1958 (Kroyanker 1991, 332–334). The hotel's founder was Hans (Tzvi) Kroch, a wealthy Jew from Leipzig who immigrated to Argentina during the Second World War and came to the state after its birth. In the coming lines, we present the circumstances surrounding its establishment within the geographical and historical reality of Jerusalem at the time.

The Holyland Hotel was built in the late 1950s on an open hill in what was southwest Jerusalem at the time, south of the Bayit Vegan neighborhood and north of the Arab village al-Maliha.[72] Parts of the hill apparently belonged to the Arab village until 1948.[73] The point was four kilometers away from the Central Business District of Jerusalem as the crow flies, a fact that illustrates the seclusion of the area relative to the settled parts of the city; it was also a mere 1,300 meters from the border between Israel and Jordan.[74] The area, at an average height of 770 meters, rose above the road that passed at its feet from the south, later Golomb Road, connecting Kiryat Hayovel and Ir Ganim, public housing neighborhoods designed for new immigrants that had begun to emerge to the south and west.[75]

The Holyland Hotel's location was chosen by Hans Kroch. Born into a wealthy Prussian Jewish family whose interests included commerce, banking, and real estate, Kroch had been encouraged by the Nazis to leave the country in order to get his partners, located outside of the country, to sign an agreement to transfer his part of the business to the Reich. The entire family escaped from Europe to Argentina, except for Kroch's wife, who stayed in Germany as a hostage and eventually died in a concentration camp. In Argentina, his son Yaakov joined a Zionist youth movement; immigrating to Israel in June 1948, he was killed in battle against the invading Egyptian army next to the Nitzanim kibbutz in the country's south.[76]

Hans Kroch first arrived in Jerusalem in the shadow of these tragic circumstances, hoping to establish a memorial to his son. In order to overcome the bureaucracy, Kroch looked for contacts. As a German Jew, he turned to another German Jew, Teddy Kollek, then director general of the Prime Minister's Office. He asked Kollek for help in purchasing a lone hill in Jerusalem's south in order to build a hotel. As Teddy Kollek states, an "old and direct *yekke* [German Jew], dressed in the style of Leipzig in the 1920s, who was proud of what he'd done in the Leipzig fair some decades earlier" stood before him. "He came here with a lot of money and wanted this land, at the end of the world. It seemed crazy to build a hotel there, and if someone had wanted to do it, he should be encouraged and helped."[77] A further statement teaches us that Kollek saw Kroch's request as an opportunity to bring him to places that were close to the border that had not yet been settled. Kollek brought Kroch to the hilltop and showed him what to buy and where to build the hotel. "As a good *yekke*, he accepted my recommendation."[78]

Due to the locale's seclusion, the future hotel's accessibility and connection to the city and the developing urban roads was a central question even before construction began. An examination of the road network in West Jerusalem in the state's early years shows that it developed in a southwesterly and westerly direction as a result of the city's expansion. Major streets had been paved to the south of the hilltop due to the construction of neighborhoods such as Katamonim, Kiryat Hayovel, Kiryat Menachem, and Ir Ganim; to its north, the development of the Mount of Remembrance and Mount Herzl and the massive building in the north part of Kiryat Hayovel led to the paving of other major roads. Thus the area of the Holyland Hotel remained disconnected, secluded in between two main axes of development in the city's west.

From the beginning, Kroch was aware of the accessibility problem, and sought a solution. Kroch apparently understood that the only way to promote an access road to the hotel was for him to take on part of the expense. In the end, Kroch was involved in the paving of two access roads to the hotel—from the south and from the north. In late 1952 (nearly six years before the hotel opened), Kroch's participation in funding the lower access road from Malcha Way (from the south) was reported as: (1) one third of each expense and (2) a loan to the municipality for one third of each expense. The loan was given to the municipality for a period of seven years with no interest and for payments of 2,000 Israel lira per year, which would begin two years after the road was completed.[79] A few months later, in early 1953, it was reported that Kroch had agreed to give the municipality 10,000 Israel lira as a donation and 10,000 Israel lira as a seven-year loan for the upper access road from Bayit Vegan (from the north).[80] In parallel to the purchase of the land and construction of the hotel, at the initiative and pressure of Kroch and as part of the expansion of Jerusalem as described above, paving of the upper road (from the north) was completed by the time hotel guests arrived when the hotel opened its doors right before the state's first decade celebrations in 1958.[81]

The size of the original land Kroch purchased from the Government Development Authority in late 1956 was 25 acres divided into two main plots: first Kroch bought the land for building the hotel and afterwards he bought an additional plot of land to expand the hotel's garden.[82] In mid-1957, the land was registered in the Land Registry and Regulation division under the name of the company founded by Kroch, the "Holy Land Corporation,"[83] and the building permit was given a few weeks later.[84] The follow-up on the lower road, from the south, was apparently around one year after the opening of the hotel, in mid-1959. For this Kroch turned once again to Teddy Kollek for help, who was, as stated, the director general of the Prime Minister's Office and the head of the Israel Government Tourist Corporation (and later the mayor of Jerusalem, as we will see in the next chapter). Kroch needed two to four acres in addition to the plots he had already bought in order to complete the road's route.[85] Paving appears to have been completed in the early 1960s.[86]

An additional perspective on the hotel's seclusion is seen in Kroch's treatment of the question of a synagogue for the hotel. According to oral testimony, Kroch felt it important that the hotel have a synagogue with prayer services on Sabbath and holidays. For the services on Sabbath in the early years, Kroch paid ten men (the quorum necessary to hold prayer services) from the housing projects built to the south to be at services.[87] For the Yom Kippur holiday, Kroch is known to have invited taxi drivers and their families to stay at the hotel in order to ensure that there was a prayer quorum.[88] The synagogue started off in one of the abandoned Arab buildings left in the area next to the hotel; when this building proved too small, too hot in the summer, and freezing cold in the winter, the prayers were moved to the hotel itself.[89]

In the early 1960s, Kroch initiated another plan to develop and expand the hotel into an apartment hotel. This suggestion was never implemented, but it illustrates

Kroch's pioneering and innovative spirit in tourism. His hope (as expressed in a loan request to the Israel Government Tourist Corporation) was to initiate a special type of accommodation in Jerusalem, not found in Jerusalem until then. Small residential buildings around the central hotel would give the tourist coming with family a different type of accommodation—a homey and intimate atmosphere that also included services on the standard of a first-class hotel. Kroch had seen this type of hotel in his travels. The planned expansion of the hotel included another thirty buildings which would be leased to foreigners for a period of 99 years payable in foreign currency and the leasers would make the buildings available to the hotel when they were not in Israel. The Holy Land Corporation believed that these buildings, overlooking a spectacular view and next to a swimming pool with guaranteed entertainment, would attract many tourists and vacationers from overseas and would extend the duration of the stay of these guests in Jerusalem.[90] The proposal to build the villas was endorsed by Teddy Kollek, who recommended that the Israel Government Tourist Corporation provide a loan.[91]

It appears that on the eve of the city's reunification, in 1967, the Holyland Hotel had established itself in the city and Kroch could expect the full realization of his vision. In 1964, Kroch's special venture in memory of his son was completed with the construction of a model of Jerusalem at the end of the Second Temple period. This model was the crown jewel of the hotel's cultural endeavors and brought it singular fame. The model became a hugely successful attraction, drawing hundreds of thousands of visitors since its completion. Entry to view the model was for a fee—though, interestingly, only after reunification of the city, when it was once again possible to visit the sites in any case.[92]

In 1964, construction on the swimming pool was also completed, and the first season of the Holyland Hotel's sport club began. The club was open to members and hotel guests alone and club-goers had a plethora of services available to them: a newly established tennis court, a swimming pool (one of the first hotel pools in the city), a boating lake, and a miniature golf course. Tennis and swimming instructors were available to guests for training and practice.[93] These activities made the Holyland Hotel a pioneer, the first hotel built in a style and spirit unknown in the city until then. The Holyland Hotel was in effect the first hotel in the city to allow its guests a stay in a quaint, quiet, and pastoral atmosphere, inside the city and with a high standard of service.

Conclusion

Over the period of partition in Jerusalem, the city's two halves developed along very different lines.

In the eastern city, the holy and historical sites continued to serve as a central draw for pilgrims and tourists, contributing to the accommodations and other tourism services. East Jerusalem was, in fact, the tourism magnet to the Jordanian kingdom in the time of the partitioned city. An elaborate new hotel in the eastern city was established and the majority of the area's income and employment came from the tourism sector.

However, the central Jordanian regime saw the evolution of Jerusalem's political status as a threat to the Hashemite monarchy and therefore took no pains to develop it, leaving it with a lesser status than other cities. Though Jordan saw a great influx of tourists, and though the majority of its tourism focused around East Jerusalem, the city's tourist industry grew somewhat but did not fully capitalize on its resources.

In contrast, the western part of the city underwent a revolution. With close to no historical and religious sites left, efforts were made to shape a national capital in which the governing institutions and national symbolic buildings would be located. Thus during partition three loci of Jewish sovereignty developed: Yad Vashem and Mount Herzl, representing Holocaust and rebirth; the national center, the halls of power of the Jewish state as a governing body; and the education and cultural center. Binyanei Ha'uma, intended to be a new cultural institution, was established, holding two important exhibitions. While these changes were of a political nature, other changes in the city were more closely tied to tourism. Tour routes and alternative pilgrimage sites formed, and attempts were made to revive archaeological sites. New hotels cropped up in the western city. So West Jerusalem in 1967 was a thriving, modern city with a new locus of economic activity.

The changes in West Jerusalem had a dual purpose. On the political level, the goal was to establish the city as indisputable capital, containing the state's governing buildings and cultural centers. The hope was that the world at large and Jewry would accept this location—with or without the religious sites—as the center of the Jewish nation. Tourism would, it was hoped, both encourage immigration from the U.S. and Western Europe and reach "ambassadors" who could conduct public relations for the country. On another level entirely, many of the changes aimed to draw more people to the city for economic reasons. The state hoped to attract visitors both Jewish and non-Jewish and, while impressing upon them that the heart of the Jewish state was in Jerusalem, benefit from a growing tourist sector and economy.

Ultimately, tourism during the years of partition focused far more on Jordan than Israel—and, by extension, more on East Jerusalem than West Jerusalem. However, during that time, Israel was laying groundwork for the years ahead, planning and building the secular sites that would serve it later on. Upon reunification, the western city already had its own secular character, alongside the historical-religious nature of the eastern section.

The Six-Day War which broke out in Jerusalem in June 1967 would create a new religious, geopolitical, and urban reality in a matter of days, making both parts of the city one geographical unit once again. This new reality would usher in a new era in Jerusalem.

Notes

1 The West Bank, also known as Judea and Samaria, is a 5,860-km^2 area to the west of Jordan and to the east of the Green (ceasefire) Line. The territory was first ruled by Jordan, which annexed it in 1950; in the Six-Day War it was conquered by Israel's army.

2 On the chain of events that led to the declaration of West Jerusalem as capital of the State of Israel see Bialer 1985, 163–191; Lorch 1989, 377–403.

3 The central claim of the Jordanians was that they could not guarantee the security of Jews and Israelis passing in the midst of the hostile population of the Old City. See Benvenisti 1976, 80–81.

4 Overview of the Jordanian urban outline based on Hashimshoni, Schweid, and Hashimshoni 1974, B:83–84.

5 For more on the Jordanian government's attitude to East Jerusalem, the steps it took amongst Christian communities in general, and the excitement stirred up by the pope's visit to East and West Jerusalem in particular, see Gilbert 1996, 265–267.

6 In the years following the Second World War there was a dramatic rise in international tourist traffic around the world, particularly in the developed world.

7 According to a conversation with Awni Inshewat, general manager of the Seven Arches Hotel (formerly the Intercontinental), August 9, 2012.

8 Holocaust and Heroism Remembrance Law—Yad Vashem 1953, Law Book No. 132, August 28, 1953.

9 The hall, planned by architects Arieh Elhanani, Arieh Sharon, and Benjamin Idelson, stood on an area of 850 square meters, and was in fact a massive cube whose bottom, more than two meters in height, was made of large basalt stones with a large concrete roof laid on top. For more on the symbolism of the various items in the Hall of Remembrance, see Brog 2006, 120–122.

10 The Hall of Names (1968), the Pillar of Heroism (1970), the Holocaust History Museum (1973), the Warsaw Ghetto Square (1975), the Monument to the Jewish Soldiers and Partisans Who Fought against Nazi Germany (1985), the Children's Memorial (1987), the Valley of the Communities (1992), and the Cattle Car Memorial (1995). In spring 2005, the new historical museum at Yad Vashem was inaugurated. See Brog 2005, 42–63.

11 Brought in Brog 2006, 112; Shenhavi is quoted from a letter sent to Prof. Dinaburg (Dinur), October 6, 1952, Foreign Ministry file, 2388/16, Israel State Archives, Jerusalem.

12 For a review and evaluation of the path in the context of Israeli nationalism, see Feldman 2007, 1147–1174.

13 Dr. I. E. Nebenzahl, director of the Jerusalem Development Department at the Jewish Agency, July 7, 1949, lecture at the Jewish Agency in the series "Wisdom of the Economists," S21, 402, Central Zionist Archives, Jerusalem.

14 Transcript of a radio interview with Mayor Daniel Auster on the subject "Jerusalem Rises from the Ashes," July 6, 1950, 2095, 29–42, Jerusalem Municipal Archives, Jerusalem.

15 Alexander Ezer (Yevzerov; 1895–1973), born in Ukraine, was one of the pioneers of the Zionist movement in Siberia. In 1920 he went to China and established its first agency of the World Zionist Organization mission and in 1921 he emigrated from there to Palestine. He was the founder and editor of the economic journal *Mischar V'ta'asia* ("Trade and Industry," 1923–1934). From 1926, he also published an economic newspaper in English, *Palestine and Near East*, later renamed *Palestine and Middle East*, which was published until 1944. In 1949, with the establishment of the Binyanei Ha'uma Company, he was chosen general director. He was one of the directors of the "Conquest of the Desert" exhibition in 1953 and the "First Decade" exhibition in 1958 (discussed later in the chapter). In 1954 he was responsible for tourism under the auspices of the government and beginning in 1956, with the establishment of the IGTC (the Israel Government Tourist Corporation) was appointed a consultant for the company. See Shavit, Goldstein, and Be'er 1983, 377; Tidhar 1949, C, 1348–1349.

16 Mr. Ussishkin, address at the ceremony for the opening of the Alexander Ezer Hall in Binyanei Ha'uma, July 15, 1974, A458, 27, Central Zionist Archives, Jerusalem.

17 A. Yevzerov and V. Tornovski to the Jerusalem Economic Development Company, undated, S21, 99, Central Zionist Archives, Jerusalem.

18 "Facts and Figures for the Establishment of the Center for Conventions and Exhibitions in Jerusalem (by the Binyanei Ha'uma Company)," December 1949, unsigned, S21, 403, Central Zionist Archives, Jerusalem; "Binyanei Ha'uma under Construction—Accredited reports about the progress of the endeavor," November 1, 1950, issue no. 1, year 1, S21, 403, Central Zionist Archives, Jerusalem.

19 On the phenomenon of international fairs and the large public events that took place primarily in Tel Aviv during the Mandate period, see Helman 2000, 120–157. On the convention centers, festivals, and fairs as a global phenomenon, the modern history of their development, their place in cultivating national and local pride, and the way in which they served as an impetus for promoting tourism in various places in the world in the past and today, there is extensive academic literature. See for example Hall 1992; Law 1993, 39–68; Petersen 1989.

20 Zeev Rechter (1899–1960) was born in Kovalevka, Russia. In 1919, he came to Palestine onboard the ship *Ruslan*. He studied architecture and was considered the first to build column buildings in Tel Aviv (1933). From 1934 he devoted himself to establishing public buildings. The first was the Kalia Hotel, on the shores of the Dead Sea, and afterwards dining halls in kibbutzes and hospitals such as Elisha on the Carmel. Later on he planned Binyanei Ha'uma and Heichal Hatarbut (the sanctuary of culture) in Tel Aviv (1957, with Dov Carmi). See Shavit, Goldstein, and Be'er 1983, 469.

21 S. Dor, "The Nation's Glory without the External Glory: A Conversation with Architect Z. Rechter" [in Hebrew], *Maariv*, May 5, 1950. A critique of the style claimed that it was hard to avoid the heavy and unpleasant presence of the building standing impenetrable atop a high hill. The large façade window also did not leave space for the human scale. Rechter was apparently influenced by a Swedish architect named Gunnar Asplund who designed some impressive buildings in Stockholm based on clean and right-angled geometric shapes, exaggeration in dimensions, and flush and elongated walls. The shape of the building was typical of the heavy and ungainly architecture of many public halls planned in the 1950s primarily in western and Eastern Europe. See: Shechori 1987, 46–48.

22 Y. Ben-Ari, "Binyanei Ha'uma in Jerusalem: A Conversation with Architect Z. Rechter," *Hador*, November 19, 1950.

23 The signing of Binyanei Ha'uma's charter took place at a festive meeting of the Jewish Agency plenary, with the participation of the president, prime minister, ministers, Knesset members, Jewish Agency board members, heads of financial institutions, many invitees, and journalists. See Binyanei Ha'uma Company, *Jerusalem Assembly Building*, booklet published in honor of the signing of the charter of the Buildings of the Nation, January 25, 1950, KH4, 6236, Central Zionist Archives, Jerusalem. A press release was also given to the media at the time. See for example B. Koralnik, "Binyanei Ha'uma's Charter to Be Signed Today" [in Hebrew], *Maariv*, January 25, 1950.

24 Facts and figures about the congress and exhibition building in Jerusalem (by the Binyanei Ha'uma Company Ltd.), December 1949, unsigned, S21, 403, Central Zionist Archives, Jerusalem; Z. Gold, Jerusalem Development Department, memorandum to the prime minister, Jerusalem, August 18, 1949 A-458, 1, Central Zionist Archives, Jerusalem.

25 "Binyanei Ha'uma under Construction—Accredited reports about the progress of the endeavor," year 1, issue 1, November 1, 1950, page 4, S21, 403, Central Zionist Archives, Jerusalem.

26 "Words in Memory of Father," Beit Hakerem, Jerusalem, unsigned, December 22, 1974, A458, 27, Central Zionist Archives, Jerusalem.

27 A. Ezer, general director of the Binyanei Ha'uma Company, to the director the subdivision for construction and building materials, Department of Trade and Industry, Jerusalem, January 31, 1951, 48–23, 4493, 8, Israel State Archives, Jerusalem.

28 Dov Yosef, minister of trade and industry, memorandum on the "Conquest of the Desert" exhibition, Jerusalem, November 18, 1952, 48–23, 4512, 29, Israel State Archives, Jerusalem.

29 Conquest of the Desert exhibition, progress report no. 1, February 1952, 48–23, 4512, 29, Israel State Archives, Jerusalem; "Conquest of the Desert," international exhibition and nations' fair, general regulations, 1988, 19-1-29, Jerusalem Municipal Archives, Jerusalem.

30 "The Exhibition under Construction," E. Samuel, director of the exhibition's European office, exhibition pamphlet no. 3, August 27, 1953, 48–23, 4512, 29, Israel State Archives, Jerusalem.

31 W. Eytan, chairman of the board of the "Conquest of the Desert" exhibition, Jerusalem, to M. Sharett, acting prime minister, Jerusalem, December 6, 1953, 48–23, 4512, 29, Israel State Archives, Jerusalem.

32 Y. Kimmelman, "Vox Populi Vox Dei," *Yediot Aharonot*, October 16, 1953.

33 "The First Decade Exhibition"—General outline, 62, 319, Israel State Archives, Jerusalem. Brought in Limor 2002, 34.

34 Memorandum on the exhibition of achievements within the celebrations of one decade to Israeli's independence in 1958 at Binyanei Ha'uma, January 20, 1957, 62, 318, Israel State Archives, Jerusalem. For more on the "First Decade" exhibition in the life of Jerusalem, see Gilbert 1996, 264–265.

35 In 1958, Israel's Jewish population numbered 1,810,148. See Central Bureau of Statistics 1961, 12, table 6.

36 First meeting of the exhibition's board, July 8, 1957, 62, 318, Israel State Archives, Jerusalem.

37 For more on the connection between Zionism and Jewish nationalism and its religious and historical roots, see Davis 2004; Feige 2002, 22–35 and sources there; Gurevich and Aran 1991, 9–44; Rolbant 1964, 307; Shapira 2005, 1–36; Silberman and Small 1997; Zerubavel 1995.

38 Memorandum from meeting of the planning committee for Binyanei Ha'uma, S. Livertov, June 29, 1951, 48–36, 7302, 17, Israel State Archives, Jerusalem; Y. Tzuriel, acting director of the tourism center, Jerusalem, to Y. Rishin, director of the publicity division for the "Conquest of the Desert" exhibition, Binyanei Ha'uma, Jerusalem, October 21, 1953, 48–23, 4512, 29, Israel State Archives, Jerusalem.

39 W. Eytan, chairman of the board of the "Conquest of the Desert" exhibition, Jerusalem, to M. Sharett, acting prime minister, Jerusalem, December 6, 1953, 48–23, 4512, 29, Israel State Archives, Jerusalem.

40 For a full overview of the criticism of the First Decade exhibition, see Limor 2002, 60–81.

41 The similarity between *asor*, decade, and *ason*, catastrophe, was a wry commentary on the exhibition.

42 "The Catastrophe Exhibition" [in Hebrew], *Haolam Hazeh*, issue 1087. Brought and analyzed in Limor 2002, 64–72. Limor emphasizes in her research that the reviews reflected in the press should be examined against the backdrop of the political line represented by each of the papers. *Haolam Hazeh*, for example, which adopted a blunt style and was the most biting of the critics, exploited the exhibition to attack the government and saw the faults as symptoms of the deficiencies of the state as a whole. The paper's critique of the national exhibition joined its attacks on the establishment, on Ben-Gurion, and on what it called the "Mapai Commissars" regime.

43 A. Ezer, memorandum to the board of directors of the Binyanei Ha'uma Company regarding establishing the company for events, August 1, 1965, A-458, 7, Central Zionist Archives, Jerusalem.

44 P. G. Natan, head of the Government Information Bureau for Tourists, Jerusalem, to the director of the Jerusalem Development Department, December 13, 1948, S21, 105, Central Zionist Archives, Jerusalem.

45 Press release, Government Information Bureau for Tourists, Jerusalem, to the Department of Tourism, Jerusalem, December 21, 1949, Israel State Archives, Jerusalem.
46 P. G. Natan, Government Information Office for Tourists, Jerusalem, to C. Gavriyahu, the Jerusalem Development Department, the Jewish Agency, Jerusalem, July 29, 1949, S21, 105, Central Zionist Archives, Jerusalem.
47 M. Setner, "Development and Construction in Jerusalem during the First Knesset Term," February 1949–July 1951, Jerusalem, Ministry of Finance and Ministry of Commerce and Industry, July 24, 1951, 71, 1084, 9, Israel State Archives, Jerusalem; Ben-Arieh and Wager 1994, 96.
48 Report of the Commission for Inquiry on Jerusalem, B, August 2, 1953, 43, 5430, 17, Israel State Archives, Jerusalem.
49 Mr. Tzuriel, Tourism Center, Ministry of Commerce and Industry, Jerusalem, to the Government Information Bureau for Tourists, Jerusalem, September 3, 1953, 48, Gal-9, 7307, Israel State Archives, Jerusalem. For figures regarding the comings and goings at Mandelbaum Gate in the first half of the 1960s, see Rolbant 1964, 310–313. Mandelbaum Gate was the only onshore crossing in Jerusalem between Israel and Jordan through which tourists could visit both parts of the city. On Mandelbaum Gate see Selzer and Tamir 2006, 29–32.
50 A. Lipshitz, chairman of the hotel, café, and restaurant association in Jerusalem, to A. Azar, responsible for tourism, Jerusalem, February 8, 1955, 48, Gal-9, 7307, Israel State Archives, Jerusalem.
51 Rolbant 1964, 329; Y. Forder, chairman of the board of the Israel National Bank (Bank Leumi), speech at the economic club in Jerusalem, January 6, 1964, 80, Gal-1, 4650, Israel State Archives, Jerusalem.
52 The country's income in 1963 was 5,949,000,000 Israel lira, or approximately two billion dollars. See Central Bureau of Statistics 1967, 141, table F/1.
53 On David Ben-Gurion's place in the return to biblical origins, see Shapira 2002, 121–146; Tzahor 1996, 140–149.
54 One of the high points in the history of early Israeli archaeology and its link to Zionism and Jewish nationalism were no doubt Yigal Yadin's famous findings, including the Bar Kokhba scrolls, Masada, Hazor, and other places. See Elon 1981, 280–289.
55 The revival of historical sites and buildings for visits and for various needs is a known tourism strategy in the tourist-historic city, and constitutes an important component in the model of the development of a tourist-historic city related in the academic literature. See Ashworth and Tunbridge 2000, 85–87; in the context of Mandate-era Jerusalem, see Cohen-Hattab 2004, 279–302.
56 In the assembly of the Zionist General Council that took place in August 1948, the Committee for Jerusalem resolved to establish the Jerusalem Development Department. The Jewish Agency administration appointed Rabbi Ze'ev Gold, one of the "Mizrachi" leaders, to head the new department. The department began its work in September 1948 and was in existence until 1952. For details on the department's activities, see the introduction to the list of files in the archive of the Jerusalem Development Department, 1948–1952, 2000, 3, Central Zionist Archives, Jerusalem.
57 The Jewish Agency for Israel, the Jerusalem Development Department, interim report on development of Jerusalem for September 1948–September 1950, S21, 400, Central Zionist Archives, Jerusalem.
58 Memorandum of a meeting in which the renewal of work on the Tombs of the Sanhedrin and the preservation of other ancient monuments in Jewish Jerusalem were discussed, Department of Antiquities, April 28, 1949, S21, 312, Central Zionist Archives, Jerusalem.
59 Y. Shenberger, Department of Antiquities, to I. E. Nebenzahl, Jerusalem Development Department, Jerusalem, October 23, 1949, S21, 312, Central Zionist Archives, Jerusalem. On the Tombs of the Sanhedrin during the Ottoman period see Ben-Arieh

1986, 37–39. For an item on the beginning of excavations in the Tombs of the San-hedrin, see "In Jerusalem" [in Hebrew], *Haaretz*, December 2, 1949. For more on the Tombs of the Sanhedrin, see Bar 2007, 116–120.

60 For a selection of studies dealing with the connection between death and cemeteries and modern nationalism and tourism, see Lennon and Foley 2000; Lloyd 1998; Seaton 1999, 130–158; Towner 1996, 51–52. One interesting expression of the tradition of cemetery visits as part of modern tourism is that it began to develop in the time of British rule in relation to the military cemetery on Mount Scopus in Jerusalem. For this, see Cohen-Hattab 2006, 164–165.

61 "Burial Caves in the Sanhedria Neighborhood," no author given (estimated summer 1951), S21, 312, Central Zionist Archives, Jerusalem; "Jewish Graves in Sanhedria," no author given (estimated summer 1951), S21, 312, Central Zionist Archives, Jerusa-lem. For a summary of excavations done at the site see Kloner and Zissou 2003, 264–266, and sources there.

62 Memorandum from meeting of the subcommittee on Sanhedria, Department of Antiq-uities, Jerusalem, November 21, 1949, S21, 312, Central Zionist Archives, Jerusalem.

63 I. E. Nebenzahl, Jerusalem Development Department, Jerusalem, to Treasury, Jerusa-lem, November 8, 1949, S21, 312, Central Zionist Archives, Jerusalem.

64 Memorandum from meeting in which the preservation and enhancement of the ancient monuments in Jewish Jerusalem were discussed, Department of Antiquities, Jerusa-lem, November 13, 1949, 1878, 29–42, Jerusalem Municipal Archives, Jerusalem.

65 The mausoleum hewn in stone between the King David Hotel and the Yemin Moshe neighborhood discovered by Conrad Schick in 1892. At first it was believed to be the tomb of Herod mentioned in Josephus' *Wars of the Jews*, but other researchers claimed that in all probability Herod's Family Tomb should be looked for to the north, closer to the Sultan's Pool. There are even those who believe that the building is north of Damas-cus Gate. The elaborate quarrying work proved that this was a burial place of people of means and status. "Herod's Family Tomb," no author listed (estimated summer 1951), S21, 312, Central Zionist Archives, Jerusalem. For a description of the archaeological findings at the site and sources see Kloner and Zissou 2003, 219–222.

66 The Muslim cemetery in Mamilla was the only cemetery that remained in the western city after partition. On the Muslim cemeteries in Jerusalem in the nineteenth century, see Ben-Arieh 1986, 66–67.

67 A massive stone column lies in the Russian Compound, still in the quarry in which its hewing was begun. Its length is roughly twelve meters. The finding of the column proves that there were those would work on building columns in their place before disconnecting them from the bedrock. Based on its size and shape, it was first estim-ated that it belonged to the Second Temple period, possibly to one of Herod's palaces. A similar column was found in the quarry at Machane Yehuda in 1934 during the digging of foundations for a home. See "Ancient Columns in their Quarry Sites," no author given (estimated summer 1951), S21, 312, Central Zionist Archives, Jerusa-lem. More recently it has been claimed that it is possible that the column is from a later era and it was one of the columns for the Nea Ekklesia Church built in Jerusalem in the late Byzantine era; see Tsafrir 2005, 27–30 and sources there.

68 In Abu Tor, in the southeast of the city near the railway station, a Greek monastery was found on a hill known to Christians as the "Hill of Evil Counsel." According to a tradition from the Middle Ages, at the time of Jesus the home of High Priest Caiaphas stood here. In the New Testament (Matt. 26:3–8), it is told that in the house gathered "the chief priests…and the elders of the people…and consulted that they might take Jesus by subtilty, and kill him." From here comes the name "Hill of Evil Counsel." In the courtyard of the Greek Monastery at the peak of the hill, remains of a church with an underground chapel attributed to the early seventh century were found. "Deir Abu Tor," no author given (estimated summer 1951), S21, 312, Central Zionist Archives, Jerusalem.

69 In the west of Jerusalem, between Romema and Beit Hakerem, a hill known by the name Sheikh Badr stands. In the summer of 1949, fragments of bricks and tiles with the seal of the tenth Roman Legion were found at the site. These remnants and remnants of walls that protruded at a few points proved that the remains of a settlement were buried there. Thus before the Jewish Agency began to build Binyanei Ha'uma, it was required to carry out an archaeological excavation at the site. The excavation was done under the auspices of the Israel Exploration Society and the Department of Antiquities. The most ancient remnants found there were pits hewn in stone from the end of the Second Temple, dug most probably in order to provide building materials for the city, particularly in the time of Herod, who constructed many buildings in Jerusalem. After the destruction of the Temple, the area was in the hands of the tenth legion, which used the place for the brick industry. Later on, the Romans prepared the land for a different purpose, possible for housing or for a different industry. At the site there were also the remnants of a Byzantine church and monastery. Sheikh Badr, no author given (estimated summer 1951), S21, 312, Central Zionist Archives, Jerusalem. For more on the archaeological findings in this area see Avi-Yonah 1949, 19–24.
70 Progress report and conclusions of the interoffice committee for the improvement of historical sites, October 1, 1950, 43.06, 5451, 6, Israel State Archives, Jerusalem.
71 Hotel, Café, and Restaurant Owners' Association, Jerusalem, to the Government Tourist Bureau, January 21, 1949, S21, 105, Central Zionist Archives, Jerusalem; consultation regarding hotels and tourism, Jerusalem Development Department, Jerusalem, January 30, 1949, S21, 105, Central Zionist Archives, Jerusalem.
72 As we saw in Chapter 3, Bayit Vegan was one of the five "garden suburbs" built in Jerusalem during the British Mandate period and planned by architect Richard Kaufmann. On the garden suburbs, see Biger 1977, 108–131. Al-Maliha was an Arab village located in southwest Jerusalem, northwest of Beit Safafa, which was abandoned during the 1948 war.
73 According to a 1924 map, planting and crops appear to the north and west of the site on which the hotel would be built and a road descended to the southwest from Bayit Vegan close to the point. See Figure 4.2.
74 The figures and measurements were done by Survey of Palestine, Jerusalem, 1:10,000, Sheet 3, 1945; Department of Surveys, Jerusalem, 1:10,000, 1962; see Figure 4.2.
75 Survey Israel, aerial photograph mm/2379/32, March 1958.
76 Giora Alon, *Memories of Eretz Hatzvi*, Jerusalem, August 5, 1994, Hillel Charney private archives.
77 Giora Alon, *Memories of Eretz Hatzvi*, Jerusalem, August 5, 1994, quoting Teddy Kollek, Hillel Charney private archives.
78 A personal communication from Hecht found in Hillel Charney's personal archive. Hillel Charney, Kroch's grandson, relates that his grandfather had not worked in hotels beforehand, and that in any event, this was not his goal. He defined the building as an assembly house, a place the extended family could come to once a year. Accordingly, the hotel was indeed established as a family business, with the extended family as shareholders. See H. Charney, Project Manifesto, press release, July 19, 1994, Hillel Charney private archives.
79 Y. Kariv, mayor, to A. Hartman, director of the Ministry of Labor, Jerusalem, October 30, 1952, Holyland Hotel Box, Jerusalem Municipal Archives, Jerusalem.
80 H. Steinfeld, director of the Israel Hotel Development Company founded by the Finance Department of the Jewish Agency, to the Jerusalem municipality, January 14, 1953, Holyland Hotel Box, Jerusalem Municipal Archives, Jerusalem; city engineer, Jerusalem municipality, to the municipal treasurer, August 5, 1953, reports that Kroch transferred 20,000 Israel lira for his part in building the Kroch road.
81 Dr. H. Steinfeld, manager of the Holyland Hotel, to Gershon Agron, mayor, April 7, 1958, Holyland Hotel Box, Jerusalem Municipal Archives, Jerusalem.

82 Protocol from meeting no. 100 of the Government Development Authority, Jerusalem, October 30, 1956, page 8, request no. 38, 43, C-8, 5444, Israel State Archives, Jerusalem; protocol from meeting no. 101, November 6, 1956, request no. 122, page 22–23, 43, C-8, 5444, Israel State Archives, Jerusalem.

83 Land registry extract, State of Israel, Department of Justice, Land Registry and Regulation Division, volume 16, page 81, June 10, 1957, Israel State Archives, Jerusalem. The land had trees planted, the owners were Chaya Devorah Yaakov Yehuda and Moshe Shneerson, and the buyer's name was Holy Land Corporation.

84 Building Permit no. 10115, local committee for building and planning cities, Jerusalem Municipal Council, Jerusalem, July 25, 1957, Jerusalem Municipal Archives, Jerusalem.

85 H. Kroch, Holyland Hotel, Jerusalem, to T. Kollek, Prime Minister's Office, Jerusalem, April 5, 1959, 43, C-11, 6375, Israel State Archives, Jerusalem.

86 No evidence about the completion of paving has been found but the road appears on a map from 1962. See Department of Surveys, Jerusalem, 1:10,000, 1962.

87 Personal communication from Nahari found in Hillel Charney's personal archive.

88 Personal communication from Hecht found in Hillel Charney's personal archive.

89 Personal communication from Solomon found in Hillel Charney's personal archive.

90 Y. Kollek, from Kollek and Weil attorneys, Jerusalem, to A. Iraon, director of the Tourism Development Company, Jerusalem, January 23, 1962, 43, C-11, 6375, Israel State Archives, Jerusalem.

91 T. Kollek, Prime Minister's Office, Jerusalem, to A. Iraon, Israel Government Tourist Corporation, August 25, 1961, 43, C-11, 6375, Israel State Archives, Jerusalem.

92 Tsafrir 2011, 47–86 and many sources there. As part of the real estate project and the destruction of the hotel, the model was transferred to the renewed Israel Museum and is one of the most important sites in Jerusalem today.

93 Publicity brochure, May 22, 1964, 43, C-11, 6375, Israel State Archives, Jerusalem.

References

Amiran, David. 1986. "The Geographic Development of Jerusalem, 1860–1985" [in Hebrew]. *Ariel* 43: 9–70.

Ashworth, Gregory John and John. E. Tunbridge. 2000. *The Tourist-Historic City: Retrospect and Prospect of Managing the Heritage City.* Amsterdam and New-York: Pergamon.

Avi-Yonah, Michael. 1949. "Excavations at Sheikh Bader" [in Hebrew]. *Bulletin of the Jewish Palestine Exploration Society* 15 (1–2): 19–24.

Azaryahu, Maoz. 1995. *State Cults: Celebrating Independence and Commemorating the Fallen in Israel 1948–1956* [in Hebrew]. Sde Boker: Ben–Gurion University of the Negev Press.

Azaryahu, Maoz. 2002. "(Re)locating Redemption—Jerusalem: The Wall, Two Mountains, a Hill and the Narrative Construction of the Third Temple." *Journal of Modern Jewish Studies* 1 (1): 22–35.

Azaryahu, Maoz. 2005. "Mt. Herzl: A Historical Outline of Israel's National Cemetery in Jerusalem" [in Hebrew]. *Horizons in Geography* 64–65: 369–383.

Bar, Doron. 2004. "Re-Creating Jewish Sanctity in Jerusalem: The Case of Mount Zion and David's Tomb between 1948–1967." *The Journal of Israeli History* 23 (2): 233–251.

Bar, Doron. 2005. "Holocaust Commemoration in Israel during the 1950s: The Holocaust Cellar on Mount Zion." *Jewish Social Studies* 12 (1): 16–38.

Bar, Doron. 2007. *Sanctifying a Land: The Jewish Holy Places in the State of Israel 1948–1968* [in Hebrew]. Jerusalem: The Ben-Gurion Research Institute and Yad Izhak Ben-Zvi.

Baram, Moshe. 1981. *Not in a Furrow* [in Hebrew]. Tel Aviv: Am Oved.

Ben-Arieh, Yehoshua 1986. *Jerusalem in the Nineteenth Century: The Emergence of the New City*. Jerusalem and New York: Yad Izhak Ben-Zvi.

Ben-Arieh, Yehoshua and Eliyahu Wager. 1994. "Stages in the building and development of Israeli Jerusalem between the years 1948 and 1967." In *Divided Jerusalem, 1948–1967*, edited by Avi Bareli, 91–114. Jerusalem: Yad Izhak Ben-Zvi.

Benvenisti, Meron. 1976. *Jerusalem, The Torn City*. Minneapolis: University of Minnesota Press.

Bialer, Uri. 1985. "Jerusalem 1949: Transition to Capital City Status" [in Hebrew]. *Cathedra* 35: 163–191.

Biger, Gideon. 1977. "'Garden Suburbs' in Jerusalem—Planning and Development under Early British Rule, 1917–1925" [in Hebrew]. *Cathedra* 6: 108–131.

Brog, Mooli. 1996. "On the History of the Representation of the Holocaust and Heroism at Yad Vashem" [in Hebrew]. *Bishvil Hazikaron* 12: 14–17.

Brog, Mooli. 2003. "Victims and Victors: Holocaust and Military Commemoration in Israel." *Israel Studies* 8 (3): 65–99.

Brog, Mooli. 2005. "Landscape of Memory: Monuments for the Holocaust and Heroism at Yad Vashem" [in Hebrew]. *Ariel* 170: 42–63.

Brog, Mooli. 2006. "Landscape of Memory and National Identity: The Holocaust Commemoration at Yad Vashem 1942–1966" [in Hebrew]. Jerusalem: PhD diss., the Hebrew University of Jerusalem.

Central Bureau of Statistics. 1961. *Israel Statistical Yearbook 1959–60* [in Hebrew]. Jerusalem: Central Bureau of Statistics

Central Bureau of Statistics. 1967. *Israel Statistical Yearbook 18* [in Hebrew]. Jerusalem: Central Bureau of Statistics.

Central Bureau of Statistics. 1968. *Israel Statistical Yearbook 19* [in Hebrew]. Jerusalem: Central Bureau of Statistics.

Cohen-Hattab, Kobi. 2004. "Historical Research and Tourism Analysis: The Case of the Tourist-Historic City of Jerusalem." *Tourism Geographies* 6 (3): 279–302.

Cohen-Hattab, Kobi. 2006. *Tour the Land: Tourism in Palestine during the British Mandate Period, 1917–1948*. Jerusalem: Yad Izhak Ben-Zvi [in Hebrew].

Cohen-Hattab, Kobi. 2007. "Tradition and Innovation in the Formation of National Identity in West Jerusalem during the First Decade after the Establishment of the State of Israel" [in Hebrew]. *Zion* 72 (2): 189–217.

Davis, Thomas W. 2004. *Shifting Sands: The Rise and Fall of Biblical Archaeology*. New York: Oxford University Press.

Efrat, Elisha. 1967. *Jerusalem and the Corridor: Geography of a Town and Its Environment* [in Hebrew]. Jerusalem and Tel Aviv: Achiasaf Publishing House.

Efrat, Elisha. 1973. "Changes in Jerusalem's Design Concept in the Past Fifty Years (1919–1969)" [in Hebrew]. *Ma'alot* D (6): 9–20.

Efrat, Elisha. 1976. *Town and Urbanization in Israel* [in Hebrew]. Tel Aviv: Achiasaf Publishing House.

Elon, Amos. 1981. *The Israelis: Founders and Sons*. Tel-Aviv: Adam Publishers.

Feige, Michael. 2002. *One Space, Two Places: Gush Emunim, Peace Now and the Construction of Israeli Space* [in Hebrew]. Jerusalem: The Hebrew University of Jerusalem Magnes Press.

Feldman, Jackie. 2007. "Between Yad Vashem and Mt. Herzl: Changing Inscriptions of Sacrifice on Jerusalem's 'Mount of Memory.'" *Anthropological Quarterly* 80 (4): 1147–1174.

Ganchovsky, Dov. 1994. "The Economy of the Divided City" [in Hebrew]. In *Divided Jerusalem, 1948–1967*, edited by Avi Bareli, 166–188. Jerusalem: Yad Izhak Ben-Zvi.

Gilbert, Martin. 1996. *Jerusalem in the Twentieth Century*. London: Chatto & Windus.

Golani, Motti. 1992. *Zion in Zionism: The Zionist Policy and the Question of Jerusalem 1937–1949* [in Hebrew]. Tel Aviv: Ministry of Defense.

Gold, Dore. 2007. *The Fight for Jerusalem: Radical Islam, the West, and the Future of the Holy City*. Washington, DC: Regnery Pub.

Gonen, Amiram. 2003. "The Emergence of a Geographical Heartland in Israel" [in Hebrew]. In *Economy and Society in Mandatory Palestine, 1918–1948*, edited by Avi Bareli and Nahum Karlinsky, 439–488. Sde Boker: Sde Boker Research Center.

Gosenfeld, Norman. 1973. "The Spatial Division of Jerusalem, 1948–1969." Los Angeles: PhD diss., University of California.

Gurevich, Zali and Gideon Aran. 1991. "About the Place (Israeli Anthropology)" [in Hebrew]. *Alpayim* 4: 9–44.

Hall, Colin Michael. 1992. *Hallmark Tourist Events: Impacts, Management and Planning*. London: John Wiley and Sons.

Hall, Colin Michael. 2002. "Tourism in Capital Cities." *Tourism (Zagreb)* 50: 235–248.

Hashemite Kingdom of Jordan, Department of Statistics. 1962. *Statistical Yearbook* 13. Amman: Hashemite Kingdom of Jordan.

Hashemite Kingdom of Jordan, Department of Statistics. 1964. *Statistical Yearbook* 15. Amman: Hashemite Kingdom of Jordan.

Hashemite Kingdom of Jordan, Department of Statistics. 1965. *Statistical Yearbook* 16. Amman: Hashemite Kingdom of Jordan.

Hashimshoni, Avia, Yossi Schweid, and Tziyon Hashimshoni. 1974. *Jerusalem Master Plan, 1968* [in Hebrew]. Jerusalem: Jerusalem Municipality.

Hattis Rolef, Susan. 2000. "The Knesset Building at Givat Ram—Planning and Construction" [in Hebrew]. *Cathedra* 96: 131–170.

Hattis Rolef, Susan. 2002. "Planning the Knesset building: Additional Comments and Corrections" [in Hebrew]. *Cathedra* 105: 171–180.

Helman, Anat. 2000. "The development of Civil Society and Urban Culture in Tel Aviv during the 1920s and 1930s" [in Hebrew]. Jerusalem: PhD diss., the Hebrew University of Jerusalem.

Hopkins, Ian W. J. 1969. *Tourism in Jerusalem: A Report for the Ministry of Tourism*. Israel: Durham.

Huminer, Esther. 1997. "The Establishment of Jerusalem as the Capital of the State of Israel and Its Development as a Capital City in the Early Years" [in Hebrew]. Jerusalem: Master's thesis, the Hebrew University of Jerusalem.

Katz, Kimberly. 2005. *Jordanian Jerusalem: Holy Places and National Spaces*. Gainsville: University Press of Florida.

Katz, Yossi. 2003. "Position of the British, the UN, and the Zionist Leadership in Regard to the Partition of Jerusalem" [in Hebrew]. In *Jerusalem and the British Mandate: Interaction and Legacy*, edited by Yehoshua Ben-Arieh, 133–166. Jerusalem: Mishkenot Sha'ananim and Yad Izhak Ben-Zvi.

Katz, Yossi and Yair Paz. 2004. "The Transfer of Government Ministries to Jerusalem, 1948–49: Continuity or Change in the Zionist Attitude to Jerusalem?" *The Journal of Israeli History* 23 (2): 232–259.

Kendall, Henry. 1948. *Jerusalem—The City Plan: Preservation and Development During the British Mandate, 1918–1948*. London: H.M.S.O.

Kimhi, Israel, Benjamin Hyman, and Gabriele Claude. 1976. *Jerusalem 1967–1975: A Socioeconomic Survey* [in Hebrew]. Jerusalem: The Hebrew University of Jerusalem.

Klein, Chaim H., ed. 1973. *The Second Million: Israel Tourist Industry, Past-Present-Future* [in Hebrew]. Tel Aviv: Amir.

Kloner, Amos and Boaz Zissou. 2003. *The Necropolis of Jerusalem in the Second Temple Period* [in Hebrew]. Jerusalem: Yad Izhak Ben-Zvi, the Israel Exploration Society.

Kroyanker, David. 1991. *Jerusalem Architecture—Periods and Styles: Modern Architecture outside the Old City Walls 1948–1990* [in Hebrew]. Jerusalem: Maxwell-Macmillan and Keter.

Law, Christopher M. 1993. *Urban Tourism: Attracting Visitors to Large Cities.* London: Mansell.

Lennon, J. John and Malcolm Foley. 2000. *Dark Tourism: The Attraction of Death and Disaster.* London and New York: Cengage Learning EMEA.

Levine, Ayala. 2006. "The 'Netzer Aharon' Monument: On Marginalization and Repression in Israeli Memory-work" [in Hebrew]. *Zmanim* 95: 38–43.

Limor, Galyah. 2002. "The First Decade Exhibition: The Exhibition that Disappeared" [in Hebrew]. Jerusalem: Master's thesis, the Hebrew University of Jerusalem.

Lloyd, David William. 1998. *Battlefield Tourism: Pilgrimage and Commemoration of the Great War in Britain, Australia, and Canada—1919–1939.* Oxford, UK: Berg.

Lorch, Natanel. 1989. "Ben-Gurion and Jerusalem as Israel's Capital" [in Hebrew]. In *Jerusalem in Zionist Vision and Realization,* edited by Hagit Lavasky, 377–403. Jerusalem: The Zalman Shazar Center for Jewish History, the Historical Society of Israel, and the Center for the Zionism and the Yishuv, the Hebrew University of Jerusalem.

Maitland, Robert and Brent W. Ritchie. 2009. *City Tourism: National Capital Perspectives.* Wallingford, UK: CABI.

Ministry of Education and Culture and the Department of Antiquities. 1956. *A Short Guide to the Rock-cut Tombs of Sanhedriya* [in Hebrew]. Jerusalem: Turim Press.

Naor-Wiernik Michal and Doron Bar. 2012. "The Competition for the Design and Development of Herzl's Tomb and Mount Herzl, 1949–1960" [in Hebrew]. *Cathedra* 144: 107–136.

Narkiss, Uzi. 1975. *The Liberation of Jerusalem* [in Hebrew]. Tel Aviv: Am Oved.

Natan, Samuel. 1973. "First Steps" [in Hebrew]. In *The Second Million: Israel Tourist Industry, Past-Present-Future,* edited by Chaim H. Klein, 33–40. Tel Aviv: Amir.

Petersen, David C. 1989. *Convention Centers, Stadiums and Arenas.* Washington: Urban Land Institute.

Prime Minister's Office. 1957. *The Government's Yearbook 1956* [in Hebrew]. Jerusalem: The State of Israel Government Press.

Prime Minister's Office. 1966. *The Government's Yearbook 1965* [in Hebrew]. Jerusalem: The State of Israel Government Press.

Ramon, Amnon. 1987. *Divided Jerusalem: The City Line—1948–1967* [in Hebrew]. Jerusalem: Yad Izhak Ben-Zvi.

Rolbant, Samuel, ed. 1964. *Jerusalem—Paths to Economic and Social Advancement* [in Hebrew]. Tel Aviv: Midoa, Institute of Economic and Sociological Research, Urban Problems Unit.

Roman, Michael. 1967. *Socioeconomic Survey of Reunited Jerusalem* [in Hebrew]. Jerusalem: The Maurice Falk Institute for Economic Research.

Roman, Michael. 1989. "The Shift of the Demographic and Economic Center from Jerusalem to Tel Aviv during the Mandate" [in Hebrew]. In *Jerusalem in Zionist Vision and Realization,* edited by Hagit Lavasky, 217–234. Jerusalem: The Zalman Shazar

Center for Jewish History, the Historical Society of Israel and the Center for the Zionism and the Yishuv, the Hebrew University of Jerusalem.

Schwartz, Kobi. 2004. "Political-educational Tourism: German Tourism to Israel in the 1950s and 1960s" [in Hebrew]. Tel Aviv: PhD diss., Tel Aviv University.

Schweid, Yosef. 1994. "The Urban Development and Architecture of Jerusalem in the Years 1948–1967" [in Hebrew]. In *Divided Jerusalem, 1948–1967*, edited by Avi Bareli, 115–132. Jerusalem: Yad Izhak Ben-Zvi.

Seaton, A. V. 1999. "War and Thanatourism: Waterloo 1815–1914." *Annals of Tourism Research* 26 (1): 130–158.

Selzer, Asaf. 2006. *The Reflection of the State and Its Space in a National Festival—Israel's Tenth Anniversary Events (1958–1959)* [in Hebrew]. Jerusalem: PhD diss., the Hebrew University of Jerusalem.

Selzer, Asaf and Yoram Tamir. 2006. "From a Home to a Border Crossing Area" [in Hebrew]. *Etmol* 187: 29–32.

Shalom, Zaki. 1993. "Israel's Struggle to Thwart UN Resolutions on the Internationalization of Jerusalem in the 1950s" [in Hebrew]. *Iyunim Bitkumat Israel* 3: 75–97.

Shapira, Anita. 2002. "Ben-Gurion and the Bible: The Creation of a Historic Narrative?" [in Hebrew]. In *A Century of Israeli Culture*, edited by Israel Bartal, 121–146. Jerusalem: The Hebrew University of Jerusalem Magnes Press.

Shapira, Anita. 2005. *The Bible and Israeli Identity* [in Hebrew]. Jerusalem: The Hebrew University of Jerusalem Magnes Press.

Shapiro, Shachar. 1973. "Planning of Jerusalem—The First Generation (1918–1968)." In *Urban Geography of Jerusalem: A Companion to the Atlas of Jerusalem*, edited by David Amiran *et al.*, 139–147. Berlin and New York: W. de Gruyter.

Shavit, Yaacov, Yaacov Goldstein, and Hayim Be'er. 1983. *General Biographical Lexicon of Palestine, 1799–1948* [in Hebrew]. Tel Aviv: Am Oved.

Shechori, Ran. 1987. *Zeev Rechter* [in Hebrew]. Jerusalem: Hakibbutz Hameuchad.

Shoval, Noam. 2009. "Tourism in Jerusalem, 1967–2000." In *Planning and Conserving Jerusalem: The Challenge of an Ancient City*, edited by Eyal Meiron and Doron Bar, 389–407. Jerusalem: Yad Izhak Ben-Zvi.

Shoval, Noam and Kobi Cohen-Hattab. 2001. "Urban Hotel Development Patterns in the Face of Political Shifts." *Annals of Tourism Research* 28 (4): 908–925.

Silberklang, David. 2003. "Much More Than a Monument: The History of Yad Vashem" [in Hebrew]. *Yad Vashem and Jerusalem*, 6–7.

Silberman, Neil Asher and David B. Small, eds. 1997. *The Archaeology of Israel: Constructing the Past, Interpreting the Present*. Sheffield: T&T Clark.

Strom, Elizabeth. 2001. *Building the New Berlin: The Politics of Urban Development in Germany's Capital City*. Lanham and Oxford: Lexington Books.

Tidhar, David. 1949. *Encyclopedia of the Pioneers and Builders of the Yishuv* [in Hebrew]. 19 vols. Tel Aviv: Sifriyat Rishonim.

Towner, John. 1996. *An Historical Geography of Recreation and Tourism in Western World 1540–1940*. Chichester: John Wiley.

Tsafrir, Yoram. 2005. "Procopius on the Nea Church, the Cardo, and the 'Finger of Og' in Jerusalem" [in Hebrew]. *Cathedra* 115: 5–30.

Tsafrir, Yoram. 2011. "Designing the Model of Jerusalem at the Holyland Hotel: Hans Zvi Kroch, Michael Avi-Yonah, and an Unpublished Guidebook" [in Hebrew]. *Cathedra* 140: 47–86.

Tzahor, Zeev. 1996. "Ben-Gurion as a Shaper of Myth" [in Hebrew]. In *Myth and Memory: Transfigurations of Israeli Consciousness*, edited by David Ohana and Robert S. Wistrich, 136–155. Tel Aviv: Hakibbutz Hameuchad.

Yizrael, R. 1986. "Jerusalem's Urban Line and the Jerusalem Corridor" [in Hebrew]. In *Jerusalem: A City United, Ariel* 44–45, edited by Ely Schiller, 17–26. Jerusalem: Ariel.
Zerubavel, Yael. 1995. *Recovered Roots: Collective Memory and the Making of Israeli Nation Tradition*. Chicago: University of Chicago Press.

Archives and Collections
Central Zionist Archives, Jerusalem.
Hillel Charney Private Archives.
Israel State Archives, Jerusalem.
Jerusalem Municipal Archives, Jerusalem.

5 Tourism in the reunited city (1967–2000)

The final battle in Jerusalem during the Six-Day War took place on Wednesday, June 7, 1967. Israel's minister of defense, Moshe Dayan, and the commander-in-chief of the Israel Defense Forces, Yitzchak Rabin, entered the Old City through Lions' Gate. Exiting their vehicle, they marched with their large entourage to the Temple Mount area. There, they turned to the Western Wall plaza, where Moshe Dayan declared:

> This morning, the Israel Defense Forces liberated Jerusalem. We are uniting the divided capital of Israel and we have returned to our holy places; we have returned never to be separated from them again. To our Arab neighbors we extend, at this time, a hand in peace. To members of other religions, Christians and Muslims, we promise faithfully to protect your full freedom and religious rights. We have not come to Jerusalem to conquer sites holy to others or to restrict the freedom of other religious groups, but to guarantee the unity of the city and to live together with others in friendship.
>
> (Quoted in Benvenisti 1976, 122)

With these words Moshe Dayan expressed the Israeli government's desire to reunite Jerusalem under Israeli sovereignty and to open the united city to all visitors.

The Six-Day War brought about the political unification of the two parts of Jerusalem for the first time in the history of the State of Israel, leading to dramatic changes in the city's status. The removal of the border dividing Jerusalem made freedom of movement between the east and west possible. Very quickly, tourists domestic and foreign flocked to Jerusalem's gates; the highlight of their visits was the Old City and the now unrestricted religious sites.

The military victory and the confidence which accompanied it generated a growing demand for development and building throughout Jerusalem. Israel was overcome by the feeling that it was possible to do anything, and at any cost.

Many building plans were submitted, some requiring demolition of entire areas and a fresh start. Work in the Old City, the museum district, promenades, the city center, open spaces and lookouts, the Old City basin, and the cultural mile changed the city's landscape. In response to the rapid changes, the question of preservation of historical places appeared on the public agenda. At the same time, tourism plans were developed to maximize the city's potential, and hotels began to crop up around Jerusalem. These ultimately led to another public debate, this time surrounding high-rise construction and its effects on the city's skyline.

But beyond tourism's importance in the physical changes taking place in the city, it was once again used for political means. Israel recognized tourism as an economic boon, but also knew that its political implications were crucial in the transition to a unified city: First, it would help buttress territorial control. Second, Israel could better justify its rule over the unified city if it demonstrated that all factions thrived under its control. Finally, it could draw in Jews the world over, inspiring them to tie themselves to the state. In certain cases, agents in Israeli society attempted to leverage tourism in order to increase national pride or claim land for their own.

Ultimately, the growth of tourism was highly influenced by geopolitical factors, which brought about changes in tourism services' supply and demand. Among these factors were the outbreak of the first Intifada at the end of the 1980s, the Gulf War (1991), the peace talks between Israel and the surrounding countries that followed (1993), and the second Intifada (2000), which dealt tourism in Jerusalem a severe blow—both in terms of numbers and in terms of public image.

Growing tourism in a time of instability

The years between 1967 and 2000 were considered years of prosperity for international tourism. Tourism in Israel and Jerusalem also flourished during these years, though there were ebbs and flows resulting from the geopolitical situation in the Middle East (Mansfeld 1996, 265–278). During this period more than 80 percent of the tourists who came to Israel visited Jerusalem, making Jerusalem and the Old City the leading tourist attractions in the country (as measured by numbers of visitors; Shoval 2009, 390).

The year 1978, approximately a decade after the Six-Day War, was the first time that one million tourists entered the country. During the 1980s, fluctuations in the number of tourists meant that inbound tourism ranged from one million to one and a half million per year. The continuous trend of growth and improvement continued during the first half of the 1990s; in 1994, for the first time, over two million tourists came to Israel. However, three years later, in the wake of Palestinian suicide bombings in Israel—most notably in Jerusalem—the number of tourists fell once again.

During the last two years of the 1990s, in the spirit of optimism as the Millennium approached, there was a revival in tourism, and in the year 2000 the number of visitors to Israel reached a peak of 2,672,000. The outbreak of the second Intifada that same year had only a slight effect on the number of tourists, but afterwards the numbers decreased dramatically. In 2002 only 862,000 foreign tourists came, the lowest number since 1976 (see Figure 5.1).

The years that followed saw an impressive recovery, with tourism returning to the state that had existed prior to the outbreak of the Intifada and even surpassing it: in 2008 the number passed the three million mark for the first time (Central Bureau of Statistics and the Ministry of Tourism 2009).

Nir Barkat, current mayor of Jerusalem, has a vision of reaching ten million annual tourists in Jerusalem within a decade. At present, this is unrealistic due to the relations between Israel and its neighboring countries; however, those numbers should be realistic looking at destinations such as Barcelona (13 million), Paris (fifteen million), and Rome (12 million; Cohen-Hattab 2009; Dumper 2002, 139–170).

Practically speaking, during the past 45 years, tourism has grown in Jerusalem, notwithstanding lulls during periods of violence. This growth was accompanied, and is still partially accompanied, by a number of major developments in Jerusalem's urban area, presented below.

Renewal of tourism in the united city

Immediately following the cessation of hostilities in June 1967, the Israeli Ministry of Tourism took steps to ensure renewed tourism in Jerusalem. This was motivated by economic factors, but other considerations also had a role: first, the desire to demonstrate to the world that Israel was capable of guaranteeing free access to the holy places and governing the united city; second, a wish to provoke commitment and identification on the part of Jews the world over.

To accomplish this, the ministry combined the tourist resources from Jordanian rule with those existing in Israel. Accordingly, the following steps were taken (Prime Minister's Office 1968–1969, 489):

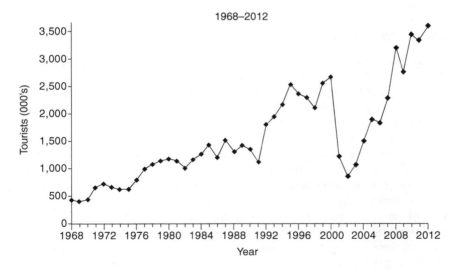

Figure 5.1 Inbound tourism to Israel 1968–2000.

- The Ministry of Tourism granted temporary licenses to approximately 50 Arab travel agencies in the eastern part of the city, all of whom worked in Jerusalem and its surroundings. These travel agencies did not affiliate with their Israeli counterparts; in fact, beginning immediately after the 1967 war they protested any attempts to involve them in the Israeli economy or administration.[1] The same was true for hotel owners.
- There were 34 hotels with 1,800 hotel rooms as well as dozens of youth hostels for Christian pilgrims in East Jerusalem. West Jerusalem contained 1,200 hotel rooms. Most of the hotels were not destroyed during the war and were ready to resume functioning. The Ministry of Tourism gave East Jerusalem's accommodations temporary permits for six months of operation and ranked them according to the Israeli Ministry of Tourism quality standards. Later on they received permanent permits.
- Immediately following the cessation of hostilities, the Ministry of Tourism published many new walking tour routes in Jerusalem and trained new tour guides. Arab tour guides who had worked in the city under Jordanian sovereignty were also given licenses (Prime Minister's Office 1968–69, 490).
- East Jerusalem was quickly included in "A" (high priority) development territory, which meant substantial benefits to investors developing hotels and tourist sites (Prime Minister's Office 1969–70, 299–301).

With these initial activities, the state signaled its interest in cultivating tourism in the united city. At the same time, the city began to evolve; restoration, construction, and change became commonplace, shaping a Jerusalem that was more attractive to tourists and better equipped to welcome them in.

A new city emerges

The Old City as a focus of tourism

At the end of the Six-Day War, the borders and roadblocks which had divided the eastern and western parts of Jerusalem were removed. To some extent, Jerusalem returned to its pre-1948 state, when the Old City was Jerusalem's major tourist attraction. Indeed, the new "tourist map" placed the Old City in the center as the united city's principal attraction.[2]

The preservation and restoration of the Old City and its surroundings were the basis of the planning that had begun during the British Mandate period. Israel took advantage of the new situation and continued implementing the major tenets of the British period—but in a new reality, in which the Old City and the sites within it were open to all visitors. Among the goals: the restoration of the walls and gates; establishing a national park around the walls; rebuilding the Jewish Quarter, destroyed following the 1948 war; renovating infrastructure (sewage, water, electricity, and telephone lines) in the various quarters; paving the alleyways with stone; and installing public lighting (Kroyanker 1988, 50).

Development included renovation of the marketplace in the Old City's Muslim Quarter as a tourist center for business as well as renovation of the Via Dolorosa to make it suitable for the larger groups of pilgrims that began to arrive following the war. The extensive construction and development which began immediately after the Six-Day War in the Old City and its surroundings caused an uproar in the Christian and Muslim worlds alike over Israel's right to build in East Jerusalem; the issue was frequently raised on the agenda at the General Assembly and in the United Nations' Security Council, despite the fact that much of the development was carried out in collaboration between the local Muslim Waqf and the Jerusalem Foundation.[3]

Rebuilding the Jewish Quarter

One of the principal achievements in the restoration of the Old City after the Six-Day War was the reconstruction of the Jewish Quarter.[4] After the war, the Jewish Quarter's residents were evacuated and the government announced that it would occupy the Jewish Quarter for one year for surveying and planning purposes. Based on this, the government expropriated 29 acres, most of which had belonged to Jews before 1948, including the area around the Western Wall, with the exception of the Wall itself.

The Old City planning staff conducted many detailed surveys and published its final plans early in the 1970s (Gardi 1972; Sharon, Brutzkus, and Sharon n.d.). The planners were challenged by the emotional uniqueness and historical significance of the Jewish Quarter; this was compounded by the fact that it was inseparable from the texture and distinct character of the Old City. The master plan for the Jewish Quarter envisioned a residential area, a center of Jewish public and religious institutions, and a central area which would attract tourists and visitors. The plan was multifaceted and included residential and commercial areas, public buildings and open spaces. Areas were clearly defined and space was carefully demarcated, indicating distances to the Western Wall in which no building would be permitted as well as the height of building allowed within the Jewish Quarter.

According to the plan, three parallel streets would cross the Jewish Quarter from north to south: Chabad Street, Hayehudim Street (a continuation of the Old City marketplaces), and Misgav Ladach Street (see Figure 1.1). In order to create a link between the various points of the Jewish Quarter, two central traffic routes would be constructed perpendicular to the main arteries. One of the routes would be for tourists and commerce and would have commercial façades. The other would be designated for most of the institutions in the center of the Quarter. Both of these routes would meet at the Western Wall plaza, and be joined together by steps and observational lookout points, emphasizing the connection between the Jewish Quarter and the Western Wall.

The plans dictated that the residential areas be built around small internal passageways. The developers hoped to achieve a division between the residential area and the commercial and tourist sides of the Jewish Quarter; their hope was to protect the privacy of residents as much as possible while at the same time transforming the area into a dynamic and vital tourist site. To achieve this, areas were set aside for public squares and gardens, and the link between them would be a large square at the center of the Jewish Quarter east of the Hurva Synagogue. A park was planned near the southern wall very close to the Jewish Quarter and a "rooftop walkway" connected to the marketplaces of the Old City and provided green space for the Jewish Quarter and for the Old City (Avigad 1980; Naor 1987, 270–463; Netzer 1976, 117–125; Ricca 2007; Slae 2009, 85–108).

The principle inherent in the plans was the protection of the Jewish Quarter's unique character and the existing urban texture: limiting the Jewish Quarter to pedestrians, preserving the complex of passageways and historical structures of the Quarter, restriction of building to small units, and creating clusters of buildings. The goal of this carefully regulated construction was to preserve the visibility of the skyline and traditional rooftops; maintain terraced buildings consistent with the existing topography; limit the number of floors; preserve traditional elements such as arches, domes, and passageways above the alleyways; and build using the traditional stone (Bar Dor 1992, 49–52; Slae 2009, 85–108).

By law, before new construction could begin in the ravaged Jewish Quarter, preliminary excavations had to be carried out. "Ironically," Yadin (1975) points out, "these were indirectly brought about by the systematic destruction of the Jewish Quarter, including its numerous synagogues, during the period of Jordanian rule." Until 1969, "the upper city" had been something of an archaeological vacuum. Previous findings were primarily post-biblical and extremely meager, leading Kathleen Kenyon (in the 1950s and 1960s) and others to surmise that biblical accounts of Jerusalem were mere legend. Archaeologists in the post-1967 digs expected to find remains primarily from the Crusader Period and onwards.

In 1969, Hebrew University archaeologist Nahman Avigad began the first Israeli dig in the Jewish Quarter, moving from one site to another according to construction plans (Avigad 1975; Mazar 1975). In principle, every empty site was to be excavated prior to new building. Every old building that could be saved would be, particularly in the narrow passageways that were designated as part of the preserved urban fabric. Thus, most of the excavations took place around the ruined center of the Quarter, or the "Pilgrims' Path."

During the first three seasons, from 1969 to 1971, nine sites were excavated, almost 20 percent of the total area of the Jewish Quarter—one of the largest excavations ever conducted in Israel. Discoveries included fortifications and structures from the First and Second Temple periods (ca. 800 BCE–70 CE), the Byzantine Cardo (main street of Jerusalem between the fourth and seventh centuries), and the Nea Church complex (dated to the sixth century). The German Templar Church and the Hospice and Hospital of St. Mary provided excellent examples of Crusader architecture. Also found were relics of Ayyubid fortifications and a Turkish bazaar opposite the Templar Church. Open archaeological parks and underground museums were later constructed to display the findings.[5]

Because basic master and outline plans existed before the excavations began, the authorities had already committed themselves to establishing a sizable residential community and several large institutions. For example, a large campus was allotted to Yeshivat Hakotel[6] in 1968. After the spectacular finds in the Jewish Quarter during the 1969–1971 excavations, an attempt was made to convince the yeshiva to accept an alternate location, but the administration refused. A compromise was finally reached, whereby the excavations were preserved in an underground museum, and the yeshiva was supported by huge concrete pillars. Of course, this delayed construction and raised its price considerably (Kroyanker 1988, 128, 151–154; Slae, Kark, and Shoval 2012). If all of the excavations' findings had been preserved in sites that were open to the public, no room would have been left for a residential neighborhood or shops.

Design of the Western Wall plaza

The Western Wall, the only significant remnant of the Holy Temple, has been seen as symbol of all that the Jewish people lost and a symbol of their yearning, continuity, and determination. This yearning was not satisfied until after the Six-Day War, when for the first time in its history the Western Wall and the adjacent plaza were under Jewish control and Israeli sovereignty. The liberation of the Western Wall was considered one of the most important triumphs of the war; in the first days after the war, the Western Wall was imprinted in national memory as the embodiment of Jewish sovereignty in the land of Israel, as the reflection of Israeli control over Jerusalem, and as a powerful expression of Jewish unity. After many generations in which Jews were denied access to the Wall for prayers the restrictions were removed, and in June 1967 the liberated Western Wall became accessible and available to all who wished to pray (Ben-Dov, Naor, and Aner 1983, 140–158).

The large number of visitors expected at the plaza was one of the major reasons for the swift decision—made on the fourth day after the war—to demolish the Mughrabi neighborhood. Residents of the neighborhood were descendants of Muslim immigrants from North Africa who, encouraged by the Turkish Sultan, settled in Jerusalem during the second half of the nineteenth century. They lived in an area which extended from west of the plaza to the open area facing the Western Wall.[7] Before 1948, the Jews had had to accept a small prayer area of a few square meters under the protectorate of the Arab Mughrabi neighborhood, which not infrequently disturbed the prayers and desecrated the area.

The practical considerations for the decision to tear down the Mughrabi neighborhood were augmented by the nationalistic feeling that emerged in Israel in the immediate aftermath of the war; for some, this included the desire to settle historical accounts with those who had persecuted and humiliated the Jewish people for many years at the holiest of places.

Clearing the area around the Wall created a large open space which was later paved. The eastern section, close to the Wall itself, was designated as a prayer plaza; the western section was a space for visitors. The visitors' square ulti-mately became a site for Memorial Day ceremonies and for Israel Defense Forces' induction ceremonies. As such, the Wall acquired another significant role of a public-national nature in addition to its symbolic status as a central site of Jewish pilgrimage (Cohen-Hattab 2010, 125–139).

From the time the large open plaza was created adjacent to the Wall, it was considered temporary. The planning of the permanent space became the topic of a protracted public controversy. During the first decade after the Six-Day War several ideas and detailed architectural plans were suggested. These different ideas and plans for the plaza found expression in the tension that developed in Israel between religion and nationality, between those who saw the Western Wall as a religious site exclusively for prayer and those who saw it as a place with historical and national significance and as such wished it to be recognized as a tourist site. The difficulty arriving at a decision regarding the plans resulted in none of the plans being adopted; instead, the temporary state of the plaza became permanent (Cohen-Hattab forthcoming).

Nevertheless, the Western Wall quickly became the major tourist attraction in Israel. Surveys during the 1990s show that among both tour groups and indi-vidual tourists, the Western Wall was the primary attraction in the city, with 90 percent of Jerusalem's tourists coming to the Wall. The Wall is also considered the leading attraction for domestic tourists in Israel and estimates are that it hosts ten million visitors each year (Prime Minister and Tourism Office 2008, 49–54; Shoval 2009, 395).

The Old City walls and the Tower of David Museum

Within the undertakings intended to make the Old City a center of urban tourism, the Old City walls were gradually restored and its gates and surrounding parks repaired. All seven gates were refurbished and three other gates which had been closed prior to the Six-Day War—Zion Gate, Jaffa Gate, and the New Gate—were reopened (Berkovitz 2000, 82). A walkway was built along the entire length of the walls around the Old City, with the exception of the eastern part next to the Temple Mount/Haram al-Sharif. The route of the walkway, which is approximately 3,400 meters in length, was divided into four major sections, each having its own separate entrance and exit. Tourists on the walkway can see the Old City and the new city from a variety of different angles (Ellenblum and Ramon 1995).

The Old City citadel, first established by King Herod more than two thousand years ago, is one of the largest and most impressive sites along the wall (Tower of David 1985). It was last used as a military structure when the city was divided; at that time its courtyard became a Jordanian Legion base which set up defenses opposite no-man's land. Shortly after the unification of the city in 1967, Jerusalem's municipality, with the support of the Jerusalem Foundation, carried out thorough archeological excavations in the fortress courtyard. At the same time, at the initiative of the Jerusalem Foundation, a museum—the Tower of

David Museum—was established there with a permanent exhibit of the chronicles of Jerusalem throughout the ages (Amiran and Eitan 1970, 9–21; Solar
1983, 72).

Change outside the city walls

The Old City basin national park and the "cultural mile"

The establishment of Jerusalem's Old City basin (today's "Holy Basin") as a
national park, with important national and religious sites considered the "cultural
cradle" of the three monotheistic religions, was done in the spirit of the British
"green belt" (Kendall 1948, 4–20). The national park highlights and emphasizes
the uniqueness of the Old City, shields it from nearby construction, and distances
it from the danger of encroaching modern roads. The area's design helps protect
the natural scenery and the historic basin, which surround the historical area
(Berkovitz 2000, 82; Dvir 1972, 140). Among the national park's planning principles were the creation of a wide walkway along the entire length of the walls
and the avoidance of multi-level roads, arteries, and intersections (Dvir 1969).

The worst damage sustained during the era of partition was to the buildings
located in the historical city outside of the walls, from the length of the border
and no-man's land, extending from Sheikh Jarrah in the north to Abu Tor in the
south. In order to repair the damage after the city's unification, the neighborhoods of Yemin Moshe and Mishkenot Sha'ananim were regenerated and the
former no-man's land in the Valley of Hinnom was included in the national park.
These were important parts of what became known as the "cultural mile"—a
term Teddy Kollek used, evoking the cultural mile in Glasgow. Jerusalem's cultural mile includes a continuum of parks and buildings containing cultural and
communal activities, extending from Jaffa Gate and the Sultan's Pool for
approximately one mile, all the way to the Jerusalem Theatre.[8]

MAMILLA: LINKING THE OLD AND NEW CITIES

A noteworthy project was initiated in the 1960s even before the Six-Day
War—and completed only recently, almost 40 years later: the Mamilla complex.
The development is situated on the border between the Old City and the western
part of the city, which over 150 years of highs and lows in modern Jerusalem's
development has reflected the changes in the city.[9] This area has two sections: a
Jewish neighborhood built during the late nineteenth and early twentieth centuries and abandoned in 1967 and a 700-year-old Muslim graveyard.

Mamilla's restoration and renewal was one of the government and municipality's first objectives after the Six-Day War. The purpose was to unite the city,
creating a continuous link between the Old City and the western city center.
Mamilla was planned to serve a multitude of urban purposes, integrating economic, social, tourism, and visual dimensions of a united Jerusalem (Kroyanker
2009, 166).

The project's progress over four decades reflects the stages of urban planning as well as the conflicts that that have taken place in Jerusalem during this period.

After the Six-Day War, in efforts to unify the divided city, one of the major actions taken was the removal of concrete walls which had divided the Mamilla complex and the Old City. The government and municipality then began to formulate plans and policies for refurbishing areas along the damaged border, which had become one of the city's central areas overnight. In 1970, the government appropriated the area and established the municipal government's Karta company, which was charged with evacuating, planning, and developing the area. At the end of a long process, 350 families vacated Mamilla and were transferred to other neighborhoods around the city (Kroyanker 2009, 368).

Planning of the complex was assigned to architects Moshe Safdie and Gilbert Weil, who created a detailed three-dimensional plan which included underground roads but no particular emphasis on preserving and renovating existing buildings (Safdie 1989). After years of debate in public planning committees, the modified plan was implemented over a 20-year period and consisted of five major components built between 1995 and 2007: a road crossing the Mamilla Valley; an underground parking lot next to Jaffa Gate; the "David's Village" neighborhood on the slope south of the complex; the "David's Citadel" Hotel on King David Street; and a pedestrian shopping district on Mamilla Street used for commercial purposes, housing, and hotels. Implementation of the plans took

Figure 5.2 The Mamilla project.

almost four decades, with heated disputes and long delays. During this period residents of Jerusalem lived in the shadow of massive urban upheavals in this sensitive area between the Old City and the new city, upheavals that without a doubt damaged the functioning of the city's services as well as its image (Kroyanker 2009, 369–371).

The final result of the Mamilla project is an integrated commercial street physically connected to both the Old City and the new city. Along with institutions of higher education and hospitals, the Mamilla complex serves as one of the few meeting grounds for Jerusalem's diverse population. Its commercial nature and location on the seam of the city make it a singular example in Jerusalem—and in Israel—of the increasing use of tourism as a driving force in renovating the city center, similar to the Darling Harbor in Sidney, Australia, and the Inner Harbor of Baltimore, Maryland in the United States.

One structure whose various changes reflect the development of tourism in Jerusalem and the Mamilla complex in particular is the Fast Hotel. As we saw earlier, the Fast family had opened the hotel in the early twentieth century; after the British conquest in 1917, the Fast family was forced to leave the hotel (see Chapter 3). In the early 1920s, the building was leased from the Armenian Church by Jewish businessman George Barsky, who reopened it as a hotel and changed the name to the Allenby Hotel. In 1929, the hotel returned to the ownership of the Fast family, who ran it until the end of the Second World War. During the 1930s, it housed the German consulate for a time, with a Nazi flag displayed on its façade. During the Second World War the building was used as a club for Australian soldiers (the Australian Soldiers Club); after that, the British Mandate's Ministry of Commerce used the building until 1948.[10] After the 1948 war the magnificent building remained abandoned near the no-man's land along the border. During the 1950s, with the large-scale immigration to the State of Israel, Jewish immigrants took over the building. These immigrants faced economic difficulties and security problems in the location for 19 years. After the Six-Day War, the building was expropriated and its residents evacuated. In 1975, the building was demolished and the complex underwent various planning stages. Finally, in the middle of the 1990s, one of the first projects in Mamilla was the dedication of a hotel built on the ruins of the former Fast Hotel.[11] The Fast Hotel may be the most potent illustration of Jerusalem's constant upheavals, with its repeated changes in identity and purpose over the past century.

Restoration of the city center

The Mamilla complex, which links business and tourism, the Old City and the West Jerusalem's city center, meets the western edges of the city center, also known as "the triangle" (Jaffa Road, King George Street, and Ben-Yehuda Street). Since the 1920s, this has been the heart of Jerusalem's business district. Over the years, however, and especially during the years the city was divided, emphasis was placed on planning west of the city center, leaving the center of the city itself unchanged. The center remained rife with dilapidated buildings of two to six floors, narrow streets with no division between pedestrians and vehicles, old-fashioned storefronts, and ragged signs. Plans to develop Jerusalem initiated in the 1970s aimed to change the city center's damaged image, breathing new life into it, making widespread changes, building new roads, and removing some of the existing fabric (Kroyanker 2011).

The growing demand for extensive development and building after the Six-Day War was reflected in the many plans submitted to the municipal authorities, who wished to demolish entire areas in order to redevelop them. In the master plan for Jerusalem adopted in 1968 many of the older neighborhoods in the center of the city were designated for demolition. A new network of roads and a large commercial center were planned in the area.

However, the designated area contained buildings of historical and architectural significance. The plan to develop and build extensively in the area served to raise public awareness about the importance of preservation, ultimately preventing implementation of the program. The demolition of the Talitha Kumi orphanage in the center of the city (1980) and the Alliance Française technical school next to the Machane Yehuda marketplace (1969) were important warning signs. Both the general public and the municipal leaders gradually recognized that preserving even relatively new historical buildings—buildings that were 100 years old outside of the Old City—had great significance for Jerusalem's legacy. Once the process of preservation and restoration began in the Nachalat Shiva, Ohel Moshe, Zichron Moshe, and Mazkeret Moshe neighborhoods, these and many other areas eventually became vibrant places of interest, attracting many visitors to the new city.[12]

NACHALAT SHIVA: THE CASE FOR PRESERVATION

The chronicles of Nachalat Shiva illustrate the transformation that Jerusalem underwent from the 1960s until the present. Built in the late 1860s, Nachalat Shiva was one of the first Jewish neighborhoods outside of the Old City. The neighborhood has maintained its uniqueness ever since, boasting small homes of one or two stories, tile roofs, internal courtyards, and narrow passageways.

The first master plan for Jerusalem, prepared by Clifford Holliday in 1930, targeted many of the old Jewish neighborhoods, among them Nachalat Shiva, for reconstruction. This program was never implemented but remained legally binding; it was re-authorized in 1944 in Henry Kendall's master plan. This plan also labeled most old Jewish neighborhoods as congested. Because of their poor physical condition and overcrowded housing they were considered unfit for habitation and therefore designated for demolition and rebuilding. The program contained other guidelines, including a freeze on any new building so that no other economic factors would complicate the situation. This would make it possible, when the time came, to vacate residents and rebuild the area (Hyman 1994; Kendall 1948; Shapiro 1973). These decisions regarding demolition and building freezes, paradoxically, are what made possible the preservation and reconstruction of the neighborhood.

The building plan made for Jerusalem's center at the beginning of the 1970s included demolition of the Nachalat Shiva neighborhood and the adjacent court-yard (the Feingold houses). The basis of the plan was a change in the image of Jerusalem's center, giving it an appearance befitting the capital of Israel. Within the plan, Nachalat Shiva was meant to become a large, impressive urban park surrounded by multi-story buildings which would serve as a commercial center with offices (Kroyanker 1988, 256–266). However, new ideas began to influence urban planning in Jerusalem. In the Western World, the preservation trend gained momentum; avoiding demolition of the old for the sake of the new, taking into account the advantages of preserving the legacy of the past, became widespread (Lichfield 1988; Shoval 1998).

Nachalat Shiva ultimately benefited from recognition as a neighborhood with great historical importance: it was the first neighborhood outside of the walls to be built on private initiative (rather than an external philanthropist) and the third neighborhood built outside of the Old City. The renewal plans earmarked Nach-alat Shiva as a focal point of urban activity. The opening of new businesses in the area, especially restaurants, cafés, galleries, and boutiques, was a positive development.

The neighborhood's location in the heart of the urban hub, along with the special character of its buildings and passageways, were well suited to youth and tourists. Nevertheless, the accelerated commercial activity required direction. The plan formulated a list of permitted businesses—primarily stores, cafés, and restaurants—and required that each business owner coordinate activities with the planning commission.

Within this restoration, extensive work was done. The dilapidated infrastructure of the neighborhood, barely touched since the days of the British Mandate, was renewed. Façades and streets were restored, lighting was installed, street fixtures were mounted, and, wherever possible, later additions to buildings were removed. At the center of the reconstruction was the conversion of Yoel Solomon Street into a pedestrian walkway similar to its older neighbors, Ben-Yehuda Street, Dorot Rishonim Street, and Luntz Street. Yoel Solomon Street is a regular commercial street, with a great deal of traffic running between Hillel Street and Shammai Street. Most of the businesses, cafés, pubs, and commercial centers are in this area (Kimhi 1989, 67–69).

The pedestrian walkway in Nachalat Shiva and on the nearby streets reflected new ideas, predominant in the West during the 1950s and 1960s, of creating commercial and shopping centers without vehicles (pedestrianization). These ideas came to Jerusalem 20 years later (Kroyanker 1988, 275). The plans for the restoration of Jerusalem's city center formulated in the late 1990s adopted the principle of limiting cars and encouraging walking and public transportation in the city center (Kutz 2011, 180–185; Manor 2011, 163–178).

Restoration and renewal of the innermost city center in the western part of Jerusalem is progressing and currently nearing completion. It is particularly visible today, now that the light rail traverses the city center along the entire length of Jaffa Road (Israel Government Tourist Corporation 1995; Kroyanker

2003). Completion of the restoration in the different urban complexes will doubtless transform the Old City and parts of the new city into the united city's Central Tourist District (CTD; Shoval 2009).

While restoration of historic Jerusalem was underway, more revolutionary changes were also in motion: the construction of new cultural institutions such as the museum on Givat Ram.

The formation of the museum district

Urban tourism in recent decades has displayed a growing interest in museums and their design and collections (Hamnett and Shoval 2003). Museums have become a major attraction in the tourism industry; this is true of post-1967 Jerusalem, too, where their development was accorded a prominent place. The most significant museum in Jerusalem during this period was the Israel Museum at Givat Ram, considered one of the largest and notable museums in Israel. Inaugurated in 1965, the museum was founded by Teddy Kollek, Jerusalem's mayor.

Kollek managed to solicit donations for his new undertaking from collections from around the world. The museum contains over 500,000 pieces of art representing major world cultures from antiquity until the present; its collections include archeology, ethnography, Judaica, Israeli art, and international art (Katz 1968, 13–38; Kollek and Goldstein 1994, 320–328; Snyder 2005, 6–21). One noteworthy wing of the museum, a major attraction for visitors, is the Shrine of the Book, which holds outstanding archeological findings: the Dead Sea Scrolls, ancient biblical parchments, and the Aleppo Codex.[13]

The location of the museum and of the Shrine of the Book was a deliberate choice, as noted in the previous chapter. Its proximity to Israel's governmental institutions creates a cultural-educational center which includes the Hebrew University at Givat Ram. After the city's reunification the entire area served as the heart of the museum district. The Shrine of the Book's placement adjacent to the museum and next to the Knesset was also meant to be symbolic of the connection between modern Israel and historic Israel. It is clear that the constellation was created to give historical and archeological legitimacy to the new Israel.

Two new museums opened next to the Israel Museum in the 1990s—the Bloomfield Science Museum and the Bible Lands Museum—enlarging the museum district. Future plans include construction of a new Nature Museum in the area as well.

Creating observation points: the promenades in Armon Hanatziv

Preserving open spaces, maintaining verdant views, and creating observation points have become significant components of contemporary urban tourism, especially in natural or appealing urban settings. Cities with a coast or riverbank make those features central elements of tourism (Towner 1996; Williams 1995). The natural setting in Jerusalem is neither seashore nor riverbank; the city is instead surrounded by desert and mountains. Yet the setting and the city are worth viewing, and can be seen from the promenade overlooking the Old City and its environs from the south, considered a key site in Jerusalem today.

In essence, two promenades exist, the Haas Promenade and the Sherover Promenade. The first, built on the slopes of Armon Hanatziv (East Talpiot), was opened to the public in 1986. The second, adjacent to it, was inaugurated in 1989. The design of the park on the Armon Hanatziv promenade was assigned to Lawrence Halprin, a well-renowned American landscape architect, and Israeli architect Shlomo Aronson. Completion and development of the promenade was funded by Gita Sherover. The Sherover Foundation's contribution was dedicated not only to construction and maintenance but also to the activities that take place at the promenade (Aronson 1994, 106–107; Kollek and Goldstein 1994, 321–326). The site is a focal point for visitors and residents alike, a place where a variety of events and activities are held. However, the dream of a meeting place for Jews and Arabs has been only partially realized; repeat disturbances and even a number of stabbing incidents over the years have made the location less desirable.

Tourism in the newly reunited city

Tourism plans

Tourism development plans created for Jerusalem over the years have focused primarily on the increase in the number of hotel rooms. This stems from the understanding that an adequate reserve of hotel rooms is crucial in order to increase the number of tourists who come to Israel without reducing the amount of time the average tourist stay in Jerusalem, Israel's most important tourist destination. In this regard, all of the national tourism development programs after 1967–1970 (Ministry of Finance 1970)—those from 1975 (Litersdorff and Goldenberg 1976), 1987 (Mazor 1987), and 1996 (Goldenberg 1996)—considered an increase in number of hotel rooms to be essential. Most plans listed a number of hotel rooms necessary but did not determine where these rooms should be located. The first plan to deal with the hotels' locations was published in 1977 (Jerusalem Municipality and Ministry of Industry, Trade, and Tourism 1977).

The first detailed plan for tourist development in Jerusalem, which included the urban interior structure, was published at the end of the 1980s. Its goals included increasing European and domestic tourism to Jerusalem, developing tourism related to international conferences, and planning for seasonal fluctuations in tourism. The development strategy included four major areas: the city center, the eastern section of Jerusalem, the area around Binyanei Ha'uma, and the southern part of the city (Machene Allenby and the Armon Hanatziv promenade). The plan surveyed the existing state of tourism and defined operative goals as per hotels, leisure activities, and cultural activities (Weinshel and Friedman 1988).

In the national master plan of tourism and recreation drafted in the 1990s, Jerusalem was positioned as the major tourist attraction in Israel and the reason most tourists come to the country. In the pervasive stable geopolitical atmosphere of that period, the plan forecast five million tourists by 2020, Jerusalem being the major attraction "based on its cultural and religious heritage, its historical importance, and the spiritual experience inherent in visiting the Holy Land" (Ministry of Tourism, Ministry of the Interior, and Israel Land Authority 1996, 64). The plan recommended adding 10,000 hotel rooms in the city and another 3,000 on the outskirts of the city. The plan also took into account the physical and natural scenery which had developed in the city, as well as the atmosphere: a unique cultural environment from historical, national, and religious perspectives combined with desert and green areas around the city.

The master plan, therefore, emphasized that the city must take precautions to guarantee the visibility of green areas and open valleys as well as the cultural and built heritage. The plan suggested policy that included preference to tourism over other interests in the case of conflicted use of space; careful attention to protecting the image and appearance of Jerusalem at the major entrances to the city; maintaining open views in areas of particularly striking scenery; use of local stone in building; opening new tourist complexes; renovating the center of the city; protecting and renovating historical structures; and converting some historical structures into hotels. This plan was the first to include "sustainable development" as it related to urban tourism development. As we will see, some of the ideas which appeared in the plans have been implemented over the years in the expanded city.

In the geopolitical stability which prevailed in the city in the late 1990s following the Oslo Accords (1993) and in anticipation of the Millennium celebrations, the minister of tourism and the mayor of Jerusalem established a steering committee to promote tourism in Jerusalem. Their goal: to prepare a working plan for tourism development in Jerusalem between 1993 and 2000. Among the committee's recommendations, it stated that

> the improvement of Israel's standing internationally in the last three years has created an opportunity to dramatically expand tourism, in anticipation of the expected improvement of relations with the neighboring countries, both in everything pertaining to Arab–Muslim tourism which is expected to arrive and in everything pertaining to tourism that will result from open borders between the countries in the area.
>
> (Ministry of Tourism, Jerusalem Municipality, Jerusalem Development Authority 1993, 12–14)

The Ministry of Tourism and Jerusalem's municipality established a steering committee for the promotion of tourism to Jerusalem, based on "the existing potential of tourism to Israel and on the belief that it would be possible to reach, with suitable preparation, 2.5 million tourists by 1996, 3 million tourists by 1998, and 3.5 million by the year 2000" (Ministry of Tourism, Jerusalem Municipality, Jerusalem Development Authority 1993, 14). Implementation of the committee's recommendations would, in the opinion of committee members, "transform Jerusalem, the capital of Israel, to an economic stimulus for developing tourism in Israel as a whole and transform Jerusalem, when peace arrives, to the most important tourist destination in the Middle East" (Ministry of Tourism, Jerusalem Municipality, Jerusalem Development Authority 1993, 17). These words were meant to underscore the strong connection that the government saw between Jerusalem's religious, geopolitical, and urban uniqueness and its place as a central anchor of tourism in the State of Israel.

The outbreak of the second Intifada, the Al-Aqsa Intifada, in September 2000, brought some of these plans to an abrupt halt, with a dramatic decline in the entire tourism enterprise in Israel and in Jerusalem in particular. Only a few years later, with the gradual conclusion of the Intifada, was tourism to Jerusalem rekindled—and only then did the implementation of plans developed during the mid-1990s become possible.

Hotels: growth in the western city, stagnation in the eastern city

As we saw, very few hotel rooms were built in the western part of the city during the period between 1948 and 1967; great efforts were made to remedy this situation after the 1967 war. The tremendous increase of tourism to Jerusalem led to extensive building of large hotels—many of which left their mark on the Jerusalem skyline, particularly in the western part of the city. One hotel which stands out above the skyline is the Leonardo Plaza Hotel (previously the Sheraton Plaza); another is the Crown Plaza (formerly the Hilton) at the city's western entrance.

An examination of hotel construction between 1967 and 2000 reveals that most of the city's hotel rooms were in the eastern section through the end of the 1960s. In the early seventies, the number of rooms in both sections of the city was about the same—approximately 1,700 each. From then on the gap between the eastern and western parts of Jerusalem grew. By the middle of the 1970s, 58 percent (3,200 of the 5,460 rooms) were in the western part of the city; in the 1990s the proportion grew to 72 percent (5,179 rooms of the 7,196 rooms). So while the mid-1970s saw an increase of about 600 rooms in East Jerusalem, a steady decrease ensued. By the year 2000, 78 percent, or 7,127 rooms of a total 9,107, were in the western part of the city.

Fluctuations in average bed-nights

Another development was the gradual decline in the average number of nights tourists remained in the city, from 3.7 days in the eighties to 2.7 days in the year 2000. There was a similar decline in the average number of nights Israeli tourists stayed in the city, from 2.2 in the 1980s to 1.6 in the 1990s (Central Bureau of Statistics and the Ministry of Tourism 2001). This development characterizes international urban tourism in general and is explained by the increase in vacations, on one hand, and the decrease in time spent in any single location, on the other. The phenomenon is related both to changing work patterns and to improvements in transportation, which make it possible to take more frequent vacations for shorter periods of time (Shaw and Williams 2002).

An additional detail arises from this analysis: between 1980 and 2000 there was a noticeable change in the proportion of nights spent in hotels in Jerusalem as opposed to the two other foci of tourism in Israel: Tel Aviv and Eilat (Jerusalem Institute for Israel Studies 2001, 287). In 1980 tourist bed-nights in Jerusalem made up approximately 24 percent of all nights spent in Israel; bed-nights in Tel Aviv comprised 20 percent and Eilat, 11 percent. During the next two decades there was a major change in the division; by 2000, 18 percent of the nights were spent in Jerusalem, 19 percent in Tel Aviv, and the 32 percent in Eilat.

A careful examination of the relative proportion of nights spent in hotels reveals a more complex picture: for two decades, Jerusalem retained its lead in the number of days tourists spend in the city; 30 percent of the total nights were spent there. Tel Aviv in the early 1980s boasted about 24 percent of tourism and at the turn of the century, 16 percent. Eilat in the early 1980s had 10 percent, compared to 17 percent two decades later. Thus practically speaking Jerusalem maintained its standing relative to the total number of nights inbound tourists spend in Israel.

The greatest change was actually in the proportion of nights Israelis spend in Jerusalem as opposed to other cities. What was 8 percent in the early 1980s declined to 5 percent by the year 2000. The proportion of nights Israeli tourists spent in Tel Aviv also declined during these years. In contrast, the number of days Israelis spent in Eilat rose dramatically, from 16 percent in the early 1980s to 46 percent in the year 2000. The proportion of nights Israelis spent at Dead Sea hotels also rose dramatically. It appears that an important contributing factor to the change in the proportion of nights spent in Jerusalem—from 24 percent of all the nights early in the 1980s to 18 percent in the 1990s—is related to the rise in the standard of living in Israel, which enabled more and more Israelis to vacation in resort hotels. The number of nights spent in Jerusalem declined as a result of Israelis' changing vacation patterns and not that of foreign tourists. Thus in the last few decades, despite the fluctuation in the numbers of tourists, Jerusalem's place has remained prominent among the foreign tourists who continue to come to the city.

Hotels on the former border

A geographic analysis of the rise in tourism services in the western part of the city demonstrates that the building of hotels along the former border was a priority after the Six-Day War. Tourism, it appears, was used to bridge the gap between the two parts of the city. Creating employment opportunities for Jerusalem's Arab residents and catering to people of all faiths, tourism is considered less sensitive for the residents of East Jerusalem than other developments. Following the Six-Day War, large swaths of the area formerly known as no-man's land were destroyed, and a "living bridge" between the Jewish city center in the west, the Old City, and the Arab city center in the east was created (Margalit 1994, 110–112). One of the major avenues to achieve this has been the building of hotels and tourist services in the area, a step which often led to controversy over the height of buildings and the nature of Jerusalem's skyline, as we will see below (Shoval and Cohen-Hattab 2001, 908–925).

The area around Mandelbaum Gate—used during the partition period as a border crossing—sheds light on these developments. For a number of reasons, municipal planning authorities saw many advantages in using the "seam" extending north of Damascus Gate, in the area of Beit Yisrael and Sheikh Jarrah, for hotels. The area is located near major tourist attractions: the Old City, Mount Scopus, and the Mount of Olives. It has easy access to commercial areas, public transportation, and institutions. It is also close to the major Arab businesses in the eastern section of Jerusalem. Moreover, the area has exceptional views. There are many hotels nearby, mainly on the eastern side. The location has several benefits: the concentration of hotels and tourist services is convenient; the land is available for building since it belongs to the Israel Land Authority; the use of the area for hotels is neutral and suitable for a border area; development of a commercial area would potentially bring together the city's two populations. Commercial developments at this location would be valuable to tourists (Jerusalem Municipality 1981). In this sense, tourism can facilitate the unification of the city. Thus three large hotels—with a total 1,400 rooms—have been built in the area: the Novotel, Olive Tree, and Grand Court.

Since 2000, several other projects have been completed in the former border area, most prominent among them the Mamilla project, as we saw earlier (see Figure 5.3; Kroyanker 2009).

The expanding use of tourism to rehabilitate the border area in Jerusalem is not surprising; it has been similarly employed worldwide over the past three decades. Tourism has been widely used in the post-industrial age as a stimulus for renewing city centers (Falk 1992; Law 1992; Owen 1990; Robertson 1995). An interesting case for comparison is the area of the Potsdamer Platz in Berlin (Strom 2001). The central part of Berlin until its destruction in 1945, it became a border area between the American and Russian occupations; when the Wall was constructed in the 1960s, it ran straight through this area. After the reunification, this area became the largest focus of urban renewal in Berlin and a symbol of the new unity and vitality of both Germany and Berlin. The names of the complexes alone—Sony Center, Daimler City—make it clear that large international companies were the driving force in revitalizing this area. These projects, like Mamilla, are complexes which integrate land for offices, housing, hotels, and leisure, and their names have come to represent the link between the two parts of Berlin.

The development of a cluster of tourist services on Jerusalem's border area, especially the Sheikh Jarrah area in the north and Mamilla near Jaffa Gate, is the product of urban development. It also, to a great extent, reflects the many geopolitical changes which the city experienced during the twentieth century: from the Ottoman Empire to the British Mandate (1917), Jordanian-Israeli rule

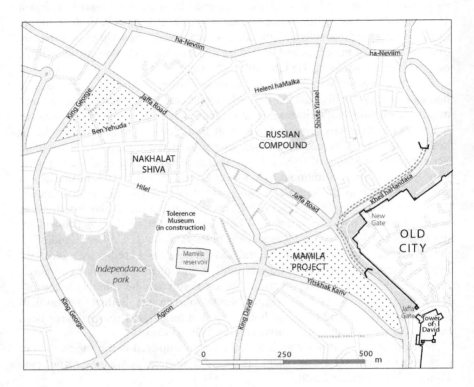

Figure 5.3 The Mamilla project and the city center.

(1948–1967), and finally Israeli sovereignty over the politically unified city. Hotels such as the Jerusalem Citadel and the Waldorf Astoria, as well as the Mamilla project, are symbols of the urban center's rebuilding. While Jerusalem began its transformation to a tourist city during the British Mandate period, its natural development was temporarily prevented; in recent decades, the city has been completing its transformation into a tourist city (see Ashworth 1989; Ashworth and Tunbridge 2000).

Distribution of Jerusalem's hotels

In the year 2000 there were almost 10,000 hotel rooms in Jerusalem (including Christian hostels), four-fifths of them in the western part of the city. A geographic glance at the distribution of tourist services reveals the growth of hotels in six prominent clusters (see Figure 4.3).

• The first cluster is the Old City, which consists mostly of hostels and hotels managed by various Christian groups as well as hostels serving backpackers (Maoz 2007; Noy 2007).

- A second cluster is located in the central business district of East Jerusalem, which extends from the triangle of Sultan Suleiman, Salah al-Din, and Nablus roads. This cluster developed when the city was divided, with most of the tourist attractions located on the Jordanian side and most of the hotels on the western side. At the time, there was a pressing need to build hotels on the Jordanian side of the city to accommodate the tourists who arrived. Today this group of hotels specializes principally in European organized tour groups. However, since the unification of the city there has been a decline both in the number of tourists and the standard of the hotels.
- Another cluster of hotels is located along the national watershed line that runs north to south to the west of the Old City, from the Ariel Hotel to the Leonardo Plaza Hotel. This cluster has two advantages: the view of the Old City on one hand and proximity to established neighborhoods on the other.
- An additional cluster is located in the center of the city, overlapping with Jerusalem's old business center. This area also contains a high concentration of hostels.
- Another prominent cluster of hotels is located at the entrance to Jerusalem.
- The last cluster to be created, chronologically, is in the area of the seam between the eastern and western parts of the city, as described above (Shoval 2001, 83–92; Shoval and Cohen-Hattab 2001).

Thus the era after the 1967 war was one of great building and change; while hotel construction was seen all over, it appears that the western part of the city saw more of the change—and more of the benefit.

The conflict over the skyline

After the Six-Day War, the area around the walls and the Old City basin became a magnet for investors wishing to exploit the enormous potential for business and tourism. Investors and international hotel chains fought to build as close as possible to the walls.[14]

The metamorphosis of the Fast Hotel discussed earlier serves as an interesting illustration, both of building hotel facilities close to the "seam" and of the dispute regarding building height which accompanied it. In 1969, the building was sold to an independent investor on condition that he demolish the existing structure and build a new, modern hotel. The architect, David Resnick, suggested building a 22-story hotel with 220 rooms. This reflected the planning philosophy at the time, which espoused building modern towers around the Old City, creating a new skyline, and expressing the spirit of new technology in contrast with the traditional building of the Old City. Those who opposed the plan claimed that it set a dangerous precedent, one that would be followed by other plans to establish multi-story buildings in sensitive areas around the wall. The Fast Hotel plan was rejected; other designs were submitted with a requirement that the building not be higher than the Walls. The plan that was ultimately approved was largely of glass, with the walls of the Old City reflected in it.[15]

The reincarnation of the former Fast Hotel is only one example of the central-ity of hotels in the conflict over the skyline in Jerusalem in the 1970s, which became one of the most raging controversies in the city's chronicles (Erlich *et al.* 1984, 32–35; Turner and Hasson 2004, 237–260). These struggles ultimately prevented the construction of other large hotels around the Old City walls.

In the absence of an approved master plan, the municipal engineering depart-ment announced that high-rise buildings would have an overpowering effect on the city, damaging its appearance (Jerusalem Municipality 1973). The municipal engineer determined that the continued development of high-rise projects would lower the status of Jerusalem's important public institutions in the eyes of visi-tors and residents alike. He asserted that the feeling of open space and escape from crowded urban life was critical. Construction of tall buildings, he felt, would dwarf such spaces, making a sense of openness impossible. (The effect of the Leonardo Plaza Hotel on Independence Park illustrates this point effect-ively.) As a result, the urban planning commission has, since the mid-1970s, generally not permitted high buildings around open public areas.[16]

Twenty-first-century Jerusalem places a premium on tourism, prioritizing hotel construction and tourism plans to ensure that it welcomes as many people as possible into its gates. But Israel's motivations for this have not been purely economic; as we have seen time and again, tourism is as much a means to a political end as it is about financial gain.

The Israeli government's growing use of tourism for political purposes in the united city

While earlier in the book we studied the use conflicting societies made of tourism for political gain, in the period following the Six-Day War it was none other than the Israeli government that shaped its tourist industry to reflect its ideology. As we have seen, tourism and the socioeconomic conditions in which it functions are highly politicized, with many factions in any given location vying for power and control (Matthews and Richter 1991; Norkunas 1993). In such power struggles, it is not uncommon for governments to make use of tourism for political purposes to promote their ideology (Kim *et al.* 2007; Richter 1989). When this occurs, an ideology designed to advance polit-ical goals and/or cultural images pervades the country's entire tourist infra-structure, including and above all its tourist-directed media: visual, oral, and written (Butler 1990).

The complex relationship between ideology and tourism is amplified in times of conflict and war (Hall 1994). Contrary to conventional wisdom, tourism does not grind to a halt in periods of political or even of military instability. A review of tourism in conflict zones reveals that conflict situations do not always lead to a dwindling of tourist activity. Moreover, in conflict situations tourism's polit-ical and ideological role gains added significance, with its use becoming even more sophisticated. In fact, tourism in these cases frequently evolves into an increasingly finely honed tool designed to promote specific beliefs (Sönmez

1998). However, it is not always the government which uses tourism to promote political goals. In conflicts, opposition parties and minority groups may also make use of tourism to strengthen their influence or make a particular point. In such cases, however, the use of tourism generally assumes the form of a negative strategy, which seeks to undermine tourism and thus weaken the regime (Aziz 1995).

During the period between 1948 and 1967, when the city was divided, the bids for influence using tourism continued, but each of the sides concentrated on drawing dividends without much interference from other parties. For example, the Jordanian monarch tried to establish his position in the Arab world as the protector of the holy sites in Jerusalem, and the newly established State of Israel tried to create the amenities and symbols necessary to consolidate Jerusalem's position as capital.

The end of the Six-Day War created opportunities for the victors. For the first time in modern history, the State of Israel—along with the Jewish religious establishment and various other institutions—assumed total responsibility for shaping the reality in the united city. Questions regarding Jerusalem's status arose later on, following political negotiations with the Palestinian leadership in the 1990s.

Israeli authorities recognized the advantages of tourism for Jerusalem beyond the economic. It was hoped that by demonstrating proficiency in creating and managing tourist sites, including sensitive religious ones, the government would reinforce its hold over the city in the eyes of the world. Furthermore, it could be used to fortify and even expand territorial control. Finally, the Israeli government wished to inspire national identity in Jews the world over through tourism.

Two main stages in the use of tourism to strengthen territorial control over the areas formerly under Jordanian control can be identified. Each stage concluded with violence between Jerusalem's Israelis and Palestinians.

The first stage took place in the 20 years following 1967, ending symbolically with the outbreak of the first Intifada in 1987. This stage was characterized by the intense and direct involvement of the State of Israel in shaping the reality and image of Jerusalem as a city and a tourist destination.

The second stage began in the years following 1987, though its symbolic and practical start can be pinpointed as 1991. During this second stage, the Israeli government's activities did not cease, but they were more limited. The year 1991 marked the opening of political negotiations between Israel and the Palestinians at the Madrid Convention. These negotiations were followed by the Oslo Accords in September 1993. The political process made it harder for Israel to enact significant changes in East Jerusalem's status quo and, as a result, this stage also showed a rise in the role of local and international NGOs in Jerusalem. The year 1991 also marked the first settlement activity in the City of David (the core of ancient Jerusalem; see below), which led to one of the more interesting uses of tourism to promote political goals and cultural agendas. The second stage terminated in 2000, with the outbreak of the second Intifada.

We focus here on the activities of two NGOs—Elad and the Simon Wiesenthal Foundation—both of which became active in Jerusalem during the last two decades. These two case studies demonstrate the growing use of tourism for political purposes, both as a tool for territorial domination and for the formation of national identity.

The City of David

The City of David, ancient Jerusalem's urban center, is located near the Gihon spring, the ancient city's main water source. Twentieth-century archaeologists tied the area to King David and his successors and it therefore holds great significance for the Jewish people. The site's slogan—"Where it all began"—successfully drives home this point. The City of David was declared an official Israeli archeological site in 1974, as part of the establishment of the larger national park surrounding the walls of the Old City (Noy 2012). The City of David national park is located south of the current Old City's walls, inside the large and densely populated neighborhood of Silwan. As is the case with many heritage sites, this site combines tourism, archeology, and tradition in a highly ideological and controversial fashion (see, for example, Duke 2007; Poria and Ashworth 2009).

The location of a Jewish heritage site in a densely populated Palestinian neighborhood in East Jerusalem suggests a potential area of friction and even hostility. This is compounded by the large number of visitors who frequent the site—mostly local and international Jewish groups—amounting to over 400,000 visitors annually in recent years (Noy 2012).

Furthermore, it is Elad,[17] a non-governmental organization with a strong national-religious Jewish focus, that runs the site. Elad was established in 1986 and its ideological goals, as stated on its website, include: "continuing King David's legacy as well as revealing and connecting people to Ancient Jerusalem's glorious past through four key initiatives: archaeological excavation, tourism development, educational programming, and residential revitalization."[18] In 1997, Elad became the sole agent legally authorized to operate the City of David's national park and the main sponsor of the extensive excavations taking place in and around the site. This is a singular case; amongst the dozens of national parks run by the Israeli Nature and Parks Authority, the City of David is the only one whose operation was assigned in its entirety to a private organization. This is due to the difficulty the Israeli government found in operating a site in so sensitive an area, located in proximity to the Temple Mount/Haram al-Sharif.

The privatization of a heritage site's management and development has been challenged in court by various Israeli organizations, with no success thus far (Noy 2012). These organizations claim that over the last decade Elad's personnel has been responsible for all of the site's activities, including selling tickets, guiding tours, securing the premises, funding the archeological excavations, and so on. Thus visitors who purchase tickets are in effect sponsoring the organization—and furthering its ideological goals, namely the Judaization of East Jerusalem.

The area surrounding the City of David is controlled by Israel and indirectly by Elad. However, the desire to control territory is most probably not Elad's foremost goal; it would appear that the organization's main aim is to present its Jewish national and religious narrative regarding the past and the future of Jerusalem. The importance of the specific location derives from the site's authenticity, with ongoing archeological excavations bringing to light increasing evidence in support of the Elad narrative. This narrative may also reflect the views of many Jews in Israel as well, if the number of visitors is evidence of the narrative's popularity.

The Museum of Tolerance

The Simon Wiesenthal Center (SWC) in Los Angeles is a Jewish human rights organization founded in 1977 and headed by Rabbi Marvin Hier. In 1993, the Center opened a "Museum of Tolerance" in Los Angeles. The museum features multimedia exhibits on contemporary human rights crises and salient local civil rights matters as well as anti-Semitism and the Holocaust.

In the early 1990s, the organization resolved to open a second branch of the Museum of Tolerance in Jerusalem. The initiative has had the support of several Jerusalem mayors including Teddy Kollek, Ehud Olmert, and Uri Lupolianski. The search for a suitable location for the museum took years (Shoval and Strom 2009). Various sites were considered, but the municipality advocated a site in the city center—a parking lot on Jerusalem's Hillel street adjacent to Independence Park (see Figure 5.3) and the open plaza next to Beit Agron across the street that currently serves as the location of an impromptu flea market. The Wiesenthal Center hired architect Frank Gehry to design the complex.

The projected costs for construction were estimated at no less than $150 million; the aim was to raise another $50 million for the endowment, relying entirely on private donations.[19]

In order to approve the plan for the museum, the master plan for the immediate area had to be changed. Moreover, despite the fact that all building in Jerusalem is required to be in local Jerusalem stone, giving the city its distinctive appearance, Gehry's design was exempted from that requirement. Normally such authorization can take ten years, but in this specific case, the change was approved in just nine months. The municipality had a great interest in furthering the project, which was to include the participation of high-profile international organizations and individuals (the Wiesenthal Center and Frank Gehry) in an urban regeneration project.

In the interest of streamlining the approval process, the municipality curtailed the public's right to respond to the plans, which may explain in part the negative reception it received in the local and national media when it was finally presented. Some commentators focused on the signature Gehry design. Architecture writer Esther Zandberg called it "the next architectural oddity," and questioned why Jerusalem, a city with a range of urban development needs, would focus its efforts on such a questionable landmark.[20] For others, the entire concept was troubling, as it was hard to conceive of a museum proclaiming the feel-good values found in the Los Angeles museum in a city like Jerusalem, where violence and strife are still part of daily reality. The project constituted, according to one commentator, "the limits of tolerance,"[21] and Meron Benvenisti, a newspaper columnist and former deputy mayor, claimed, "It is difficult to imagine a project so hallucinatory, so irrelevant, so foreign, so megalomaniac, as the Museum of Tolerance."[22] The fact that the museum was the product of an American rabbi and American philanthropy led many Israelis to perceive it as the latest incarnation of "the American uncle," that well-intentioned, well-endowed, patronizing relative—or even an example of "American Jewish cultural imperialism."[23] Other Israelis, noting the poverty that plagues Jerusalem, wished that these well-meaning American donors would look to other, more worthy, local projects.[24]

Two more profound problems, however, haunted the project: its content and its location. The content question arose early on, and came from the leadership of Yad Vashem, recognized by Israeli law as the official and definitive Jewish Holocaust memorial since its establishment in 1953. Noting that the Los Angeles Museum of Tolerance focused on the Holocaust, the Yad Vashem leadership was concerned that the Jerusalem branch would become a competitor. Due to Yad Vashem's well-established status and many supporters in Israeli society,[25] the Museum of Tolerance was forced to declare that it would not involve itself with Holocaust-related issues or with the 1933–1945 period.[26] Just what the museum would display has never been clearly articulated. Indeed, there is evidence that the initiators of the museum together with the Jerusalem Development Authority were in search of meaningful content, and contacted, among other organizations, the executive director of the Hebrew University of Jerusalem, requesting the transfer of some of the National Library's most important collections to the planned museum.[27] This effort has not, thus far, yielded results, but it may serve to illustrate the problematic nature of a museum seeking an identity.

The second problem arose from the fact that the area allocated in the center of Jerusalem for the Museum of Tolerance was a former Muslim cemetery with dozens or hundreds of graves—a fact that was known when the specific location was chosen, since the site served for centuries as the main Muslim cemetery in Jerusalem. The Palace Hotel had been built on part of the graveyard by the Supreme Islamic Council in the 1930s (see Chapter 3). After 1948, responsibility for the site was transferred to the Israeli Custodian of Absentee Property, who later handed it over to the Jerusalem municipality. The municipality built Independence Park and a parking lot on part of the site.

In February 2006, the Supreme Court halted museum construction at the site as a result of appeals by various Muslim organizations. Experts hired by the Wiesenthal Center countered that the hotel built by the Supreme Islamic Council and a planned Muslim University during the British Mandate period attested to the fact that the cemetery had been abandoned and was no longer considered holy.[28] Critics, however, noted the irony in planning an institution claiming to focus on tolerance while dismissing cultural sensitivities; in this, they felt, legal approval might be less significant.

At present, advocates of the Museum of Tolerance have managed to overturn the Supreme Court decision. Meanwhile, however, architect Frank Gehry has resigned from the project, ostensibly for financial reasons but more likely due to the potential negative media coverage. The architects who replaced Gehry eventually resigned as well as a result of disputes with the Wiesenthal Foundation.

It is unclear when and how construction of the museum will resume. What is noteworthy is the fact is that a prime location of symbolic significance in the city center was given to an American foundation, which was supported not only by museum advocates but by urban development interests as well. The Wiesenthal Center was eager to increase its presence in Jerusalem, largely because Jerusalem has such a symbolic resonance for the Center's primary constituency, the Jewish Diaspora, and primarily American Jews. For Jerusalem's leaders, finding a central site in which the project would have the greatest economic spillover effect was crucial, even when the choice of site raised other complications (Shoval and Strom 2009).

Tourism in Jerusalem in the years following the Six-Day War was understood by Israeli authorities and the local population to have a profound influence on its global image and its ties with Jews the world over. Furthermore, it could be used to reinforce control over territory in dispute; thus the use of tourism as a tool evolved over the period, with both the government and organizations employing it for their own ends.

Conclusion

After the 1967 victory, tourism in West Jerusalem went from holding a marginal place to being vital for the united city. At the time of unification, the eastern and western parts of the city each had their own character. Today, a few decades after the territorial unification of the city, the two sections complement one another and comprise a single tourist entity dependent upon political stability as well as peace and economic prosperity.

Today's Jerusalem bears little resemblance to the Jerusalem of 1967. Tourism has been used to effect urban renewal along the former border, with new hotels and complexes bridging the gap between the two. Restoration and construction are rampant in the city: a growing number of hotels, a museum district, new parks, renovated religious sites, a new Old City, and a new city center have transformed the landscape. With the planning came the public debates about the nature of the city's skyline and preservation of historic sites and buildings.

But tourism was also used to create a sense of a "united Jerusalem" under Israeli sovereignty. This served the city and the government in its standing within the global community and garnered support from Jews the world over. When Israel's government could prove its worth in managing religious sites for all faiths, it could justify its sovereignty over the city; when it drew in Jews, it encouraged them to identify with the country's ideals and vision; when necessary, it could even use tourism to reinforce its hold on territory in conflict.

Furthermore, NGOs began to see the advantage in tourism, leveraging it to further their own goals and ideals.

Tourism in Jerusalem after 1967 did not develop in a vacuum. Tourism develops to a great extent within the larger world. Tourist destinations have undergone changes and today, more than in the past, the focus is on historic sites and historic cities. As tourists become better educated, there is more interest in cultural heritage, museums, and historical sites. At the same time there has been a steady increase in business-related tourism and conferences. All of this is compatible with what Jerusalem has to offer. However, despite Jerusalem's evolution and inherent potential as a tourism destination, it did not realize its potential during the years immediately after unification. In recent decades, and especially from the 1970s and on, tourism flourished all over the world, and therefore, the fact that Jerusalem saw only a modest growth in tourism is surprising. There are certainly no fewer sites of interest to tourists in Jerusalem than in cities such as Barcelona, Prague, or Athens; similarly, there is no one—Jewish, Christian, or Muslim—who has not heard of the city. In the next chapter, we take a closer look at the challenges tourism faces and the ways to maximize the immense potential it has for Jerusalem.

Notes

1 Letter from the tourism and travel agencies' union to the acting director of the Ministry of Tourism, October 25, 1967, Ministry of Tourism File, 3497/9, Israel State Archives, Jerusalem.
2 In a survey conducted at the end of the 1990s, of the ten most visited sites in Jerusalem for free independent travelers (FIT), half were located in the Old City, four near it, and only one in the New City—the Ben-Yehuda pedestrian mall and Nachalat Shiva neighborhood. For organized tours, the picture was different; the leading sites included both the sites of the Old City and more remote locations, such as Yad Vashem and the Mount of Olives observation point. See Shoval 2009, 395.
3 For more details on the political disputes in the international arena regarding East Jerusalem after the Six-Day War, as well as the construction and development in the Old City and its surroundings, see Berkovitz 2000, 57–130.
4 During the 19 years of Jordanian occupation, most of the Jewish Quarter was destroyed. In the urban outline prepared by International Brown Engineers, the company recommended the destruction of most of the houses in the Jewish Quarter and their replacement with new houses and parks. In 1966, evacuation notices were sent to residents of the Jewish Quarter in which they were instructed to leave the Old City walls within seven days so that the dilapidated buildings could be torn down. See Kroyanker 1988, 137–138.
5 Slae, Kark, and Shoval 2012. See excavation sites in Figure 5.3.
6 The "Western Wall" *yeshiva*, or Jewish center of religious studies.
7 For more on the evacuation and demolition of the Mughrabi neighborhood from the perspective of the Muslim Waqf, see Reiter 1997, 87–95.
8 Kroyanker 1988, 195–208. See his "Cultural Mile" map with the recreational and cultural centers that developed therein, page 185.
9 The majority of the review of the Mamilla project is based on Kroyanker 2009.
10 Kroyanker 2005, 158–159. For further details on the city during British rule see Cohen-Hattab 2007, 175.

11 Kroyanker 2009, 42. Construction of the new hotel was tied to the dispute regarding high-rise construction and the struggle over Jerusalem's skyline that developed in the years following the Six-Day War. For a more detailed discussion, see below.

12 Jerusalem Municipality 1992; Kroyanker 1988, 50–53, 304–339; Yelinek 2011, 106–161 and the many sources on the subject found there.

13 The Dead Sea Scrolls, also called the Judean Desert Scrolls and the Qumran Scrolls, are scrolls that were found in the Judean Desert's Qumran caves and in other sites in the region in digs that took place there between 1947 and 1956. The discovery of the scrolls is considered one of the most important archaeological findings in the country. The scrolls have great religious and historical significance, as their estimated date of composition is in the second and first centuries BCE and thus, aside from a single fragment of the priestly benediction in silver, they are the oldest Hebrew biblical source found. Although some of the writing in the sources was damaged and cannot be restored, most were well-preserved due to the dry climate in the Dead Sea region. Most of the scrolls are written in Hebrew, and a few in Aramaic and Greek. Among other things, the scrolls shed light on the people of the "Judean Desert sect" or "Qumran sect," one of the Jewish sects during the Second Temple period. See Broshi 1991 and Cohl 1997. It should be noted that the Jordanians had a claim to ownership of the hidden scrolls, stating that the place in which the scrolls were found was under their rule. See Katz 2005, 132–135.

14 Kroyanker 1993, 177. The King David Hotel, the King Solomon Hotel, the Laromme (now Inbal) Hotel, and the American Hyatt chain are part of a long list of construction and expansion plans that included adding buildings with dozens of stories submitted in those years.

15 The existing building was planned by architect Eldar Sharon and is four and a half stories high, so that it does not tower over the Old City wall across the street. See Kroyanker 2009, 42. Later on, the hotel's name was changed to "Jerusalem Pearl." For more on the hotel under the administration of the Dan hotel chain see Portugali 2000, 239–244.

16 Jerusalem Municipality 1973. On the different ideas for building high-rises in Jerusalem in the modern era and the chronicles of the dispute on the subject, see Kroyanker 1993, 173–196, who notes that roughly 35 buildings were proposed for the center of Jerusalem in the euphoric atmosphere of the 1970s, but a combination of economic factors and the opposition of the planning authorities and the public prevented their construction.

17 Hebrew acronym of *el Ir David*, "to the City of David."

18 www.cityofdavid.org.il/en/The-Ir-David-Foundation.

19 Interestingly, $5 million was authorized for the project in the U.S. foreign aid budget in the 2005–2006 fiscal years, although it is unclear whether this money has actually been allocated. The Simon Wiesenthal Center has been very successful garnering political and financial support for its efforts among elected officials in California; this $5 million would seem to be an example of the organization's political strength (Shoval and Strom 2009). The project's fundraising efforts got off to a promising start in 2001 with a dinner in honor of Gary Winnick, chairman of telecom giant Global Crossing, who had pledged $40 million in Global Crossing shares to the project. Fortunately, the Wiesenthal center had cashed in these shares before Winnick and his firm became engulfed in controversy and eventually declared bankruptcy. Plans to name the center for Winnick, however, were dropped.

20 "The Next Architectural Oddity" [in Hebrew], *Haaretz*, September 2, 2002.

21 C. Ben David, "The Limits of Tolerance," *Jerusalem Post*, Magazine edition, November 22, 2002.

22 M. Benvenisti, "A Museum of Tolerance in a City of Fanatics" [in Hebrew], *Haaretz*, May 12, 2002.

23 Samuel G. Freedman, "Frank Gehry's Mideast Peace Plan," *New York Times*, August 1, 2004.

24 Esther Zandberg, "The Terminators" [in Hebrew], *Haaretz*, May 2, 2004.
25 Y. Melman, "Hier's Higher Connections" [in Hebrew], *Haaretz*, December 1, 1999.
26 Meron Benvenisti, "The Hypocrisy of Tolerance" [in Hebrew], *Haaretz*, February 9, 2006.
27 Udi Nisan, former director of the Jerusalem Development Authority, personal communication.
28 David Kroyanker, "Is a Jewish Museum Forbidden and a Muslim University Permitted?" [in Hebrew], *Haaretz*, January 1, 2006.

References

Amiran, Ruth and A. Eitan. 1970. "Excavations in the Courtyard of the Citadel, Jerusalem, 1968–1969 (Preliminary Report)." Israel Exploration Journal, 20 (1–2): 9–17.

Aronson, Shlomo. 1994. "Scenic Echo at the Promenade" [in Hebrew]. *Itzuv* March 1994, 106–107.

Ashworth, Gregory John. 1989. "Accommodation and the Historic City." *Built Environment* 15 (2): 92–100.

Ashworth, Gregory John and John. E. Tunbridge. 2000. *The Tourist-Historic City: Retrospect and Prospect of Managing the Heritage City*. Amsterdam and New York: Pergamon.

Avigad, Nahman. 1975. "Excavations in the Jewish Quarter of the Old City, 1969–1971." In *Jerusalem Revealed: Archaeology in the Holy City 1968–1974*, edited by Yigael Yadin, 41–51. Jerusalem: The Israel Exploration Society in cooperation with the "Shikmona" Publishing Company.

Avigad, Nahman.1980. *Discovering Jerusalem*. Jerusalem: "Shikmona" in cooperation with the Israel Exploration Society.

Aziz, Heba. 1995. "Understanding Terrorist Attacks on Tourists in Egypt." *Tourism Management* 16 (2): 91–95.

Bar Dor, Yoel. 1992. "Restoration of the Jewish Quarter" [in Hebrew]. In *Jerusalem: Selected Essays*, edited by Ely Schiller, 49–52. Jerusalem: Ariel.

Ben-Dov, Meir, Mordechai Naor, and Zeev Aner. 1983. *The Western Wall*. Tel Aviv: Ministry of Defense.

Benvenisti, Meron. 1976. *Jerusalem, The Torn City*. Minneapolis: University of Minnesota Press.

Berkovitz, Shmuel. 2000. *The Battle for the Holy Places: The Struggle over Jerusalem and the Holy Sites in Israel, Judea, Samaria and the Gaza District* [in Hebrew]. Or Yehuda: Hed Arzi Publishing House.

Broshi, Magen. 1991. *The Shrine of the Book*. Jerusalem: The Israel Museum.

Butler, Richard. W. 1990. "The Influence of the Media in Shaping International Tourist Patterns." *Tourism Recreation Research* 15 (2): 46–53.

Central Bureau of Statistics and the Ministry of Tourism. 2001. *Tourism and Hotel Services Statistics Quarterly* [in Hebrew]. Jerusalem: State of Israel Central Bureau of Statistics and the Ministry of Tourism.

Central Bureau of Statistics and the Ministry of Tourism. 2009. *Tourism and Hotel Services Statistics* [in Hebrew]. Jerusalem: State of Israel Central Bureau of Statistics and the Ministry of Tourism.

Cohen-Hattab, Kobi. 2007. "The Development of the Hotel Industry and Tourist Accommodation in Mandatory Jerusalem" [in Hebrew]. *Eretz-Israel* 28: 404–411.

Cohen-Hattab, Kobi. 2010. "Struggles at Holy Sites and Their Outcomes: The Evolution of the Western Wall Plaza in Jerusalem." *Journal of Heritage Tourism* 5 (2): 125–139.

Cohen-Hattab, Kobi. 2013. "Public Involvement and Tourism Planning in a Historic City – The Case of the Old City of Jerusalem." *Journal of Heritage Tourism* 8 (4): 320–336.

Cohen-Hattab, Kobi. (Forthcoming). "Designing Holiness: Architectural plans for the design of the Western Wall Plaza after the Six-Day War" In *Holy Sites and Holy Conflict in the Holy Land*, edited by Arieh Saposnik. Cohl, Alan. 1997. "Meaning and Myth: The Architecture of the Shrine of the Book." *Architecture of Israel* 31: 67–73.

Duke, Philip. 2007. *The Tourists Gaze, the Cretans Glance: Archaeology and Tourism on a Greek Island*. Walnut Creek, CA: Left Coast Press.

Dumper, Michael. 2002. *The Politics of Sacred Space: The Old City of Jerusalem and the Middle East Conflict*. Boulder and London: Lynne Rienner.

Dvir, Arye. 1969. *The National Garden in Jerusalem: Preliminary Proposal* [in Hebrew]. Tel Aviv: National Parks Authority.

Dvir, Arye. 1972. "The National Park, Jerusalem" [in Hebrew]. *Kadmoniot (Israel Exploration Journal)* 5 (3–4): 140–142.

Ellenblum, Ronnie and Amnon Ramon. 1995. *The Walls of Jerusalem: A Guide to the Ramparts Walking Tour*. Jerusalem: Yad Izhak Ben-Zvi.

Erlich, E., Y. Ya'ar, A. Rachmimov, and Abba Elchanani. 1984. "Symposium on Hotels in Jerusalem" [in Hebrew]. *Tvai* 22: 42–47.

Falk, Nicholas. 1992. "Turning the Tide: British Experience in Regenerating Urban Docklands." In *European Port Cities in Transition*, edited by B. S. Hoyle and David Pinder, 116–136. London: Belhaven.

Gardi, Shalom. 1972. *Program and Principles of Planning: Outline Scheme for the Jewish Quarter in the Old City of Jerusalem* [in Hebrew]. Jerusalem: Company for the Reconstruction and Development of the Jewish Quarter in the Old City of Jerusalem.

Goldenberg, J. 1996. *National Master Plan for Tourism Enterprises and Recreational Areas (#12)* [in Hebrew]. Jerusalem: Ministry of Interior, Ministry of Tourism, and Israel Land Authority.

Hall, Colin Michael. 1994. *Tourism and Politics: Policy, Power and Place*. Chichester: John Wiley and Sons.

Hamnett, Chris and Noam Shoval. 2003. "Museums as 'Flagships' of Urban Development." In *Cities and Visitors: Regulating People, Markets, and City Space*, edited by Lily M. Hoffman, Dennis R. Judd, and Susan S. Fainstein, 219–235. Oxford: Blackwell.

Hyman, Benjamin. 1994. *British Planners in Palestine, 1918–1936*. London: PhD diss., the London School of Economics and Political Science.

Israel Government Tourist Corporation. 1995. "Jerusalem's City Center: Tourism Master Plan and Development Plan" [in Hebrew]. Jerusalem: IGTC.

Jerusalem Institute for Israel Studies. 2001. *Statistical Yearbook* [in Hebrew]. Jerusalem: The Jerusalem Institute for Israel Studies.

Jerusalem Municipality, Center for Historical City Planning and Ministry of Construction and Housing. 1992. *Revival of the Inner City* [in Hebrew]. Jerusalem: Jerusalem Municipality.

Jerusalem Municipality, City Planning Department, Policy and Planning Unit. 1981. *The "Seam"—Planning Guide* [in Hebrew]. Jerusalem: Jerusalem Municipality.

Jerusalem Municipality and the Ministry of Industry, Trade, and Tourism. 1977. *Accommodations and Tourist Services in Jerusalem: Development Policy and Forecast—1985* [in Hebrew]. Jerusalem: Jerusalem Municipality and the Ministry of Industry, Trade, and Tourism.

Jerusalem Municipality, Planning Unit, City Engineer Department. 1973. *Building Height* [in Hebrew]. Jerusalem: Jerusalem Municipality.

Katz, Karl. 1968. "Background to a Museum." In: *From the Beginning: Archaeology and Art in the Israel Museum*, edited by Karl Katz, P. P. Kahane, Magen Broshi, 13–31. Jerusalem, London: Littlehampton Book Services.

Katz, Kimberly. 2005. *Jordanian Jerusalem: Holy Places and National Spaces*. Gainsville: University Press of Florida.

Kendall, Henry. 1948. *Jerusalem—The City Plan: Preservation and Development During the British Mandate, 1918–1948*. London: H.M.S.O.

Kim, Samuel Seongseop, Dallen J. Timothy, and Hag-Chin Han. 2007. "Tourism and Political Ideologies: A Case of Tourism in North Korea." *Tourism Management* 28: 1031–1043.

Kimhi, Israel. 1989. "Chronicles of the Planning of Nachalat Shiva" [in Hebrew]. In *120 Years of Nachalat Shiva*, edited by Ely Schiller. Jerusalem: Jerusalem Municipality.

Kollek, Teddy with Dov Goldstein. 1994. *Teddy's Jerusalem* [in Hebrew]. Jerusalem: Keterpress Enterprises.

Kroyanker, David. 1988. *Jerusalem—Conflicts over the City's Physical and Visual Form* [in Hebrew]. Jerusalem: The Jerusalem Institute for Israel Studies and Zmora Bitan.

Kroyanker, David. 1993. *Dreamscapes: Unbuilt Jerusalem*. Jerusalem: Tower of David.

Kroyanker, David. 2003. *Jerusalem—The Light Rail: One Hundred Years of Dreams, Visions, Ideas, and Plans from the end of the Nineteenth Century until the Late Twentieth Century* [in Hebrew]. Jerusalem: Ministry of Transport.

Kroyanker, David. 2005. *Jaffa Road: Biography of a Street—Story of a City* [in Hebrew]. Jerusalem: Keter.

Kroyanker, David. 2009. *Mamilla – Prosperity, Decay and Renewal* [in Hebrew]. Jerusalem: Keter.

Kroyanker, David. 2011. *The Jerusalem Triangle—An Urban Biography* [in Hebrew]. Jerusalem: Keter. Kupferschmidt, Uri M. 1987. *The Supreme Muslim Council: Islam under the British Mandate for Palestine*. Leiden: Brill.

Kutz, Arie. 2011. "The Plan for Renewal and Densification of Jerusalem's Center" [in Hebrew]. In *Downtown Jerusalem: The Story of Jerusalem's City Center and Its Regeneration*, edited by Amnon Ramon, Aviel Yelinek, and Asaf Vitman, 180–185. Jerusalem: The Jerusalem Institute for Israel Studies.

Law, Christopher M. 1992. "Urban Tourism and Its Contribution to Economic Regeneration." *Urban Studies* 29 (3–4): 599–618.

Lichfield, Nathaniel. 1988. *Economics in Urban Conservation*. Cambridge: Cambridge University Press.

Litersdorff, Tommy and J. Goldenberg. 1976. *Tourism Master Plan for Israel—Final Report* [in Hebrew]. Tel-Aviv: Tourism Master Plan Integrated Team.

Manor, Ofer. 2011. "The Plan for Renewing the City Center—The General Planning and the Public Space" [in Hebrew]. In *Downtown Jerusalem: The Story of Jerusalem's City Center and Its Regeneration*, edited by Amnon Ramon, Aviel Yelinek, and Asaf Vitman, 163–178. Jerusalem: The Jerusalem Institute for Israel Studies.

Mansfeld, Yoel. 1996. "Wars, Tourism and the 'Middle East' Factor." In *Tourism, Crime and International Security Issues*, edited by Abraham Pizam and Yoel Mansfeld, 265–278. New York: John Wiley.

Maoz, Darya. 2007. "Backpackers' Motivations the Role of Culture and Nationality." *Annals of Tourism Research* 32 (1): 122–140.

Margalit, M. 1994. "Sewing the 'Seam'" [in Hebrew]. *Itzuv* 20: 110–112.

Matthews, Harry G. and Linda K. Richter. 1991. "Political Science and Tourism." *Annals of Tourism Research* 18 (1): 120–135.

Mazar, Benjamin. 1975. "Jerusalem in the Biblical Period." In *Jerusalem Revealed*, edited by Yigael Yadin, 1–8. New Haven: Yael University Press.

Mazor, A. 1987. *Tourism and Recreation Master Plan 1985–95* [in Hebrew]. Tel Aviv: Urban Institute and Tahal Consultants.

Ministry of Finance. 1970. *Tourism: Development Plan, 1971–1975* [in Hebrew]. Jerusalem: Ministry of Finance.

Ministry of Tourism, Jerusalem Municipality, Jerusalem Development Authority, Steering Committee on Tourism Development in Jerusalem. 1993. *Summary Report* [in Hebrew]. Jerusalem: Ministry of Tourism, Jerusalem Municipality, Jerusalem Development Authority, Steering Committee on Tourism Development in Jerusalem.

Ministry of Tourism, Ministry of the Interior, and Israel Land Authority. 1996. *National Outline Plan for Tourism and Recreation Enterprises (Tama 12)* [in Hebrew]. Jerusalem: Ministry of Tourism, Ministry of the Interior, and Israel Land Authority.

Naor, Mordechai. 1987. *The Jewish Quarter in the Old City of Jerusalem* [in Hebrew]. Jerusalem: Company for the Development and Reconstruction of the Jewish Quarter.

Netzer, Ehud. 1976. "Reconstruction of the Jewish Quarter in the Old City." In *Jerusalem Revealed: Archaeology in the Holy City 1968–1974*, edited by Yigael Yadin, 117–125. Jerusalem: Biblical Archaeology Society.

Norkunas, Martha K. 1993. *The Politics of Public Memory: Tourism, History, and Ethnicity in Monterey, California*. Albany: State University of New York Press.

Noy, Chaim. 2007. *A Narrative Community: Voices of Israeli Backpackers*. Detroit: Wayne State University Press.

Noy, Chaim. 2012. "The Political Ends of Tourism: Voices and Narratives of Silwan/the City of David in East Jerusalem." In *The Critical Turn in Tourism Studies: Creating an Academy of Hope*, edited by Irena Ateljevic, Nigel Morgan, and Annette Pritchard, 27–41. Amsterdam: Elsevier Publications.

Owen, Charles. 1990. "Tourism and Urban Regeneration." *Cities* 7 (3): 194–201.

Poria, Yaniv and Gregory Ashworth. 2009. "Heritage Tourism: Current Resource for Conflict." *Annals of Tourism Research* 36 (3): 522–525.

Portugali, Menachem. 2000. *The Hoteliers* [in Hebrew]. Tel Aviv: Dan Hotel Company.

Prime Minister and Tourism Office, ed. 2008. "The Planning Process for the Renewal and Preservation of the Old City of Jerusalem: Interim Report" [in Hebrew]. Jerusalem: Prime Minister's Office.

Prime Minister's Office, Information Center. 1968–1969. *Israel Government Year Book* [in Hebrew]. Jerusalem: Prime Minister's Office.

Prime Minister's Office, Information Center. 1969–1970. *Israel Government Year Book* [in Hebrew]. Jerusalem: Prime Minister's Office.

Reiter, Yitzhak. 1997. *Islamic Institutions in Jerusalem: Palestinian Muslim Organization under Jordanian and Israeli Rule*. London: Kluwer Law International.

Ricca, Simone. 2007. *Reinventing Jerusalem: Israel's Reconstruction of the Jewish Quarter after 1967*. New York: I. B. Tauris.

Richter, Linda. 1989. *The Politics of Tourism in Asia*. Honolulu: University of Hawaii Press.

Robertson, Kent A. 1995. "Downtown Redevelopment Strategies in the United States: An End-of-the-Century Assessment." *Journal of the American Planning Association* 61 (4): 429–437.

Safdie, Moshe. 1989. *Jerusalem—The Future of the Past*. Boston: Houghton Mifflin Company.

Shapiro, Shachar. 1973. "Planning of Jerusalem—The First Generation (1918–1968)." In

Urban Geography of Jerusalem: A Companion to the Atlas of Jerusalem, edited by David Amiran *et al.*, 139–147. Berlin and New York: W. de Gruyter.

Sharon, Arieh, David Anatol Brutzkus, and Eldad Sharon. n.d. *Outline Plan for the Old City and Its Environs* [in Hebrew]. Jerusalem: n.p.

Shaw, Gareth and Alan M. Williams. 2002. *Critical Issues in Tourism: A Geographical Perspective*. Oxford: Blackwell.

Shoval, Noam. 1998. *Tourism as a Means for Reviving Cities: Review of Academic Literature* [in Hebrew]. Jerusalem: Ministry of Tourism.

Shoval, Noam. 2001. "Segmented and Overlapping Tourist Spaces: Jerusalem and Tel Aviv as Case Studies" [in Hebrew]. Jerusalem: PhD diss., the Hebrew University of Jerusalem.

Shoval, Noam. 2009. "Tourism in Jerusalem, 1967–2000." In *Planning and Conserving Jerusalem: The Challenge of an Ancient City*, edited by Eyal Meiron and Doron Bar, 389–407. Jerusalem: Yad Izhak Ben-Zvi.

Shoval, Noam and Kobi Cohen-Hattab. 2001. "Urban Hotel Development Patterns in the Face of Political Shifts." *Annals of Tourism Research* 28 (4): 908–925.

Shoval, Noam and Elizabeth Strom. 2009. "Inscribing Universal Values into the Urban Landscape: New York, Jerusalem and Winnipeg as Case Studies." *Urban Geography* 30 (2): 143–161.

Slae, Bracha. 2009. *Planning, Preservation and Development of the Jewish Quarter 1967–1975* [in Hebrew]. Jerusalem: Master's thesis, the Hebrew University of Jerusalem.

Slae, Bracha, Ruth Kark, and Noam Shoval. 2012. "Post-war Reconstruction and Conservation of the Historic Jewish Quarter in Jerusalem, 1967–1975." *Planning Perspectives* 27 (3): 369–392.

Snyder, James S. 2005. "The Israel Museum: One Hundred Years of Beauty and Sanctity." In *The Israel Museum*, edited by S. AvRutick, 6–21. Jerusalem and New York: Harry N. Abrams.

Solar, Giora. 1983. "Restoration of the Citadel" [in Hebrew]. In *David's Tower Rediscovered*, edited by Renee Sivan, 72. Jerusalem: Hamakor Press.

Sönmez, Sevil F. 1998. "Tourism, Terrorism and Political Instability." *Annals of Tourism Research* 25 (2): 416–456.

Strom, Elizabeth. 2001. *Building the New Berlin: The Politics of Urban Development in Germany's Capital City*. Lanham and Oxford: Lexington Books.

Tower of David. 1985. *Programme Outline* [in Hebrew]. Jerusalem: Jerusalem City Museum.

Towner, John. 1996. *An Historical Geography of Recreation and Tourism in Western World 1540–1940*. Chichester: John Wiley.

Turner, Mike and Shlomo Hasson. 2004. "Building Height in Jerusalem" [in Hebrew]. In *Sustainable Jerusalem: Issues of Development and Conservation*, edited by Maya Choshen, Shlomo Hasson, and Israel Kimhi, 237–260. Jerusalem: The Jerusalem Institute for Israel Studies.

Weinshel, Ziva and Ruth Friedman, eds. 1988. *Jerusalem—Tourism Development Plan* [in Hebrew]. Jerusalem: n.p.

Williams, Stephen. 1995. *Recreation in the Urban Environment*. London: Routledge.

Yadin, Yigael, ed. 1975. *Jerusalem Revealed: Archaeology in the Holy City 1968–1974*. Jerusalem: Israel Exploration Society.

Yelinek, Aviel. 2011. "The City Center: Current Status and the Beginnings of Change" [in Hebrew]. In *Downtown Jerusalem: The Story of Jerusalem's City Center and Its Regeneration*, edited by Amnon Ramon, Aviel Yelinek, and Asaf Vitman, 106–161. Jerusalem: The Jerusalem Institute for Israel Studies.

Archives and Collections
Israel State Archives, Jerusalem.

6 The role of tourism in Jerusalem's future

Previous chapters outlined the great impact of tourism and pilgrimage on Jerusalem's economy, built environment, political conflicts, and skyline over the course of the past 150 years. As we saw, Jerusalem's symbolic importance as the center of three religions, its historical buildings, and the extensive archaeological findings render it one of the world's largest tourist attractions—potentially. Sadly, political instability in the city and region keep Jerusalem from reaching that potential.

However, despite the political issues impeding tourism's development, Jerusalem's very structure can be better planned to optimize its potential. City planners can no longer afford to sit back and watch as the city grows around its industry; they must take proactive steps in creating a setting that capitalizes on its resources and attractions. This also includes facing the difficulties posed by the political situation—most notably, the construction of the "security fence."

Below we lay out principles for tourism development in the divided metropolitan region, principles that can ensure the continuous growth of tourism and pilgrimages. Only once the authorities recognize their role in molding a city more suited to welcoming multitudes can Jerusalem and its residents truly benefit from tourism.

Current urban processes

Aside from the large-scale tourism developments initiated by the Israeli government after 1967 (described in the previous chapter), the most significant governmental activity post-1967 was the massive construction of Jewish neighborhoods in East Jerusalem (Amiran 1973). This was a manifestation of Israel's desire to put an end to the physical, administrative, and demographic division of the city and was also a clear statement that the city would not be the subject of any future negotiations (see Figure 6.1). Since 2002, the primary activity in this realm has been Israel's unilateral division of the metropolitan region, resulting from the construction of the "security fence" (see Figure 6.2). This transformation in Jerusalem's urban geography is probably the greatest structural change since the city's unification in 1967. The fence's construction—particularly in Jerusalem—reflects the fact that at present and for the foreseeable future Israel's establishment is firm in its belief: there will be no agreement regarding the division of Jerusalem (Shoval 2008).

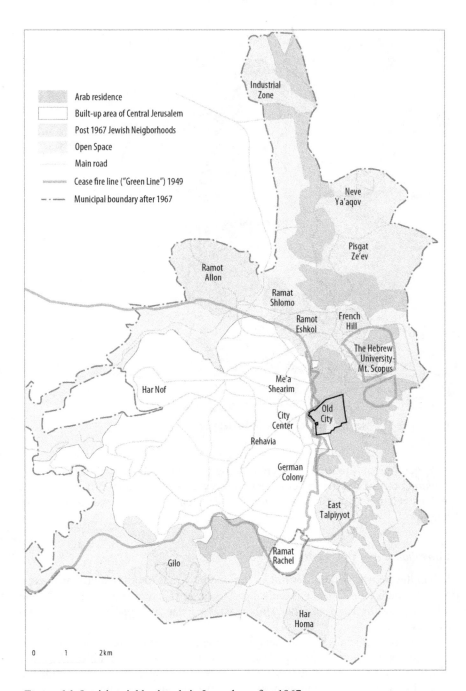

Key / Legend:

Arab residence

Built-up area of Central Jerusalem

Post 1967 Jewish Neigborhoods

Open Space

Main road

Cease fire line ("Green Line") 1949

Municipal boundary after 1967

Industrial
Zone

Neve
Ya'aqov

Pisgat
Ze'ev

Ramot
Allon

Ramat
Shlomo

Ramot
Eshkol

French
Hill

The Hebrew
University-
Mt. Scopus

Har Nof

Me'a
Shearim

Old
City

City
Center

Rehavia

German
Colony

East
Talpiyyot

Gilo

Ramat
Rachel

Har
Homa

0   1   2km

Figure 6.1 Jewish neighborhoods in Jerusalem after 1967.

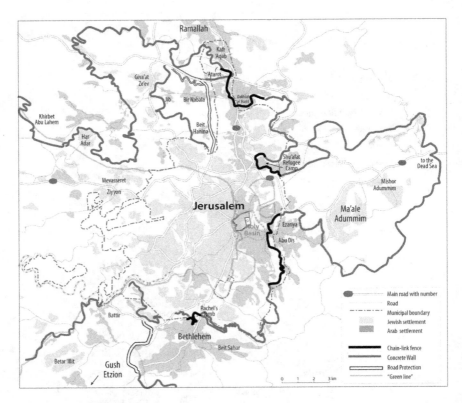

Figure 6.2 The "security fence" in the Jerusalem area.

Several urban processes that are directly and indirectly related to the fence's construction are discussed below; later on, we address the question of the fence and its relation to the future of tourism development in Jerusalem at greater length.

Consolidation of the "metropolitan X"

Urban development in the Jerusalem region today runs along two principal axes: a north–south Palestinian axis and an east–west Jewish axis (see Figure 6.3). The Old City and its environs—or "Holy Basin"—lie in the area in which the two axes overlap.

Interesting dynamics are underway on the Jewish east–west axis. Development to the east is towards Ma'ale Adumim and nearby communities; the other direction, to the west, includes plans to annex and develop areas just outside the municipal borders. The municipality's motivation in cultivating areas that are already included in the municipal borders or that will soon be annexed is clear:

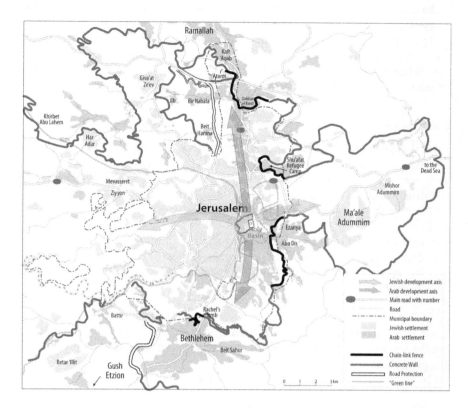

Figure 6.3 The Metropolitan "X".

people leaving the city proper are thus retained as residents. Furthermore, the municipality continues to benefit from taxes and other revenues that can boost its dwindling coffers. In contrast to Jerusalem's declining city center, Ma'ale Adumim, developing rapidly to the east, is a flourishing town, with advanced education and cultural services in addition to competitive real estate prices and fast, easy access to the city.

On the perpendicular axis, however, the situation is different: the "security fence" that will be analyzed below in essence severs the Palestinian south–north axis.

Wedged between these opposing development axes lies Jerusalem's city center. Its deterioration, seen earlier, is a result of several processes, most noticeably the ongoing suburbanization of residents and retail services, occurring much in the same manner as in all major cities in the second half of the twentieth century. Considerable resources are being invested in efforts to regenerate the city center—which is still a work in progress. At present, the hope is that the light rail or the construction of flagship museums (such as the Museum of

Tolerance), will serve as a miracle cure—in terms of both economics and image—to the struggling city center.

In contrast with the Jewish sector's suburbanization trends, in the Palestinian sector the fence is causing a reverse process, with residents moving their commercial enterprises and homes into the city to avoid remaining on the wrong side of the wall (Nasrallah 2005).

Construction of transportation arteries and ring roads

Over the last few years, several main traffic arteries have been built in Jerusalem and its environs (see Figure 6.4). Due to the city's hilly topography, such projects are costly and complicated from an engineering perspective, demanding the construction of tunnels and bridges.

Michael Dumper claims—probably correctly—that the

> new roads not only integrate the outlying Israeli Jewish settlements into the core areas of Jerusalem, but also serve to divide the Palestinian areas, breaking up the physical contiguity of those areas with each other and with the West Bank.
>
> (Dumper 1997, 99)

Even if the transportation networks were not intentionally designed to serve as a means for spatial domination, it is extremely difficult to counter the reality on the ground.

In this regard, a few developments are significant:

- The eastern ring road, parts of which are still under construction, has already been transformed on the drawing table from a traffic solution for the city into a geopolitical solution for the incorporation of the Adumim settlement bloc within the "security fence," in an effort to allow freedom of movement between Bethlehem and Ramallah and enable continuous transportation (but not territorial contiguity; see Figure 6.2).
- Construction of the fence also eliminated the planned route 45, which was intended to be the national lateral artery connecting the city with the coastal plain (Ben Gurion Airport and Tel Aviv) and the Jordan Valley.
- The Mount Scopus tunnel created a faster link to Ma'ale Adumim, easing transportation for the large Jewish population that has moved there; this undoubtedly also continues to encourage ongoing suburbanization eastwards.
- Road no. 4 (Begin Boulevard) crosses the city from north to south, extending from Malcha to Atarot and forming a direct link with Highway 443 towards Modi'in and Highway no. 1. In addition to its function for transportation, this road separates the villages of Jib, Bir Naballah, and Beit Hanina (old section) from the Palestinian continuity along Highway no. 60, encircling these communities to form an enclave bound to the north by Highway 443, as a continuation of Road no. 4. Thus the only remaining link

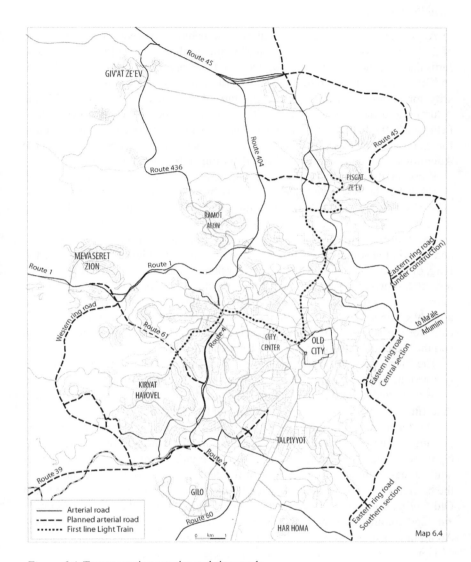

Figure 6.4 Transportation arteries and ring roads.

between these villages and Bitounia and Ramallah is one road that passes
through a tunnel underneath Highway 443.

• A new element in the cityscape worth mentioning is the light rail, which—
despite the fact that some of its routes have a north–south orientation—was
planned in the main to serve the city's Jewish sector. This is not new; separate public transportation systems (bus) have always served the eastern and
western parts of the city.

Israel's "security fence"

In August 2002, the Israeli political-defense cabinet approved the construction of 22 kilometers of the "security fence" in the northern and southern outskirts of Jerusalem. At the end of July 2003 work in those areas was completed (Michael and Ramon 2004). The outline of the "Jerusalem Envelope" was delayed primarily for political reasons, such as the fate of the fence in the area of Ma'ale Adumim and the adjacent communities. However, the government decision of February 2005, backed by "understandings" with the American administration—for example, President Bush's April 2004 letter[1]—made incorporation of the Adumim settlement bloc possible and determined the current route of the fence.

Work in the Jerusalem region is currently underway; however, in several places it has been delayed due to appeals by residents to the Supreme Court, primarily Palestinian residents for whom the fence will incur losses for various reasons.[2]

The "Jerusalem Envelope" begins in the northwest in Khirbet Abu-Lahem and ends in the southwest near the village of Battir (see Figure 6.2). It is 143 km long, of which just 18 km is made of the infamous eight-meter concrete wall (the rest in comprised of chain-link fences, trenches, dirt roads, electronic surveillance, and so on). Fifteen crossing points are planned for the wall (several are already equipped to function), among them some that were constructed specifically for tourists and pilgrims, such as the "Lazarus" crossing point in el-Azaria and the "Rachel" crossing point near Bethlehem.

The "Jerusalem Envelope" command post situated below Hebrew University's Mount Scopus campus, called "Metzudat Adumim," was deliberately built there as a wedge between Anata and a-Zaim, to prevent the creation of urban Palestinian contiguity between Ramallah and Bethlehem.

The fence currently under construction divides the city differently from the previous division (1948–1967), as this time the city core and the greater municipal area remain one political and geographic unit. Most of the Jewish hinterland, at least in terms of the number of residents, is incorporated into the city by the barrier: Giv'at Ze'ev in the north and adjacent communities such as New and Old Giv'on and Har Shmuel; in the south, Efrat and the other villages, kibbutzim, and communities that comprise Gush Etzion; in the east, the city of Ma'ale Adumim and some smaller villages and communities.

However, metropolitan Palestinian Jerusalem will be destroyed by the fence (Klein 2005). Nasrallah's harsh comments below reflect the sense of frustration and helplessness on the Palestinian side. The move is seen as yet another nail in the coffin of Palestinian autonomy in East Jerusalem, which also makes normal life in the Palestinian part of the city near impossible.

> The process of settlement construction inside and around the city's borders, followed by their actual annexation through the construction of the wall and inclusion of empty (un-built) lands as reserves for those settlements' expansion, was at the expense of the Palestinian neighborhoods and villages. This

was accompanied by the connection of the settlements to each other via a network of highways, tunnels and bridges, which has shortened distances and expanded Jerusalem's limits in all directions. The process has been coupled with the dismemberment of the Palestinian neighborhoods and their spatial and functional cohesion through Israeli spatial domination, and the use of exploitation as a means for amputating and weakening the integration of the Palestinian space. The disintegration reached a degree whereby it is possible to argue that Jerusalem's urban entity is no longer existent.

(Nasrallah 2005, 211)

One crucial issue that must be addressed is the "real" purpose of the fence. In the Israeli public and media the fence is portrayed as nothing more than a security measure—though, despite the fact that it is not yet fully operational, it is frequently deemed ineffective. This tack, positioning the fence as a military necessity, was developed by the Israeli government, probably in an effort to escape international political pressure. Furthermore, the government claims that the fence is only temporary.[3] However, any analysis of the fence's role solely as a security measure is limited, omitting its main purposes as a future political, economic (at least for customs and taxation), and demographic border. Israel's general strategy in plotting the route of the Jerusalem separation fence was most probably to take initiative in creating a border that would be as convenient for Israel as possible. The economic disparities between the two societies and Israel's wish to stop the "silent return" of Palestinians to Israel suggest that the fence will remain in place for a long time, regardless of whether security is a concern.

These reasons for the creation of a clearly defined and marked border, in addition to the enormous construction costs—estimated at $3 billion for the project as a whole—lead us to the conclusion that it is most certainly not a temporary line. It is possible that negotiations or realities on the ground will result in a modification of the current path, but the creation of a physical division does not seem to be a temporary approach. This division may not be the best option for the future of Jerusalem, as various researchers claim, but it is most probably the reality for at the next few years at least.

Analyses of the impact of the fence on the change and growth of Palestinian sectors of the city (see, for example: Brooks *et al.* 2005; Garb 2005; Garb and Savitch 2005; Khamaisi and Nasrallah 2003; Klein 2005; Nasrallah 2005) demonstrate that the fence will have a devastating impact on Palestinian society in East Jerusalem and its suburbs, particularly with regard to accessibility to medical services, education, and social and cultural life. It is interesting that, to date, no large-scale empirical research has been conducted to analyze the impact on the Jewish sectors and residents.

Optimizing tourism through planning

While tourism in Jerusalem continues to grow, the situation is far from ideal. There are a number of issues that must be addressed in order to maximize the great potential that tourism holds for the city—and, unfortunately, these issues will only grow more complicated with the completion of the security fence.

The strategic location of Jerusalem's tourist city

In one noteworthy study, three segments of tourists in Jerusalem were monitored using GPS receivers over one year (July 2010–August 2011): individual tourists who rented cars at Ben Gurion Airport, Taglit-Birthright organized groups, and backpackers. Nearly 1,000 GPS receivers were distributed to those travel groups, comprising about 8,000 tourists (thanks to a high number of organized groups). The advantage of this methodology, as noted earlier, is its high accuracy both in time and space (Shoval and Isaacson 2010).

As is clear in Figure 6.5, most tourist activity in Jerusalem takes place in the Old City and the western city center, as expected. The majority of tourist attractions are located in the Old City and its environs; most secondary tourism elements (restaurants, shops, and hotels) are located in the western city center. When the "Green Line" is artificially added (Figure 6.6) it is plain to see that most of the tourist activity in Jerusalem takes place in proximity to the city's former lines of division (1948–1967).

Thus the main economic activities related to tourism in Jerusalem are located along "tectonic fault lines" between East and West Jerusalem. This was no accident; as we saw in the previous chapter, city planners had used tourism to revive the former border. Tourism today clearly uses both parts of the city and involves both populations; it is therefore highly sensitive to political instability. Thus it is crucial that these areas function properly if the tourism industry is to thrive. Any fluctuation or disturbance in the political balance between the city's two main communities will be reflected in the tourist industry.

The question of capacity in Jerusalem: tourist arrivals and tourist bed-nights

One common fallacy about tourism is the exaggerated importance attached to the number of tourist arrivals in a destination. For the destination—as opposed to the airline—the number of bed-nights spent in a location is of far greater significance. Thus, three million tourists who stay four nights on average create twelve million tourist nights at a destination, while five million tourists who stay for two nights on average create just ten million tourist nights. From the city's perspective, therefore, the first of these scenarios is preferable.

This is one of the major problems facing historical cities and other urban destinations as a result of growing tourist demand. Several factors contribute to a decrease in the average stay: when demand is higher than supply—in this case, due to rising accommodation prices and the problem of finding enough rooms—some people resolve the problem by staying in more remote destinations or staying in the city for a shorter time. On the national level this is of lesser importance, but the local destination can lose considerable potential revenue.

Figure 6.5 Aggregate tourist time spent in cells measuring 100 by 100 meters.

Another cause for this state is the burgeoning cruise industry, a trend that the Mediterranean is witnessing as well. In the second half of the 1990s, Israel hosted about 250,000 cruise passengers each year. People disembarked at the Ashdod and Haifa ports as part of their eastern Mediterranean tour for a day-trip that included Jerusalem and Bethlehem. This kind of tourism piggybacks on local attractions and transport infrastructure, but contributes almost no revenue to destinations. This is precisely the problem facing Venice, which today has only three million tourists spending the night in the city while an additional nine million visitors spend the day there (Russo 2001).

During the millennium year some two million foreign tourists visited Jerusalem (Central Bureau of Statistics 2001), resulting in substantial congestion in the area of the Holy Basin. Churches remained open until late at night to allow the throngs of tourists to visit; occupancy in the hotels and Christian hostels was at its peak and prices were high. The overriding impression was that without greater capacity and without transportation management (Israeli and Mansfeld 2003), the city had reached full capacity in terms of the number of tourists that could be hosted—and this while movement in and around the city was almost completely unrestricted. The challenge will soon become even greater, as the future holds in store a possible political division of the metropolitan area.

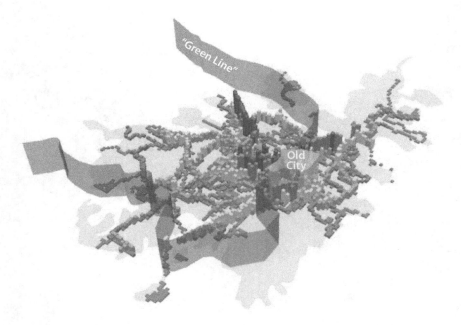

Figure 6.6 Aggregate tourist time spent in cells measuring 100 by 100 meters with the addition of the "green line".

Optimizing tourism through grassroots cross-fence cooperation: an example

The construction of the fence poses a great challenge for tourism in Jerusalem. If the two populations cannot find a way to collaborate around the barrier, both sides will ultimately lose out. However, in similar conditions, partnerships have sprung up between Israelis and Palestinians—and they can serve to illustrate the need and potential for economic interaction.

Before the most recent outburst of violent events in Jerusalem (September 2000), free passage between Jerusalem and Bethlehem was possible for Israelis and inbound tourists (see Figure 6.2), but Palestinians had to obtain a special permit to enter Israel and Jerusalem. Indeed, towards the year 2000, when Bethlehem underwent a major transformation as part of the "Bethlehem 2000" project, many tourists and Israelis visited the city. In addition, more than 2,000 hotel rooms, including the Intercontinental Hotel near Rachel's tomb (see Figure 6.7), were built.

After the onset of the violence, tourists and Israelis were not allowed to pass the checkpoint into Bethlehem; in any event, there was little demand to visit Bethlehem and the region. Incoming tourism to the area dropped significantly. As a result of Operation "Defensive Shield" (March–April 2002), agreements

Figure 6.7 Hotel Intercontinental Bethlehem.

prepared between Palestinian factions with the help of Egypt, and later the disengagement from the Gaza Strip, the overall situation in the region improved and tourism began to increase significantly. However it was clear that if tourists were unable to visit Bethlehem, a Christian pilgrimage to the Holy Land would be unattractive. Since 2004, Christian tourists have once again been allowed to enter Bethlehem, though Jewish tourists have not, due to fear of terrorist attacks or kidnappings.

As a result of this new reality, Christian groups now enter Bethlehem while their Israeli tour guide remains at the checkpoint (Figure 6.8). If the bus belongs to a Palestinian company from East Jerusalem, and particularly if the bus driver is Palestinian—the bus crosses at the checkpoint. If the driver is Israeli, the tourists are transferred to a bus that meets them from the Bethlehem side, in some instances even a bus with Israeli number plates from Jerusalem. The transfer takes place at the "300" roadblock crossing or near the crossing by the exit from the Gush Etzion tunnel road. The inspection by soldiers at the roadblock—both of the tourists and of the bus if it passes through the roadblock and returns—is not a thorough one.

Interviews conducted recently with a number of tour guides show that several methods are used to coordinate the group's passage into Bethlehem: in some cases the tour operator takes care of the details, in others an arrangement is made between the tour guide and his colleagues in Bethlehem. The most common arrangement is with store owners or large souvenir dealers in Bethlehem, who regularly call Israeli tour guides asking if they are interested in a vehicle to tour the town that week. In other instances tour groups are "ambushed" at churches such as Gethsemane in Jerusalem, where representatives of the Bethlehem

Figure 6.8 Israeli checkpoint for entry to Bethlehem.

souvenir shops frequently wait to see if the tour guides wish to arrange a visit to Bethlehem. The Bethlehem stores—generally vast premises capable of accommodating hundreds of tourists at a time—pay for the buses to Bethlehem and the local tour guides, and the Israeli tour guide receives a commission from the store owner as a percentage of the tourists' purchases. The main drawback to this arrangement is that the tour guide cannot verify whether he or she has received a fair share, though the store owners do have an interest in ensuring the satisfaction of the guides so they continue to send groups to their stores (rather than patronizing others).

It is clear, then, that the religious and cultural differences present no obstacle to tourists spending their money while visiting the area. It would appear that tourism has the ability to overcome barriers imposed by authorities when it is in the interest of all parties involved. In fact, tourism seems to be the one industry that demands cooperation—and thus it is the one realm that may be used to further partnerships or even understandings between the two opposing populations.

The place of tourism in future scenarios

It is our opinion that the completion of the "security fence" will generate far-reaching changes in the region. For example, the Palestinian road network will have to adjust due to its truncation by the fence. On the other hand, there are roads currently under construction for Palestinian use that may create new links—for example, the eastern ring road that in several years will in all probability connect the two parts of the West Bank, from Hebron and Bethlehem to

Ramallah and Nablus. Ultimately, the fence will exacerbate the separation of East Jerusalem and its population from the Palestinian inhabited network and the Palestinian economy and society.

It will come as no surprise if the fence's present path changes in the future as a result of international pressure, negotiations with the Palestinian leadership, or unilateral action by Israel recognizing that the current route's inclusion of more than 220,000 Palestinians in Jerusalem is not in its own interest. Nevertheless, the present direction is towards physical separation even if the route of the fence is modified.

Tourism is an important factor in this process; it possesses the ability to become a key element in the Jerusalem region's economic development for two important reasons. First, it is perhaps the region's only "natural resource"; second, the attractions (both material and spiritual) are abundant. Unfortunately, this resource has not yet met its full potential for various reasons—a lack of political stability, a lack of suitable infrastructure (including too few airline seats at reasonable prices), a lack of good and integrated planning and management, and finally a lack of proper marketing.

Moreover, as we saw, tourism may be the only industry that can actually serve to unify the different communities in the Jerusalem region. A thriving tourist industry is in everyone's best interest, and if the different factions can see past the underlying political conflict, they may be able to work together to further a common goal.

A broad consensus among planners and urban researchers studying Jerusalem states that it would be logical to create two municipalities as a basis for future management of the city (Auga *et al.* 2005). Hasson even argues that this move would be in Israel's interest, as otherwise one generation from now Jerusalem would perhaps remain under Israeli sovereignty, but with a Palestinian majority (Hasson 2003, 220). Thus the current situation would pose a challenge to the Jewish majority in the city within a decade or two.

Another commonly accepted idea is the need for certain mechanisms for the joint management and control of the Holy Basin due to the spatial proximity—and sometimes even horizontal overlap—of the different religions' holy places in a very small area (for example, the Room of the Last Supper and King David's Tomb). A further incentive for joint management of the Holy Basin is the fact that as the tourism core of the city, it must ensure free movement of visitors.

Despite the fact that there is an advantage to keeping the city open even if it is divided politically, it is clear that in the short and intermediate terms (maybe even in the long term as well) this will not happen for the reasons discussed earlier in this chapter. Even if the Palestinians have firm footing in Jerusalem as an outcome of future political negotiations, it is reasonable to assume that the route of the fence may change, but it seems unlikely that it will be dismantled. This means that two entities may be established in the region, entities that will be differentiated not only politically but also functionally, with limited cooperation in different areas.

Our analysis stands in contrast with the opinions of many of the writers whose work appeared in a recently published volume dedicated to this subject (Auga *et al.* 2005). These writers view the city as an open one in any political scenario. This concept is also clearly reflected by Khamaisi, who suggests political division with economic cooperation, with Jerusalem remaining an open city:

> We assume Jerusalem will be a functional open city with free movement of goods and people, and the capital of two states: Palestine and Israel, and a city with Palestinian and Israeli hinterlands. The official political and administrative border between the parts of the city will be the pre-1967 border.
>
> (Khamaisi 2003, 139)

Hasson's approach to the future of the city (2003) balances these approaches. He writes that two types of solutions have been advanced to date with regard to the Jerusalem problem: territorial separation and functional integration. In his opinion, due to the current geopolitical crisis in the Middle East, integration and cooperation across boundaries are being replaced with pleas for separation and disengagement. Territorial partition is, in his view, the only option currently viable.

However, notwithstanding his opinion that the division is inevitable, Hasson (2005) argues that there is a need for a metropolitan government, because the alternative is the perpetuation of the present situation. This would mean a lack of frameworks for coordination and cooperation on the supra-municipal level. The absence of such frameworks would carry a cost for both sides, especially in the field of tourism (Hasson 2005, 201). Political separation enhanced by the fence would increase the city's division, but the tourism industry—one of the city and region's primary resources—requires close economic cooperation and functional integration in order to flourish.

As was saw, a variety of problems ensue in the event that there is no free flow between the different parts of city, as occurred in the previous division of the city. Between 1948 and 1967, movement between the two sectors of the city was severely restricted. According to the agreement between Israel and Jordan the transit was in one direction only—from Jordan to Israel—with the exception of a few religious leaders and UN personnel. Those wishing to cross the border were forced to stay in Jordan for at least 56 hours prior to crossing over, and they also had to hold two passports, one to be stamped by the Israeli authorities and the other for the Jordanian authorities (Shoval and Cohen-Hattab 2001). Due to the difficulties in crossing from one section of the city to the other, West Jerusalem gained little from the tourism which developed in the eastern sector in this period (Cohen 1987, 162). If free passage between the two sides of the city does not exist, then those in control of more of the religious sites will be the ones making the profit, as was the case during the period of Jordanian rule.

Gonen (2005) expresses his concern that Jewish Jerusalem of the future will lose part of the expanding tourism pie to the Palestinians due to their control of a large share of the tourist sites and due to the lower salaries paid by employers.

However, Gonen's characterization does not accord with the separation map or with the scenario in which the Holy Basin would be managed jointly with free passage.

In our opinion, not only is this no cause for concern, but efforts should be made to help the Palestinians in this field for, as will be explained shortly, Israel has an interest in developing the Palestinian economy, particularly its tourism industry; Palestinian economic development is, at the end of the day, in Israel's best interest. In fact, Israel even has an interest in "losing" to the Palestinians, allowing them to develop economically and providing an incentive to preserve calm. Clearly, though, if the city is open many more tourists will visit the area and both sides will benefit.

Principles for tourism development in the divided metropolitan area

In an effort to facilitate further tourism development in Jerusalem, we believe that four steps must be taken simultaneously. These steps should be coordinated by all relevant parties—Israel, the Palestinian Authority, and key Christian entities:

1   *Free and efficient passage of tourists between the different parts of the region.*
    If security checks are conducted for people entering the Israeli side of the city, channeling the flow of visitors from one side of the fence to the other will pose a huge challenge. Tourism is an industry in which geographical freedom of movement is key; any restriction of movement affects the pockets of all involved. The rigid allocation of the area already impedes freedom of movement. Coordination of free passage (see next section) is essential, but can also serve to enhance cooperation in the area and create joint frameworks for spatial management and planning at the metropolitan level.
2   *Shared transportation and tourism management and planning in the Holy Basin and the entire metropolitan region.*
    The complex nature of the region necessitates the establishment of organizations that coordinate and promote tourism. Without it this industry—and, consequently, the two sectors or cities—will suffer immensely and will not develop as expected, since tourism and heritage are Jerusalem's primary resources.
      It should be added that such coordination is crucial due to the fact that the different religions and denominations in the city use different calendars that change over time. For example, the Muslim calendar is a lunar one and, as no days are added to adjust it to the solar calendar, there is a constant slow "reverse" movement of the festivals over the course of the year relative to the solar calendar. The Jewish calendar is also lunar but contains an adjustment mechanism so that there may be differences of a few weeks in either direction in the dates of the festivals vis-à-vis the solar calendar. The

Armenian and the Christian Orthodox churches celebrate Christmas and Easter on dates that differ from those celebrated by the Catholic and Protestant churches. Care must be taken to deal with the possible coinciding of religious festivals in Jerusalem, which could result in the congregation of large numbers of pilgrims from different religions and groups in the region. For instance, in some years Passover, with its large Jewish pilgrimage, may coincide with the Catholic Easter (or the Orthodox and Armenian Holy Fire ceremony) as well as a Muslim festival (which may occur then due to the characteristics of their calendar), which can easily attract a quarter of a million Muslim faithful to the Haram al-Sharif mosques. This situation is particularly complex in the Old City due to its dimensions.

However, as mentioned earlier, shared management, coordination, and planning is not just needed in order to enable smooth visits by the tourists; it can ensure that tourism—the number of people spending nights in the city, and not just the number of tourists arriving—grows. This could be the first step in the creation of a joint metropolitan Israeli-Palestinian administration, and the successful implementation of such a framework could lead to an extension of its mandate to other aspects of municipal governance as well.

3   *Balance of development between the Israeli and Palestinian sectors.*
Most of the tourist infrastructure in Jerusalem—hotel rooms and restaurants—is located in Israeli areas and operated by Israeli entrepreneurs. This situation must be redressed. As stated above, in our view, helping the Palestinians develop their economy would even be in the Israelis' best interests. The Israeli side would not lose existing clients if the number of bed nights increased; increased stability and a calmer atmosphere would enhance the flow of tourism to the region overall. Thus, though Israel might lose some potential revenue, as Gonen (2005) fears, its strong economy could survive such a loss and would benefit in other branches from the geopolitical stability that could be gained—not to mention the political gains that would be reflected in other branches of the economy as well.

4   *Large-scale construction of hotel rooms in the region in order to capitalize on a possible increase in demand.*
Thousands of hotel rooms must be built in the city and the region; the current situation constitutes a bottle-neck and hampers the possibility of any real increase of tourism in the city. Simply raising tourist arrivals from 2.5 million to five million tourists, for example, would not secure any real gain in tourism, since it is possible to reach the five million tourist arrivals mark but to maintain only ten million tourist bed-nights. This is precisely what will happen if the average stay falls from four nights to two as result of limited supply of accommodations. In order to increase tourist bed-nights, an additional 10,000 hotel rooms are needed in the region at the very least. It is important to note that this possible flow will probably be received by the Christian and Muslim sectors, as the Jewish sector is rather limited in size. According to Dumper (2002), Palestinian sovereignty in Jerusalem would bring large numbers of Muslims in conjunction with the Hajj, as was

the case in pre-1967 East Jerusalem, when large crowds of Muslims passed through the city as part of their journey to Mecca.

Although Israel's Ministry of Tourism and the Jerusalem municipality created plans to allocate land for hotel construction on such a scale (Shoval 2006), in recent years some of the land has been rezoned for residential construction due to the tourism crisis that followed the second Intifada (the Holyland and Haas Promenade residential projects, for example). In addition, taking into account real estate prices in the city's core and the fact that such tourism creates transportation problems, it would be wiser to direct future large-scale hotel construction to areas on the outskirts of the city. The hotels in Palestinian areas can serve the Christian and Muslim sectors, while the Jewish sector will probably continue to use the large hotels in the Jewish areas of the city.

Another reason for directing additional hotel development to the Palestinian sector is the fact that due to Israeli efforts since 1967, most of the construction took place in the Jewish parts of the city. As we saw, today some 8,000 of the city's hotel rooms are in the Jewish areas, while the eastern parts of the city offer only two thousand rooms of poorer quality, a remnant from the pre-1967 period when most of the tourist activity took place on the Jordanian side. There are an additional 2,000 beds in Christian hostels in the Old City and its vicinity (Shoval and Cohen-Hattab 2001).

The Bethlehem 2000 project proved that under normal political conditions the Palestinian Authority, with the financial assistance of the international community, is able to plan and coordinate a large development project. Such a project includes massive regeneration of historical areas, resolving tourist transportation challenges, and the construction of thousands of new hotel rooms in the city. Similar efforts should therefore be made again in Bethlehem in an effort to restore the pre-2000 situation and to add several thousand hotel rooms, probably in the less dense areas of Beth Sachour (see Figure 6.9). The magnitude of the suggested construction in Jericho and Bethlehem (see below) should be similar to the hotel compounds built in Sinai under the directive of the Egyptian Ministry of Tourism, which created some 35,000 new hotel rooms in less than ten years in the strip between Sharm e-Sheikh and Taba (Shoval and Cohen-Hattab 2008).

In addition to some development in the internal areas of East and West Jerusalem, we propose general locations for the potential of about 5,000 hotel rooms each in order to accommodate growing demand for visits, in the following places:

(a) *The area located to the east of the Mount Scopus campus of the Hebrew University* (see Figure 6.9). This location is ideal since it is in close proximity to the Old City and located just below the Mount of Olives and Mount Scopus. In addition it is a highly sensitive region—it is sometimes erroneously referred to as E1 (which actually lies further to the east). It may be one of the most problematic areas in the Jerusalem region since it is the point where the eastern ring road that will link Bethlehem and Ramallah passes as well as being the seam between Jerusalem's municipal area and the Ma'ale Adumim area. In other words, it is the exact location of the meeting point between the two main orientations of the region—north–south and east–west.

Tourism could therefore be an ideal solution for this location, as it is neutral and both sides profit from the economic outcome; it is a cooperative endeavor rather than another unilateral act on the part of the Israeli government. This feature of tourism—its ability to serve as a unifying force—is exemplified in the three hotels that were built along Route number 1 near the old seam line seen earlier (Shoval and Cohen-Hattab 2001).

(b) *The Beit Sachour and Bethlehem area*, primarily for Christian pilgrims.
(c) *Jericho*, positioned (see Figure 6.9) very conveniently for day trips to the Dead Sea, Masada, Jerusalem, and other sites. Jericho is also close to Amman. This would be an advantage at peak periods of tourism

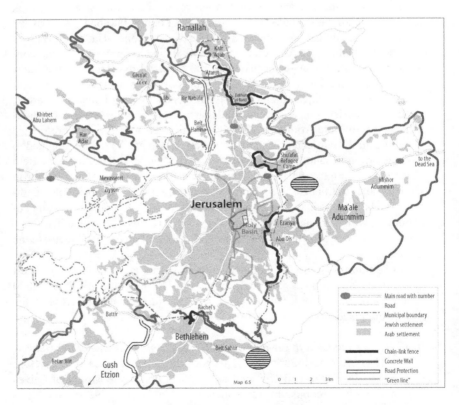

Figure 6.9 Possible locations in the Jerusalem region for massive hotel construction.

when Ben Gurion Airport is congested. Moreover, participants in the mass movement to Mecca and Medina who visit Jerusalem as well would use this as their point of entry. Concentration in the Jericho area could therefore be geared toward the Christian and Muslim sectors.

(d) *The northern part of the metropolitan region towards Ramallah.* Here, due to higher densities of residential areas, tourist accommodations could be developed for smaller groups or individual tourists in search of authentic experiences among the local Palestinian population.

It should be noted that these proposed locations are a considerable distance from Jerusalem's principal tourist sites. Moreover, studies have shown that the proximity of hotels to significant tourist sites contributes greatly to their success (Shoval 2006). This, however, applies in the main to individual tourists, whereas we are principally addressing the issue of the construction of hotels for organized groups, which is much less location-sensitive, as such groups have a tour bus and tour guide at their disposal. Thanks to the tour bus, tour groups are able to move effortlessly through the city, while the presence of a tour guide and bus driver, both of whom are familiar with the city's highways and byways, means that, unlike the individual tourist, they have no difficulty orienting themselves in the city.

Conclusion

As we have seen repeatedly in the book, Jerusalem is a tourist destination like no other: home to sites considered holy by members of three religions, it constitutes a draw for people the world over. The potential the tourism industry holds for the city's economy is tremendous—if only it were being tapped properly. This will only happen when city planners and authorities take a realistic look at current trends.

Planned geographic and structural changes are bound to present immense obstacles to the city's tourism if not properly addressed. The less-than-optimal city center, the road networks that serve Israeli but not Palestinian interests, the lack of hotel rooms, and the political instability already weaken the tourist industry; the construction of a security fence that slices the region in two can destroy it completely.

However, all is not lost, if planners can take a look at the bigger picture.

For more than 150 years, tourism has built the city; its development has been part and parcel of the city's history, its evolution has built the city's structure and infrastructure. The city has, in many ways, developed around the tourism it enjoys. It is time to turn the tables: planners must now recognize that in order to optimize tourism and, indeed, the city's economy, they must create the built environment that will most aptly serve tourism. Free passage must be ensured, tourism management must be shared by both populations, development must be balanced on both sides, and hotel rooms must be constructed on a much greater scale.

Moreover, while in the past tourism was often wielded as a political tool, a means to project a message or stake out a claim, today the situation is reversed: the political situation threatens to destroy the industry. However, if planners learn from grassroots efforts, they can leverage economic interests to create partnerships between the two conflicting populations.

In this way, tourism becomes a tool in a very different kind of political endeavor; one that unites rather than divides. Beyond its financial contribution to the city, tourism is the one industry that must include partnership and open access. When both parties work together to create an attractive and open destination, they can use tourism to bridge the divide rather than intensify it; finally, tourism can be used to improve a bleak political reality.

It is again a new dawn for Jerusalem. If both sides of the divide can work together to make the city an open and welcoming one for all, they may even lead the way for other industries, serving as an example for cooperation in other realms as well.

Notes

1 President Bush's letter was part of an exchange with Prime Minister Ariel Sharon during the year 2004. One letter states:

> As part of a final peace settlement, Israel must have secure and recognized borders, which should emerge from negotiations between the parties in accordance with UNSC Resolutions 242 and 338. In light of new realities on the ground, including already existing major Israeli population centers, it is unrealistic to expect that the outcome of final status negotiations between Israel and the Palestinians will be a full and complete return to the armistice lines of 1949....

For the full text, see the Israeli Ministry of Foreign Affairs' website, "Exchange of Letters between PM Sharon and President Bush," April 14, 2004, www.mfa.gov.il/mfa/foreignpolicy/peace/mfadocuments/pages/exchange%20of%20letters%20sharon-bush%2014-apr-2004.aspx.

2 Details on the different appeals can be found on the Israeli Supreme Court website, accessed January 14, 2014: http://elyon1.court.gov.il/verdictssearch/HebrewVerdicts-Search.aspx.

3 See the Ministry of Defense website on the subject, last modified January 31, 2007: www.securityfence.mod.gov.il/Pages/ENG/purpose.htm.

References

Amiran, David. 1973. "The Development of Jerusalem, 1860–1970." In *Urban Geography of Jerusalem: A Companion Volume to the Atlas of Jerusalem*, edited by David Amiran, Arie Shachar, and Israel Kimhi, 20–52. Berlin and New York: Walter de Gruyter.

Auga, Michèle, Shlomo Hasson, Rami Nasrallah, and Stephan Stetter, eds. 2005. *Divided Cities in Transition: Challenges Facing Jerusalem and Berlin*. Jerusalem: The Friedrich Ebert Stiftung, the International Peace and Cooperation Center, and the Jerusalem Institute for Israel Studies.

Brooks, Robert, Rassem Khamaisi, Rami Nasrallah, and Rana Abu Ghazaleh. 2005. *The Wall of Annexation and Expansion: Its Impact on the Jerusalem Area*. Jerusalem: The International Peace and Cooperation Center.

Central Bureau of Statistics. 2001. *Tourism 2000* [in Hebrew]. Jerusalem: Central Bureau of Statistics.

Cohen, Gad. 1987. "Tourists and Pilgrims" [in Hebrew]. In *Twenty Years in Jerusalem 1967–1987*, edited by Yehoshua Prawer and Ora Ahimeir, 162–167. Jerusalem: The Jerusalem Institute for Israel Studies.

Dumper, Michael. 1997. *The Politics of Jerusalem since 1967*. New York: Columbia University Press.

Dumper, Michael. 2002. *The Politics of Sacred Space: The Old City of Jerusalem and the Middle East Conflict*. Boulder and London: Lynne Rienner.

Garb, Yaakov. 2005. *The Separation Barrier and Jerusalem's Arab Neighborhoods: Integrate or Separate but Don't Postpone*. Jerusalem: The Floersheimer Institute for Policy Studies.

Garb, Yaakov and Hank V. Savitch. 2005. *Urban Trauma in Jerusalem: Impacts and Possibilities for Recovery*. Jerusalem: The Floersheimer Institute for Policy Studies.

Gonen, Amiram. 2005. "Jerusalem—How to Strengthen and Connect the Disintegrating City?" [in Hebrew]. In *Mr. Prime Minister: Jerusalem!* edited by Moshe Amirav, 153–199. Jerusalem: Carmel and the Floersheimer Institute for Policy Studies.

Hasson, Shlomo. 2003. "Jerusalem between Integration and Separation." In *Divided Cities in Transition I*, edited by Abraham Friedman and Rami Nasrallah, 217–224. Jerusalem: The International Peace and Cooperation Center and the Jerusalem Institute for Israel Studies.

Hasson, Shlomo. 2005. "Jerusalem: The Management of Urban Transformation: The Geopolitical and Political Dimensions." In *Divided Cities in Transition: Challenges Facing Jerusalem and Berlin*, edited by Michèle Auga, Shlomo Hasson, Rami Nasrallah, and Stephan Stetter, 185–204. Jerusalem: The Friedrich Ebert Stiftung, the International Peace and Cooperation Center, and the Jerusalem Institute for Israel Studies.

Israeli, Yechezkel and Yoel Mansfeld. 2003. "Transportation Accessibility to and within Tourist Attractions in the Old City of Jerusalem." *Tourism Geographies* 5 (4): 461–481.

Khamaisi, Rassem. 2003. "Urban Spatial and Functional Structure Plan for Jerusalem." In *Envisioning the Future of Jerusalem*, edited by Rassem Khamaisi and Rami Nasrallah, 103–154. Jerusalem: The International Peace and Cooperation Center.

Khamaisi, Rassem and Rami Nasrallah, eds. 2003. *Envisioning the Future of Jerusalem*. Jerusalem: The International Peace and Cooperation Center.

Klein, Menachem. 2005. "Old and New Walls in Jerusalem." *Political Geography* 24 (1): 53–76.

Michael, Kobi and Amnon Ramon. 2004. *A Fence around Jerusalem: The Construction of the Security Fence around Jerusalem*. Jerusalem: The Jerusalem Center for Jerusalem Studies.

Nasrallah, Rami. 2005. "Transformations in Jerusalem: Where Are We Heading?" In *Divided Cities in Transition: Challenges Facing Jerusalem and Berlin*, edited by Michèle Auga, Shlomo Hasson, Rami Nasrallah, and Stephan Stetter, 205–225. Jerusalem: The Friedrich Ebert Stiftung, the International Peace and Cooperation Center, and the Jerusalem Institute for Israel Studies.

Russo, Antonio Paolo. 2001. "The 'Vicious Circle' of Tourism Development in Historic Cities." *Annals of Tourism Research* 29 (1): 165–182.

Shoval, Noam. 2006. "The Geography of Hotels in Cities: An Empirical Validation of a Forgotten Theory." *Tourism Geographies* 8 (1): 56–75.

Shoval, Noam. 2008. "Transformations of the Urban Morphology of Jerusalem: Present Processes and Future Scenarios." In *Jerusalem: The Challenge of Transition*, edited by Shlomo Hasson, 90–120. Jerusalem: Floersheimer Institute for Policy Studies.

Shoval, Noam and Kobi Cohen-Hattab. 2001. "Urban Hotel Development Patterns in the Face of Political Shifts." *Annals of Tourism Research* 28 (4): 908–925.

Shoval, Noam and Kobi Cohen-Hattab. 2008. "The Role of the State and the Rise of the Red Sea Resorts in Egypt and Israel." In *Managing Coastal Tourism Resorts: A Global Perspective*, edited by Sheela Agarwal and Gareth Shaw, 235–249. Clevedon, UK: Channel View Publications.

Shoval, Noam and Michal Isaacson. 2010. *Tourist Mobility and Advanced Tracking Technologies*. London and New York: Routledge.

7   Tourism in Jerusalem

Past, present, and future

The United Kingdom's anthem is "God Save the Queen"; however, England, Scotland, Wales, and North Ireland appear at sporting events—soccer and rugby tournaments, for instance—separately. At the opening of Scotland's games, the Scottish anthem sung is "Flower of Scotland"; in Wales, the anthem is "Land of My Fathers."

The English, feeling envious, recently launched a campaign to make the hymn "Jerusalem" England's anthem. Prime Minister David Cameron himself welcomed the suggestion not long ago.[1] "Jerusalem" is a prominent and popular hymn in the Anglican Church, and is sung formally before the English team's cricket matches; it is also sung informally in the stands during England's rugby games. Moreover, it was sung in Westminster Abbey at the wedding of Prince William and Kate Middleton. And, most interestingly, "Jerusalem" was chosen as the opening hymn for the London Olympics in 2012, although "God Save the Queen" was the anthem played during the raising of the flag in salute to the queen.

Jerusalem's unique history, stemming from its religious significance for the three monotheistic religions, led to this remarkable state of affairs. The "Jerusalem" hymn does not relate to the material, worldly Jerusalem, to "Jerusalem on Earth," but to an ideal Jerusalem, "Jerusalem of Heaven," which in this case will be built in England with the return of Jesus at the end of days. Clearly, Jerusalem is a singular case, a city which lives as much in symbolism and myth as in reality.

Similarly, aside from the Vatican, no other city in the world is viewed by two nations as their capital. Here the claims are on "Jerusalem on Earth," the concrete city. Indeed, this Jerusalem is a city of fascinating heritage and architectural significance; however, in reality, it is a small city, insignificant economically, considered one of the poorer cities in the State of Israel. Yet "Jerusalem of Heaven" is no doubt the cultural and spiritual "city of the world," a city of the highest international order, whose name is known to billions of people, primarily around the monotheistic world.

There can be no doubt that on the conceptual level no city compares to Jerusalem, and indeed it is a singular case. While the city undergoes ordinary urban processes, the national struggle that takes place in it, the geography dictated by its topography, and its rich and unique past create an urban reality that is unparalleled in any other tourist city.

Our book followed two threads in its discussion of tourism in Jerusalem. First, it traced Jerusalem's urban development and the connection between the changes and the tourists who entered the city gates. Second, it examined the ways in which politics and tourism interacted, specifically the use of tourism to effect political change. In the coming pages, we briefly review the book's themes to draw final conclusions.

Urban development and tourism in Jerusalem: the past 150 years

Jerusalem's urban development was greatly influenced by the pilgrim and tourist activities that were its lot in the various periods discussed in this book. This claim holds true from far earlier in Jerusalem's cultural history; upon its consecration in the early tenth century BCE, Jerusalem began to serve as a focus of pilgrimage for religious purposes, a fact that affected the character of religious building throughout the generations in one way or another.

Since the end of the Ottoman period—primarily from the second half of the nineteenth century—the entry of global powers to the Holy Land over a relatively short period and the increase in their political influence has been evident. A concrete expression of this is without a doubt the accelerated building of consulates, churches, monasteries, hospitals, and schools by world powers and churches.

The centrality of the pilgrims and tourists in these processes is indisputable: they were the primary consumers of these services. The construction of the Russian Compound, in effect the first significant building project outside the walls of the Old City, marked the beginning of construction on the part of global powers. Pilgrims and tourists had a central role in this construction, and also served as a tool in the hands of the superpowers in establishing a hold on this part of the crumbling Ottoman Empire. Likewise, the French, German, and English construction in Jerusalem at the end of the Ottoman Empire often "used" the provision of services and protection to pilgrims to increase their influence in the city.

The increased presence of tourists, statesmen, celebrities, authors, poets, scientists, and researchers required the construction of additional tourist services, intended to support those tourists—first and foremost, accommodations. The construction of hostels and hotels in Jerusalem was, then, one of the most prominent urban developments, evident in the city's skyline from the second half of the nineteenth century.

The city's transition to British rule in late 1917 marked the end of the age of Muslim control and the beginning of Western, modern rule. One realm in which this change was noticeable was the improvement in transportation, one of the greatest technological and cultural revolutions in the country. The development and improvements in railway infrastructure and existing roads, modern communications, ports, and airports all had the wherewithal to create a far more advanced infrastructure than had existed in the country at the end of the Ottoman period. Although this system was forged due to strategic considerations on the part of the British, intended first and foremost to serve the government's activities and establish control in different spaces, the local residents and visitors to the country used it as well. In effect, tourism to Jerusalem would not have developed during the Mandate period had the British authorities not focused on developing infrastructure. Foreign and domestic tourism benefited from the technological innovations and the modernization processes that the British brought with them.

Special importance is accorded to the development of accommodations in Jerusalem during the Mandate period, as they accurately represent the new trends in tourism. The success of the hotel industry is always an important milestone in the development of urban tourism infrastructure and teaches possibly better than anything else about the tourism revolution in the city during the Mandate period: relative to the inventory of hostels and hotels in Jerusalem at the end of the Ottoman period, in the British period a number of fancy and prestigious hotels were built in which services were given on a purely European standard. The hotels became one of the symbols of Jerusalem as a social and intellectual center. The very addition of new attractions and hotels on a European scale illustrates the trends and changes that took place in the city—changes in its symbolism and the diversity of its appeal.

Jerusalem's partition after the 1948 war created a unique urban reality in the city: the eastern city continued to function as a pilgrimage and tourist site under Jordanian rule; in the western section, the State of Israel built its capital with all of the symbolic and functional meaning that that process implied. The formation of West Jerusalem's three prominent centers—the Holocaust and Rebirth center on Mt. Herzl and the Mount of Remembrance, the national center in the National Quarter with the Knesset and Binyanei Ha'uma, and the education and culture center that included the Hebrew University on Givat Ram and later on the Israel Museum—all created an essential change in the urban and symbolic landscape of West Jerusalem. During the partition years these centers began to serve as attractions for visitors to West Jerusalem. Yet, the centrality of tourism to urban development in the years of partition was most noticeable in East Jerusalem, where the religious and historical attractions of the city were located. A good portion of the eastern city's economy was based on tourism. Obviously, this was evident in the city's landscape and physical development, with the growth of tourist services and the accommodations established in the different parts of the eastern city outside of the walls in particular.

Jerusalem's reunification following the Six-Day War had two noticeable outcomes in the field of tourism: first, Jerusalem's Old City became the State of Israel's—and Jerusalem's—tourist epicenter; second, the national symbolic centers that were first created in the western city during the partition years were reinforced, now symbols of the united city. Israel's governments invested heavily in the urban infrastructure in order to advance the city's development— primarily in physically uniting the city—due for the most part to political motives, but tourism benefited as well. Many development activities took place in Jerusalem, and the results in the field of tourism were visible: the growth of the Old City as a tourist focus and the establishment of the Old City basin as a national park; the formation of the "Cultural Mile"; the revival of the expanded city center; the formation of the museum district; the preservation of open spaces and observation points; and the growth of accommodations in the western city. The last was noticeably expressed in the growth of hotels in the western city's skyline and the public dispute that accompanied it. In all of these acts, tourism served to some degree as leverage for the physical unification of the city, for urban development, and for growth.

The unique skyline that formed in Jerusalem toward the end of the millennium reflects the importance of the city in both the religious and tourist worlds; the skyline is characterized by buildings of all three religions—synagogues, churches, monasteries, and mosques—and by large-scale hotels. In this, Jerusalem, the holy city, may be comparable to none other than Las Vegas; both cities, unlike others, are characterized by skylines made up of hotels and attractions, rather than office buildings. Jerusalem's unique landscape is often celebrated in artwork and souvenirs, with its familiar domed roofs, church spires, large hotels, and stone walls.

Tourism to Jerusalem as a political tool

The use of tourism as a tool in the political struggle over Jerusalem's identity and physical space did not begin after the Six-Day War with Israel's reunification of the city; rather, it was one of the city's prominent features for generations. Even before the appearance of modern tourism, when Jerusalem was a religious pilgrimage center for believers of the three different religions, the different pilgrims were in many cases a tool in the hands of the political leadership of their time for the increase of their influence on the city. So, for instance, the Jewish pilgrimages during the time of the Temple were an instrument used by the Jewish leadership to establish its influence and hold on Jerusalem both during the First Temple period and during the Second Temple period. During the Crusades, crusaders were sent to redeem the holy places in the city from the Muslims; however, the religious mission was not isolated from the internal conflicts in the Church or the political clashes between various world powers at the time.

In contrast with earlier eras in the city, during the 150 years from the mid-nineteenth century until the early twenty-first century the political changes that took place in the city were rapid and numerous, with pilgrimage and tourism playing a crucial role. The entry of world powers to Jerusalem from the mid-nineteenth century was in no small part accomplished through the many pilgrims and tourists who had begun to visit the city. Most prominent early on was the Russian Orthodox pilgrimage, which—aside from its religious aspirations—was a political tool used by the Russian leadership to expand its influence and infiltrate the Holy Land and Jerusalem. The political conflicts in Jerusalem at the end of the Ottoman Empire were expressed not only in the physical construction of the city and the world powers' struggle over its skyline but also through the visitors themselves, who were political pawns and consumers of the various services in the city and thus had influence on the society and the urban economy.

The British, as a rule, did not tend to interfere in urban tourism and the pilgrimage industry, which was perceived as an urban religious and economic activity. Their work was primarily in the preservation of Jerusalem and in the special treatment given to holy and historical places in the city, greatly helping to advance the urban tourism industry. In this case, too, it is clear that the British activity, even if not intended to promote tourism, was used politically in order to promote their interests in the city and in the country in general. These interests were in keeping with a more open worldview, one that welcomed the Western world into the country, in contrast with the previous administration's disengagement from the non-Muslim world. Keeping public order in the holy places, introducing new norms in preserving the urban space, deploying the police for resolving violent conflict between the different religious communities, legislation, formulating urban plans, employing the Department of Antiquities—all these were done out of different British interests, with tourism benefitting after the fact. The new Western norms the British brought with them to the city as part of their colonial outlook created suitable and appropriate conditions for the increase of the tourist traffic to the city and the development of modern tourism in it.

In the period of British rule, the national conflict took an ever-growing place in Jerusalem's life and this was expressed in tourism in various ways. Thus for instance, one of the ideological battlegrounds between Jews and Arabs was the right to guide tourists coming to the country, Jerusalem in particular. The leadership of the Arab and Jewish communities made use of tour guides, among other things, in order to impart the narrative that accorded with the ideological outlook they wished to promote to tourists.

This trend of politicization of tourism continued even more intensely after the establishment of the State of Israel and the partition of Jerusalem, where in both parts of the city much urban development activity had a political bent, with tourism and the tourist industry serving as an important tool for the establishment of a political hold and control over the space. East Jerusalem continued to strengthen ties between the Hashemite royalty and the holy sites; in West Jerusalem, symbolical national institutions were built, strengthening Israeli control in this part of the city.

This trend further intensified, of course, after the Six-Day War, when the use of tourism as a political tool became the prime instrument for Israel's governments in the struggle to create a "unified Jerusalem" under Israeli rule and to establish Israeli sovereignty in the eastern part of the city. The end of the Six-Day War created irresistible opportunities for the Jewish state. For the first time in the modern era the Israeli state, the Jewish religious establishment and various organizations had a near complete ability to shape the reality in all parts of

Jerusalem. In the first 20 years after 1967, the Israeli state was intensely and directly involved in shaping the reality and image of Jerusalem as a city and a tourist destination.

This period ended with the outbreak of the first Intifada (Palestinian uprising) in 1987. In the years following 1987, a new era began in Jerusalem's tourism. The year 1991 marked the beginning of the political process between Israel and the Palestinians at the Madrid Convention, a process that continued with the Oslo agreements in September 1993. These developments made it harder for the Israeli state to effect significant changes in the status quo in East Jerusalem; as a result, this stage marked the rising role of various local and international NGOs, which became more and more active in Jerusalem. Most notably, the City of David (the ancient core of Jerusalem) effectively used tourism to promote political goals and cultural agendas.

Jerusalem past and future: from a pilgrimage destination to a tourist city

Jerusalem on Earth—that sad, neglected place—has evolved over the past 150 years, in no small part due to those who enter its gates in search of Jerusalem of Heaven. Jerusalem's nature as a city of pilgrimage and tourism accompanied this transformation, becoming one of the most prominent characteristics of its urban existence. Just as pilgrimage was one of the most significant components in the city in eras past, modern tourism became a central element in Jerusalem's development from the beginning of the modern era until today. When tourism is fully understood, when administrators recognize its place and value, they can grow the city's economy and image in ways heretofore unseen.

Here, of course, Jerusalem's Old City is worthy of special attention as the mainstay for tourism in the State of Israel. The Old City and its surroundings contain many sites of religious, archaeological, historic, cultural, and national value. It is a singular place with global significance, the seat of the three monotheistic religions, a place with a 4,000-year history of settlement, war, destruction, and rebirth, declared a UNESCO World Heritage site in 1980.

For centuries, the holy places and historical sites in Jerusalem were its primary attractions. However, beginning in the late Ottoman period and early days of the British Mandate, new types of attractions appeared in the city. The Mandate period marked the first time that the city's celebrated religious and historical sites were accompanied by other types of sites. New original attractions in the urban landscape complemented the city's historical and religious places. Museums, public exhibitions, hotels, and communal buildings were new features in Jerusalem's urban landscape during the Mandate period and even had an influence on the urban tourism map; however, they did not become central attractions in themselves but rather accompanied the city's traditional attractions. In effect, for the first time in the history of the city, "secular visiting sites" existed, sites that were not necessarily connected to the religious heritage, a trend that would grow in the years of partition and the later reunification. The built environment flourished even more following the 1948 war, when Israel, with few historic sites remaining in its territory, made great efforts to build museums, memorials, and government buildings—creating a landscape worthy of a capital city.

Even today, Jerusalem's most significant comparative advantage economically is the field of tourism. The city's historical heritage, its archaeological and architectonic assets, its holy places, its religious and national institutions, the views of the Old City, its roads, its alleys, its buildings, its many museums, its multicultural mosaic of communities, and its unique ambiance—all make up a city that should serve as a tourist mecca, contributing to a booming economy. Jerusalem was and is the primary tourist attraction to Israel, and almost every tourist who comes to Israel visits it during his or her trip.

At present, tension in the region impedes tourism to Israel—and Jerusalem in particular. However, were peace to finally come to Jerusalem, tourism could and should become the city's most significant basis for growth and prosperity. Tourism is prominent in each political negotiation about the city's future: a peace settlement would greatly augment Jerusalem's greatest comparative advantage—the field of tourism.

The question of Jerusalem's political future has been discussed by many in academia and in the public sphere, in Israeli and internationally. In light of Jerusalem's symbolic importance to the three monotheistic religions and especially in light of its transformation to a symbol of the Arab–Israeli conflict, it seems unlikely that a resolution regarding the city's future that is acceptable to all parties will be reached in the near future. However, as geographers occupied with research on Jerusalem over the past two decades, it is clear to us that in any scenario the city must remain a functionally open and unified city in order to guarantee its economic vitality and its future.

The coming years may well see another partition, instituted using a separation fence dividing the city. This can have disastrous effects on tourism and, consequently, the city's economy. However, in our opinion, a number of steps may help ease the distress: free passage between the different sections of the city, cooperative transportation and tourism management, careful and balanced tourism development in both sectors, and large-scale hotel construction. These measures can help minimize the damage caused by dividing the city.

In the face of mounting conflict and possible separation, the two sides must be willing to join forces and bridge the divide in order to maintain and develop the tourism sector. It is only with cooperation between the two factions that tourism can flourish, and the city can grow. This type of collaboration would be beneficial to those on both sides of the conflict. Such a partnership could possibly shift to other aspects of joint administration as well, setting an example of mutually beneficial collaboration that could be followed in other sectors. After centuries of using tourism to exert political control, authorities now have a unique opportunity: they can choose to wield tourism to moderate the conflict, leading the charge for reconciliation and building something new, together.

Note

1 Sunder Katwala, "Jerusalem Is David Cameron's Choice of English Anthem," dotdot-dot (blog), British Futuer, July 14, 2012, www.britishfuture.org/national-conversations/england/jerusalem-is-david-camerons-choice-of-english-anthem/; Patrick Hennessey, "David Cameron Backs Jerusalem as English National Anthem," *Telegraph*, July 14, 2012, www.telegraph.co.uk/news/politics/david-cameron/9400486/David-Cameron-backs-Jerusalem-as-English-national-anthem.html; "Should English Sports Teams Have an English Anthem?" News Blog, *Guardian*, July 15, 2012, www.guardian.co.uk/uk/blog/2012/jul/15/english-sports-teams-anthem.

Index

Page numbers in *italics* denote tables, those in **bold** denote figures.

(Bethlehem) 180, **181**; King David Hotel 42, 56, 57–8, 79n60; mid-sized and small hotels 59–60; need for construction 186–9, **188**; Palace Hotel 58–9; reunited Jerusalem 149, 151; West Jerusalem 118–21; *see also* boarding houses
Hufschmid, G. H. 57
Hussein (King of Jordan) 96, 98

inbound tourism 42–5, **43**, 111–12, **112**, 136–7, **137**
infrastructure *see* roads and transportation development
Intercontinental Hotel 98–9
Intercontinental Hotel (Bethlehem) 180, **181**
International Association of Convention Centers 109
International Brown Engineers 94
Interoffice Committee for the Improvement of Historical Sites 117
Islam 1, 51, 93; *see also* Muslims
Israel 96; government use of tourism for political purposes 156–61; sovereignty rituals 101
Israel Museum 99, 103, 110, 148

Jaffa Gate 25, 26, 36
Jansen-Verbeke, Myriam 10–11
Jericho 188–9
Jerusalem: Armenian Quarter 8; balance of development between the Israeli and Palestinian sectors 186; bed nights 45–6, *45*, **46**, 178–9, **180**; Beit Hakerem 61–2; cafés and restaurants 33, 62; changes in urban geography 46–8; Christian Quarter 8; construction of Jewish neighbourhoods in East Jerusalem 170, **171**; culture and leisure attractions 52–6; development from a pilgrimage destination into a tourist city 198–9; economic development and tourism 183; electricity 32–3; evolution of tourist services 33–6; freedom of movement 184, 185; growth and change dynamic 2; holy places and sites of interest 8, 10–11, 22–5, 47, 48–52, 93, 96, 115–18, 183, 198–9; impact of Jewish revival 8–9; inbound tourism 42–5, **43**; "Jerusalem of Heaven" image 193; Jewish Quarter 8, 12, 24, 139–41; logicality of creating two municipalities 183; maps xiv, **9**, **31**, **63**, **69**, **95**, **97**,

117, **154**, **171**, **172**, **173**, **175**, **188**; "metropolitan X" 172–4, **173**; modernization in late 19th century 21; as a multi-religious center 1; Muslim Quarter 8, 139; Old City 8, **9**, 47, 67–8, 138–9, 142, 143, 154, 198; open city concept 183–4; optimizing tourism through grassroots cross-fence cooperation 180–2; organized tourism 27–9; Palestinian economic development 185; pilgrim space development 7; political future 199; politics of tourist space segmentation 7–10; principles for tourism development in the divided metropolitan area 185–9; religious nature of 1, 6–7; roads and transportation development 26–7, **26**, 47, 174–5, **175**, 182–3, 194–5; Second World War, impact on tourism 73–4; security fence 170, 172, **172**, 176–7, 180, 182–3, 199; shared transportation and tourism management and planning 185–6; skyline 136, 140, 151, 153, 155–6, 196; strategic location of tourist city 178, **179**; study of tourism in Jerusalem 13–15; tourism as a political tool in the Jewish Arab struggle 63–75; tourism mapping in the Old City 11–13, **13**; urban development and tourism 10–11, 194–6; *see also* divided Jerusalem (1948–1967); reunited Jerusalem (1967–2000)
Jerusalem Development Department 116
"Jerusalem Envelope" 176–7
"Jerusalem" (hymn) 193
"Jerusalem (Jordan) and Region Planning Proposals" 94–5, **95**
Jesus 1, 22, 24, 25, 193
Jewish Quarter 8, 12, 24, 139–41
Jews 24; bed nights 45, *45*; guidebooks for Jewish tourists 66–8; hotels 32; souvenirs 35; tour guides' relations with Arab guides 70–1, 72–3, 197; tourism as a political tool in the Jewish Arab struggle 63–75; tourists 29, 44; violence against 51–2
Jordan 96, 184

Kaufman, Richard 61
Kendall, Henry 47, 48, 94–5
Kenyon, Kathleen 140
Khamaisi, Rassem 184
King David Hotel 42, 56, 79n60
Knesset building 9, 99, 103, 110, 111, 195

CPSIA information can be obtained
at www.ICGtesting.com
Printed in the USA
BVHW042005140219
540335BV00007B/43/P